Effective Grading

BARBARA E. WALVOORD
VIRGINIA JOHNSON ANDERSON

Foreword by
THOMAS A. ANGELO

Effective Grading

A Tool for Learning and Assessment

JOSSEY-BASS
A Wiley Company
www.josseybass.com

Published by

JOSSEY-BASS
A Wiley Company
989 Market Street
San Francisco, CA 94103-1741

www.josseybass.com

Jossey-Bass books and products are available through most bookstores. To contact Jossey-Bass directly, call (888) 378-2537, fax to (800) 605-2665, or visit our website at www.josseybass.com.

Substantial discounts on bulk quantities of Jossey-Bass books are available to corporations, professional associations, and other organizations. For details and discount information, contact the special sales department at Jossey-Bass.

We at Jossey-Bass strive to use the most environmentally sensitive paper stocks available to us. Our publications are printed on acid-free recycled stock whenever possible, and our paper always meets or exceeds minimum GPO and EPA requirements.

Library of Congress Cataloging-in-Publication Data

Walvoord, Barbara E. Fassler, date.
  Effective grading : a tool for learning and assessment / Barbara
E. Walvoord, Virginia Johnson Anderson.—1st ed.
      p.   cm.—(The Jossey-Bass higher and adult education series)
  Includes bibliographical references (p.) and index.
  ISBN 0-7879-4030-5 (pbk. : alk. paper)
  1. Grading and marking (Students)—United Staes. 2. College
students—Rating of—United States. 3. Educational tests and
measurements—United States. I. Anderson, Virginia Johnson, date.
II. Series.
LB2368.W35   1998
  378.1'67—dc21   97-41753

FIRST EDITION
PB Printing   10 9 8 7 6

The Jossey-Bass
Higher and Adult Education Series

CONTENTS

FOREWORD

Research shows, and, from practical experience, we all know that grades matter greatly. They matter greatly to college students: what and how we grade powerfully influences what and how they study and how deeply or superficially they learn. To many students, grades also represent the keys to their future professional success and material well-being. Grades matter greatly to faculty, who are trapped in the untenable role conflict of being both coaches and judges and who themselves are often judged by the grades they give. They matter greatly to administrators, who depend on grades in making fateful decisions regarding admissions, financial support, honors, and awards. And they matter greatly to researchers and assessment practitioners, who use grades as measures of student learning and success.

But most of us also know that grades are too often inadequate, imprecise, and wildly idiosyncratic indicators of learning. We worry that our grading policies may be fair but not rigorous enough, or rigorous but not fair enough. We agonize over our criteria: should we grade on effort? Improvement? Achievement? Because we're not sure what grading criteria should be, we too often grade on an unstated, shifting amalgam. We all know that a stellar grade in one course may not equal, in important ways, a mediocre grade in another. As a consequence, we realize that grade point averages—despite the patina of objectivity that quantification lends them—too often represent a meaningless averaging of unclear assumptions and unstated standards.

Students complain, cajole, pressure, and sometimes even threaten over grades. Too often they become gradegrubbers instead of learners. Far too many resort to cheating and plagiarism. Legislators and critics regularly accuse us of grade inflation. Faculty feel angry, defensive, or unsure of our judgments.

Grading makes us so uncomfortable that many faculty would rather not give grades at all, but that's rarely an option. In the halls, over coffee, and in endless meetings, we lament our situation and discuss the need for higher standards and tougher grading policies; but year after year, in most cases and most places, the confusion and discomfort continue unabated.

When it comes to grades and grading, most of us would sincerely like to do better and feel better, but most of us just don't know how.

Barbara E. Walvoord and Virginia Johnson Anderson have written a book that can help faculty, administrators, researchers, and assessment experts alike clarify and improve our grading processes and use of grades. *Effective Grading* is a thoughtful book that explores the *whys*—not just the *whats* and *hows*—of grading. It's a practical book that can help us use the power of grades to focus students' efforts and improve the quality of their learning. It's a realistic book, based on the authors' years of experience as teachers, consultants, and field researchers. It's a welcome book in that it can help reduce conflicts and misunderstandings over grades. And it's a groundbreaking book that explores ways to use grades to foster a culture of high standards, assessment, and evidence in our classrooms—a culture of higher learning.

In short, *Effective Grading* can help us do better and, having done better, legitimately feel better about grading.

I write this foreword based on my experience. It has been my privilege to read the evolving manuscript. As a college teacher, low-level administrator, assessment practitioner, and sometime researcher who struggles mightily with grading in all those roles, I've benefited greatly from the analysis, examples, and guidelines Walvoord and Anderson provide. I've changed the way I think about grades, the way I assign them, and the way I explain them, all to good effect. Consequently, I recommend *Effective Grading* without reservation.

January 1998

THOMAS A. ANGELO
Associate Professor
Educational and Psychological
   Studies Coordinator
Higher Education Program
University of Miami

To our mothers:
Marie Walvoord and Edna Contardi

To our children:
Lisa and Brian and Randy, Sherry and Billy

To our husbands:
Hoke L. Smith and Cliff Anderson

PREFACE

Despite all its problems, grading is still a deeply entrenched mode of evaluating student learning in higher education. It is the basis of a college or university's decision about who graduates. It is the most universal form of communication to employers or graduate schools about the quality of a student's learning. Grading systems implemented in classrooms powerfully shape students' expectations and experiences.

Grading is the topic faculty most frequently choose when asked which issues they want to discuss in future workshops. In our years of orchestrating and leading such workshops, we've never seen a more popular topic—or a more complex one. Teachers puzzle over myriad questions about grading:

- How can I establish standards and criteria for grading?
- Should I grade on a curve?
- Should effort and improvement count?
- How can I help my students without doing their work for them?
- Which kinds of comments and feedback are most useful for my students' essays, math problems, drawings, or clinical performances?
- How can I handle the workload?
- What should I do about students who seem narrowly focused on just getting the grade?

As teachers ourselves, of biology and English, we've spent nearly every day of our teaching lives wrestling with the problems, the power, and the paradoxes of the grading system. *Effective Grad-*

ing addresses these questions and presents suggestions for making classroom grading more fair, more time-efficient, and more conducive to learning.

Audiences and Purposes

One audience for this book is our faculty colleagues. Another equally important audience is faculty and administrators who share responsibility for assessment in departments or in general education programs. Faculty members often struggle simultaneously to create effective grading systems in their classrooms and effective "assessment" systems in their departments and general education programs. This book addresses the common questions that arise in both classrooms and institutions—how grading can be made more effective in the classroom and how it can contribute to departmental and general education assessment in ways that institutions will find useful and accrediting agencies will applaud.

Relating Classroom Grading to Institutional Assessment

Skillful teachers use grading as a rich process for learning. These faculty begin by thoughtfully considering what they want students to learn. They construct tests and assignments that will both teach and test that learning. They guide the students' learning by carefully selecting laboratory or library experiences, reading and writing assignments, classroom discussion, e-mail correspondences and Web explorations, and sequenced steps that guide students through large projects. They offer feedback to their students in the form of comments and grades. They establish fair, clear standards and criteria, and they apply those criteria consistently to student work. They make grading part of a classroom motivational structure that encourages students to focus on deep learning. They use what they learn from the grading process to improve their teaching. And they call for workshops to help them improve their grading practices.

Yet when institutions are trying to establish the assessment systems required by accrediting agencies and legislatures, the warning that "you can't use grades for assessment" is a common shibboleth. We certainly agree that, as isolated artifacts, grades are not very useful for departmental and general education assessment. We acknowledge the multiple problems that attend the grading system—grade inflation, lack of consistent standards and criteria among courses and institutions, student motivation that focuses too narrowly on grades, and so on. But the grading process, when well employed by skillful teachers, can yield rich information about student learning. Why ignore that information when the department or the general education program is assessing student learning? Why throw out the baby with the bath water? We composed a riddle to make our point: "Which assessment method has nearly universal faculty participation, enjoys superb student participation, is never accused of violating academic freedom, provides detailed diagnostic assessment of student learning, is tightly linked to teaching . . . has a tight feedback loop into classroom learning and into teacher planning, and is cheap to implement? Answer: grading, when it is well done" (Walvoord and Anderson, 1995, p. 8). This book discusses how the grading process may be made more effective in individual classrooms and how the information about student learning that the grading process yields may be used within an institution's assessment plan.

Our Approach to Grading

In order to best help the individual classroom teacher and to make grading useful for departmental and general education assessment, *grading* must be understood as a process that includes all the activities we mentioned: identifying the most valuable kinds of learning in a course, constructing exams and assignments that will test that learning, setting standards and criteria, guiding students' learning, and implementing changes in teaching that are based on information from the grading process. We urge faculty to abandon false hopes that grading can be easy, uncomplicated, uncontested, or one-dimensional. Teachers must manage the power and complexity of the grading system rather than ignore or deny it.

We adopt an approach to grading that we believe will help classroom teachers improve their grading processes and that will help institutions use the grading process within their assessment plans in ways that accrediting agencies will embrace. To accomplish these ends, we place grading within the frame of *classroom research*—a term used for a teacher's systematic attempt to investigate the relationship between teaching and learning in her or his classroom (Cross, 1990) and to use that information to improve teaching and learning. Cecilia López, associate director of the North Central Association's Commission on Institutions of Higher Education, found that the common goals of classroom research and the assessment that regional accreditation agencies want are "compatible and indeed complementary" (1996, p. 1).

Our approach is, above all, learner-centered. When dilemmas arise within the grading process, we urge faculty to first ask what learners need. Our approach also respects students as learners. Acknowledging that all human beings sometimes just want to get by with minimum effort, we believe that most students want more for themselves than that. We believe grading can be part of a rich and positive motivational system, and in *Effective Grading* we suggest how such a system may be implemented.

Our grading system can adapt to the changing roles of faculty in an era of rapid technological advances, decreasing resources, and increasing diversity in student backgrounds. We discuss how grading can serve rather than cripple a teacher's attempt to use methods that involve active learning, peer collaboration, computer-aided instruction, or distance education. The key to this flexibility is that grading must be integral to the entire process of teaching and learning—teachers must consider grading in their first deliberations about a course, not when student work is piled high on the desk.

Overview of the Contents

Chapter One discusses in detail the ways in which our approach to grading can be compatible with "assessment" for regional accreditors. Chapter Two presents twelve principles that can inform the classroom grading process. After these initial two chapters, *Effective Grading* is organized to help faculty follow a course-planning process, which begins when faculty define the kinds of learning they value most and then construct exams and assignments that both teach and test that learning (Chapter Three). Next, the teacher selects teaching methods that enhance student learning and motivation (Chapter Four). Clear criteria and standards for grading must inform not only the final marking of finished work but the entire teaching and learning process (Chapter Five). Systems for calculating course grades convey messages about learning (Chapter Six). One of the most important parts of the process is communicating with students about their work and about their grades (Chapter Seven). To sustain such an ambitious, learning-centered plan, teachers must make the grading process highly time-efficient (Chapter Eight). Finally, the thoughtful teacher uses information gleaned from the grading process to improve student learning in the future (Chapter Nine). Integration of the grading process into the course planning process helps a grading system accommodate teaching methods as varied as collaborative learning, distance education, the World Wide Web, or lecture and discussion.

Chapters Ten through Twelve describe how grading can be part of broader assessment purposes. One of these purposes is to document student learning for a faculty member's promotion, tenure, grants, or publication (Chapter Ten). A second purpose is to show how classroom grading can be a viable part of departmental or general education assessment. Chapter Eleven sets out the basic principles and gives examples. Chapter Twelve documents how one college is using our approach for assessment of its general education program.

Using This Book for Faculty Workshops

Because Chapters Three through Nine follow a course-planning sequence, we include at the end of each of those chapters suggested activities that, taken together, lead faculty members through a process of course planning that will integrate grading with teaching and learning. The activities are to help readers apply to their own course planning the suggestions presented in the chapter. Readers can complete the activities by working individually, but the activities are also designed for use in a workshop setting. Faculty might read each chapter in turn, complete the activities alone or in small groups, and then discuss their plans with each other before moving on to the next chapter.

Collegiality is built into this book, not only through the workshop activities but through the basic assumptions that underlie our suggestions about grading and assessment: (1) faculty are assessing student learning, often in rich and skillful ways, and they want to do it better, and (2) faculty working together can integrate classroom and institutional assessment processes to ask the questions that are natural to all teachers and all learners. Are students learning what they need to know? How can individual classroom teachers, departments, and general education programs best help them learn?

Acknowledgments

Thomas A. Angelo has responded to this manuscript at a number of points and has contributed important ideas to its development, though the authors, of course, take full responsibility for the ways in which we have used his suggestions. We also acknowledge our debt to the hundreds of faculty members with whom we have worked over the years, whose ideas infuse this book, whose generosity has allowed us to use their material, and whose creativity has shown us what good teaching can be.

January 1998

BARBARA E. WALVOORD
Notre Dame, Indiana

VIRGINIA JOHNSON ANDERSON
Towson, Maryland

THE AUTHORS

BARBARA E. WALVOORD is director of the John Kaneb Center for Teaching and Learning and concurrent professor of English at the University of Notre Dame, Indiana. She earned her B.A. degree (1963) in English and Philosophy at Hope College in Holland, Michigan, and her M.A. degree (1964) in English from The Ohio State University. She received her Ph.D. degree (1976) in English from the University of Iowa.

Walvoord was named the 1987 Maryland English Teacher of the Year for Higher Education by the Maryland Council of Teachers of English Language Arts. She was a founder and codirector of the Maryland Writing Project (a site of the National Writing Project) and of the Baltimore-Area Consortium for Writing Across the Curriculum. Before coming to Notre Dame in 1996, she taught English and directed writing-across-the-curriculum programs at Central College in Iowa, at Loyola College in Maryland, and at the University of Cincinnati. Each of those programs won national acclaim. Since 1972 she has been leading faculty workshops across the country on grading, assessment, teaching, learning, and writing.

Her publications include *Academic Departments: How They Work, How They Change* (forthcoming); *In the Long Run: A Study of Faculty in Three Writing-Across-the-Curriculum Programs* (1997); *Thinking and Writing in College: A Study of Students in Four Disciplines* (1991), and *Helping Students Write Well: A Guide for Teachers in All Disciplines* (2nd ed., 1986). She has also published articles and book chapters about grading, assessment, teaching, learning, and writing. Currently in progress is a six-year study of change in the teaching missions of seven academic departments at a large research university. *Making Large Classes Interactive* (1995), a thirty-minute video of which she is co–executive director, has won two national awards.

VIRGINIA JOHNSON ANDERSON is professor of biology at Towson University (TU) in Maryland. As chair of the biology department's assessment committee, she has taken an active role in campus and systemwide university assessment in Maryland, served as an assessment consultant on several National Science Foundation (NSF) projects, and presented formative assessment workshops for the American Society of Microbiologists and U.S. Peace Corps. Joining the TU faculty in 1968 as an instructor, Anderson received her B.S. degree (1960) in biology from Lamar University, her M.S. degree (1966) in science education from the University of Georgia, and her Ed.D. degree (1984) in science education from the University of Maryland.

Since 1985, Anderson has obtained over $500,000 in external grants. She directed the NSF Urban Science Teaching Project in Baltimore City from 1993 to 1996 and since 1997 has been directing the reciprocal Science Success workshops that bring teams of university scientists and science educators from across the nation into Baltimore's urban classrooms to observe, reflect, and collaborate.

Anderson has published in the *Journal of College Science Teaching*, the *Journal of Research in Science Teaching*, *Science Teacher*, the *Journal of College Composition*, and *Assessment Update*. She has presented a number of papers at science education conferences and has coauthored four book chapters with Walvoord.

CHAPTER 1

The Power of Grading for Learning and Assessment

When we (the authors) speak of *grading,* we are not referring to a process of merely bestowing isolated artifacts or final course marks. Rather, we are referring to the *process* by which a teacher assesses student learning through classroom tests and assignments, the *context* in which good teachers establish that process, and the *dialogue* that surrounds grades and defines their meaning to various audiences. Grading, then, includes tailoring the test or assignment to the learning goals of the course, establishing criteria and standards, helping students acquire the skills and knowledge they need, assessing student learning over time, shaping student motivation, feeding back results so students can learn from their mistakes, communicating about students' learning to the students and to other audiences, and using results to plan future teaching methods. When we talk about grading, we have student learning most in mind.

For example, a biology teacher asks students to complete scientific experiments and write them up in scientific report form. She chooses this assignment because it will teach and test her learning goals for the course—goals that she carefully discusses with her students and for which she asks the students to be responsible. She sets clear criteria and standards, and she communicates these to her students. Across the semester, she helps students learn the requisite knowledge and skills. She responds to drafts and to final reports in ways that help students learn from their experiences. And, after grading the set of scientific reports, she thinks, Well, the students did better than last year on experimental design, but they still didn't do very well on graphing data. I wonder if that would improve if I . . . and she plans a new teaching strategy. After turning in her final course grades, she goes to the final faculty meeting of the semester and talks with her colleagues about how skills such as graphing might be introduced earlier in the curriculum.

In short, we view grading as a context-dependent, complex process that serves multiple roles:

- *Evaluation:* the grade purports to be a valid, fair, and trustworthy judgment about the quality of the student's work.

- *Communication:* the grade is a communication to the student, as well as to employers, graduate schools, and others. Grading is also the occasion of (sometimes highly emotional) communication and is thus an important and powerful aspect of the ongoing classroom conversation among students and teachers.

- *Motivation:* grading affects how students study, what they focus on, how much time they spend, and how involved they become in the course. Thus grading is a powerful part of the motivational structure of the course, for better or worse.

- *Organization:* a grade on a test or assignment helps to mark transitions, bring closure, and focus effort for both students and teachers.

In the face of such complexity, we suggest that teachers concentrate on the power of the grading system and that they use that power for learning. We try to show concretely and practically how that may be done.

Departmental and General Education Assessment

We argue in this book that a good departmental or general education assessment program can draw upon the rich information about student learning that the grading process can produce. We define *assessment* as the systematic gathering and analyzing of information to improve student learning. The biology teacher's grading process meets our definition of assessment, and it meets many of the conditions for good assessment that are outlined in the American Association for Higher Education's *Principles of Good Practice for Assessing Student Learning* (see Appendix A). For example, assessment should

- Answer questions that people really care about
- Lead directly to improvement in teaching and learning

- Be embedded in the context of learning
- Take place repeatedly over time

We will show how an assessment program that uses the grading process can also meet the requirements of accrediting agencies. That leads to the question, What are the requirements of these agencies? *Assessment*, as these agencies define it, is not just a classroom practice; it is a national movement with a reform agenda. Its proponents have wanted to force significant changes in the way colleges and universities do business. The assessment movement is based on a paradigm that calls for an institution to

- Define its goals and objectives
- Measure whether those goals and objectives have been met
- Use that information to make improvements
- Assess how the improvements have worked

Faculty are going to have to make their peace with this paradigm and with the need to communicate to outsiders in new ways about student learning. The assessment movement is not just another fad that will go away. Every serious analysis of the current U.S. political and educational scene that we've read points to unmistakable evidence of a changed public mood (Kennedy, 1995). The Age of Accountability has arrived for higher education. No longer do boards, legislatures, and accrediting agencies trust that we faculty are doing a good job with undergraduate education; no longer are they content to leave us alone to set our tests, our criteria, and our measures of student outcomes invisibly in our private classrooms. They want to know what we're doing. State legislatures and boards are asking for mission statements, and they are beginning to base resources on the performance of the mission.

Regional accrediting agencies such as the North Central Association or the Mid-Atlantic Association have been major forces driving assessment nationally. They now require all accredited institutions to

- Assess student learning. Some measures of student learning must be *direct* (that is, the assessment directly measures the student's performance with, for example, a paper, a test, or a clinical procedure). Asking the students what they thought they learned or measuring their job placement rate or polling employers are all *indirect* measures.
- Connect assessment to the mission, goals, and objectives of the college or department.
- Attend to issues of validity and reliability.

- Demonstrate widespread faculty involvement.
- Use assessment information for improvement.
- Integrate assessment with planning and budgeting.

In order to prevent faculty from saying that they already assess student work by grading and then going about their business as usual, assessment proponents in the past have strongly maintained that institutions cannot use grades for assessment. In 1986, the American Council on Education defined *assessment* as "any measure—other than end-of-course grading—by which the college evaluates its students or programs" (El-Khawas, 1986, p. 5).

We agree that grades, particularly final course grades, *as isolated artifacts,* are not particularly useful or appropriate for most contemporary institutional assessment needs. If the criteria, standards, and context for a grade are not known to external audiences, grades convey little information. However, assessment proponents have sometimes been so busy dismissing faculty grades that they have ignored or obscured faculty grading *processes* that are integral to good assessment. In short, they have thrown out the baby with the bath water.

Assessment has been touted as something brand new that must now be created. Though the language of more recent versions has changed, the 1992–93 *Manual for the Evaluation Visit* of the North Central Association shaped attitudes that are still present when it identified *developmental stages* of an institution's progress in assessment, beginning with the stage where the institution resists and has not yet begun the assessment process. At assessment conferences, too, it has been common to hear institutions categorized as "those that have not yet started assessment," despite the fact that the students of such institutions are probably being assessed approximately fifteen times each semester—through a midterm, a final exam, and a paper or project in each of five courses.

When assessment practitioners appear to dismiss assessment already being conducted via classroom grading processes, they convey to faculty that assessment is something *else* they will have to do—something alien, imposed, external. Given such a climate of disregard for classroom activity, and given such obvious preoccupation with external tests and examiners, faculty soon begin thinking of themselves as "us" and assessment coordinators and administrators as "them."

This polarization is harmful and unnecessary. Effective assessment must arise from what happens in classrooms. If effective classroom assessment is not going on now, it is hard to believe that effective departmental or general education assessment will occur in the future.

We faculty have been doing assessment of student learning in our classrooms all along, but we have not seen the need to make it more visible or valued externally. It has been "stealth assessment," so to speak. If we as faculty do not make our learning goals, tests, criteria, and standards explicit and understandable to legislatures, boards, accrediting agencies, and other audiences in ways that meet their needs and concerns, we face the very real possibility that some of the control we currently exercise in our classrooms will be taken from us. We must deal with assessment, but we need not construct a new parallel assessment structure that ignores the assessment we already conduct.

Fortunately, bridges exist that can help us link classroom grading processes to departmental and general education assessment. There is a movement nationally, within assessment practice, to focus on classroom-based modes (Ewell, 1992). Resource 1.1 suggests sources about the so-called "classroom research" movement, where teachers systematically investigate student learning. One articulation of classroom research is the "Classroom Assessment–Classroom Research" (CA-CR) model proposed by Cross, Angelo, Steadman, and others (Angelo, 1991a, 1991b, 1995, 1996; Angelo and Cross, 1993; Cross 1990, 1995; Cross and Angelo, 1988; Cross and Steadman, 1996). CA-CR is "any systematic inquiry designed and conducted for the purpose of increasing insight and understanding of the relationships between teaching and learning" (Cross, 1990, p. 136).

Angelo and Cross's 1992 *Classroom Assessment Techniques* focuses on one aspect of classroom research: how faculty can keep their fingers on the pulse of student learning through frequent, short, ungraded assessments carried out in the classroom. For example, at the end of a class, students write for a minute or two about what was for them the muddiest point in that day's class

---

Resource 1.1.
Sources About Classroom Research.

Cochran-Smith and Lytle, 1993. Theory and practice across grade levels.
Cross and Steadman, 1996. Theory and practice, higher education.
Eisenhard and Borko, 1993. A how-to manual for teachers.
Hubbard and Power, 1993. A how-to manual for teachers.
Karabenick and Collins-Eaglin, 1995. Institutional program to get faculty involved in research.
Rowland and Barton, 1994. Institutional program to get faculty involved in research.
Schratz, 1993. Institutional program to get faculty involved in research.

session. It has been admittedly difficult to tie this *ungraded* assessment to departmental and general education assessment or to help faculty fully embed it in their course planning (Angelo, 1995). As a companion, then, we try to show in this book how *graded* student work can be used for classroom research and for assessment and how graded work can be embedded in course planning to enhance learning. The strategies we promote are an aspect of the "Classroom Research" component of CA-CR. In the hands of good teachers, the grading process can be a systematic collection, analysis, and use of data about learning.

But will assessment conducted as we recommend meet the requirements of the regional accrediting associations? The national assessment movement, like CA-CR, emphasizes careful and systematic collection and use of data about student learning. Cecilia López, associate director of the North Central Association's Commission on Institutions of Higher Education, in a 1996 paper called "Classroom Research and Regional Accreditation: Common Ground," lays out the shared elements of classroom research and regional accreditation: "From my perspective, the purposes and potential value of Classroom Assessment and Classroom Research (CA/CR) and those of assessing student learning now expected of institutions by regional accrediting associations are compatible and, indeed, complementary" (p. 1).

In sum, then, grading and assessment are not polar opposites, nor are they mutually exclusive. The way is open for faculty and institutions to avoid polarization and to integrate the classroom grading process with the kind of departmental and general education assessment that is being demanded today from colleges and universities.

Purpose of the Book

One purpose of this book, especially in Chapters One through Nine, is to help faculty improve their classroom grading processes and to make grading more time-efficient. Chapters Ten through Twelve explain in more detail how departments and institutions can tap the richness of their classroom learning and grading processes to conduct assessment that is useful to the institution and to accrediting agencies. First, however, we address classroom grading, because it yields rich information about student learning and because without skillful *classroom* assessment, it is hard to imagine how effective *institutional* assessment can take place.

PART ONE

Grading in
the Classroom

CHAPTER 2

Managing the Grading Process

"I don't give grades," announced one faculty member in the first few minutes of a workshop Walvoord was leading. The ensuing seconds of dead silence among workshop colleagues contained, among other feelings, awe and envy. When the faculty member recited the many problems with the grading system that had led him to his current stance, there were nods of agreement. However, at the end of the two-day workshop, he was still the only person present who chose to opt out of the grading system.

Grading is deeply embedded in higher education; most faculty will choose, perhaps uncomfortably, to work within its bounds. The challenge is to manage the grading process, not to avoid it.

In Chapter One we argued that grading, when well done, can serve departmental and general education assessment. Now we look at what *well done* means. This chapter analyzes those challenges and suggests twelve basic principles for managing the classroom grading process. Chapters Three through Nine then offer specific advice, organized around the course-planning process. We concentrate on steps that individual faculty members can take in their own classrooms, within the present system, despite its flaws and constraints.

To manage the grading process in their classrooms, faculty must abandon three common false hopes that belie the context and the complexity of the grading process:

1. The false hope of total objectivity in grading
2. The false hope of total agreement about grading
3. The false hope of one-dimensional student motivation for learning

These false hopes embody faculty members' wishes that grading could somehow be freed from its entanglements in the messy, difficult context of the classroom. We faculty members sometimes wish that our only obligation were to pass judgment on a student product. In our dreams, this judgment is securely grounded in incontrovertible standards. It represents an objective and accurate assessment of the product. No one challenges the grade; no one disagrees. Students, in our dreams, ignore the grades we give and concentrate solely on the joy of learning for its own sake.

This leads to our first principle for managing the grading process.

PRINCIPLE 1
Appreciate the Complexity of Grading; Use It as a Tool for Learning

Give up false hopes of a perfect, simple system. Accept that the grading system will have flaws and constraints. But focus on using the power and complexity of the grading process as a tool for learning in your classroom.

If faculty are to use grading as a tool, they need a concept of grading that acknowledges its power and complexity and that suggests additional principles for action. We suggest that grading is a socially constructed, context-dependent process that serves many roles and that, if well managed, can be a powerful tool for learning.

When we say that grading is *socially constructed* and *context-dependent*, we mean that no grade or grading system is immutably right by some eternal standard. People have constructed grading systems to meet the needs and constraints of their situations. Milton, Pollio, and Eison's review of the history of grading (1986) amply demonstrates that grades have had different forms and meanings in different eras of U.S. educational history. The same authors' questionnaire survey of more than six thousand students, faculty, parents, and business recruiters demonstrated that grades hold various meanings for each of these types of people, and they are used differently by each.

Among the respondents were more than forty-three hundred students from twenty-three colleges and universities distributed across types and regions of the United States. The meaning of grades for these students also varied depending on the students' orientation, motivation, previous experiences, and so on. So when you look out across your classroom, you see students for whom your grading system has diverse meanings. You and they are engaged in a system whose context, meanings, and characteristics are changing over time.

Guba and Lincoln (1989) posit that evaluation is not only a judgment that outsiders pass upon inert recipients; evaluation is a socially constructed process with many participants, all of whom help to make it what it is. For example, if the evaluation is to result in improvement, those who have been evaluated have to buy in; *they* have to make the changes. Guba and Lincoln suggest that evaluators abandon the false hope of achieving objective judgment and instead collaborate with the evaluees and other participants to construct a system that serves everyone's needs. The greatest good is not to arrive at an abstractly perfect evaluation—there is no such thing. The greatest good is to serve the needs of the participants and to bring about useful change. Skills in listening, negotiation, cultural understanding, and empathy thus facilitate rather than sabotage the evaluation process.

In their social context, grades play multiple roles that can be managed for the enhancement of learning. We identify four major roles of the grading process—evaluation, communication, motivation, and organization

PRINCIPLE 2
Substitute Judgment for Objectivity

Recognize that there is no such thing as an absolutely objective evaluation based on an immutable standard. Even supposedly objective multiple-choice tests are anything but. The selection of items, the phrasing of questions, the level of difficulty—all these are judgments made by the teacher according to circumstances. As a teacher, your job is to render an informed and professional judgment to the best of your ability. You will want to establish the clearest and most thoughtful criteria and standards that your professional training can supply. You will want to exercise that judgment within the context of your institution, your students, and their future employers.

PRINCIPLE 3
Distribute Time Effectively

Spend enough time to make a thoughtful, professional judgment with reasonable consistency, then move on. There are other aspects of student learning that need your time. Faculty often know from their own observations, and research (Jacobs and Chase, 1992) affirms that teachers in the same discipline will vary in the grades they give to the same student. Even the same professor, a few weeks later, may give the same paper a different grade. Repeatedly reviewing student work will not bring you to the perfectly objective grade.

PRINCIPLE 4
Be Open to Change

The social meaning of grading is changing all the time. Your grades and grading system will be interpreted and used within the system that *is*—not the one you wish for or the one you experienced as a student. For example, the "average" grade in the United States today is in the *B* range. A grade of *C* communicates, therefore, a set of meanings to employers, students, parents, and graduate schools. Because grades are useless apart from the meanings that people impart to them, we suggest you abide by the system of meanings in which you find yourself. Except when issues of integrity and ethics are at stake, it's okay to use French coins in France and Spanish coins in Spain, and it's okay to pay for a hamburger at the current inflated rates, not the rates you paid in the good old days. Grade inflation is a national problem and must be addressed by institutions in concert at the national level. Individual teachers cannot address the problem in isolation; all you can do is use the coin of the realm.

PRINCIPLE 5
Listen and Observe

Focus on understanding and managing the meaning of grades to various kinds of students. A grade does not have the same meaning for students that it has for you, and it means different things to different students. It's the meaning students attach to grades that will most affect learning. Be very clear and explicit to your students about the meanings you attach to grades and the standards and criteria on which you base your grades; don't assume they know. Observe your students and listen to them. In establishing grades, you are not invoking the immutable laws of the universe; you are invoking a set of cultural beliefs and values that will shape the learning potential of your grading process. The better you understand that culture, the better you can manage the grading process for learning.

PRINCIPLE 6

Communicate and Collaborate with Students

The grading process need not provoke antagonism. Fair and helpful evaluation of their work is something learners naturally seek and teachers naturally want to give, because it can help them both. Though external forces limit what can be done, students and teachers can influence the way grading works in their classroom. Research affirms that student-faculty and student-peer interaction powerfully influence student learning (Pascarella and Terenzini, 1991). Try to build in your classroom a spirit of collaborating with your students toward common goals. Explain the criteria and standards you hold for their work and seek their active engagement in the learning process. The following chapters offer specific suggestions for accomplishing this goal.

PRINCIPLE 7

Integrate Grading with Other Key Processes

Grading cannot be separated from planning, teaching, and interacting in your classroom. Don't shove it to the periphery; instead, we suggest making grading integral to everything else you do. Chapters Three through Nine discuss how to coordinate grading within the course planning process.

PRINCIPLE 8

Seize the Teachable Moment

Because grades are highly symbolic, because they reveal and complicate the bases of power in the classroom, because they so powerfully shape interrelationships among students and teacher, and because they often carry high stakes for learners, they will evoke strong emotions. In fact, the learning process itself, like any significant change, can evoke strong emotions in learners and teachers alike.

The years of education are often years of multiple changes for your students. These are sometimes years of great openness, great elasticity. You're in the middle of this learning and growing. You're in the kitchen, as the saying goes, so expect the heat. In fact, we suggest that you welcome the heat. Informal feedback and discussion about grades can be significant events for students, affecting their attitudes and their learning (O'Neill and Todd-Mancillas, 1992). When a student bursts into tears or shouts angrily in your office, don't be flustered or dismayed; be alert and stay focused. What do you want the student to learn in this moment? What memory do you want the student to carry away from this encounter? What values of human life do you want to communicate through this interaction? Such moments of emotional intensity may be the most powerful teaching moments of the semester.

PRINCIPLE **9**
Make Student Learning the Primary Goal

External audiences need information about a student's achievement in a course. While grades are sometimes misused in that context, such a report seems reasonable and necessary in a society where achievement, rather than birth and class, should lead to advancement. Thus you will want to make the fairest and most careful reports you can through grades, letters of recommendation, and other forms.

Sometimes the need for an external report will conflict with the needs of learners in your classroom, but often the needs will be consonant. Learners need reality checks; they need to know how a professional would judge their work. Often a tough judgment, delivered in a supportive way, can be the most helpful feedback you can offer.

When values do clash, we suggest that teachers remember to hold learning, rather than reporting to outsiders, as the most important goal of grading. A survey of more than six thousand students, faculty, parents, and business recruiters showed that while these groups believed that reporting to outsiders was a major focus of grading, they felt that learning should be the main focus (Milton, Pollio, and Eison, 1986). We suggest, then, that when dilemmas arise and values conflict, the teacher should choose the option that will best lead to student learning.

Research suggests that the grading process does significantly affect learning, in ways both beneficial and harmful (Pascarella and Terenzini, 1991). Students study for the tests we give them, seek to meet the standards and criteria we establish, and engage in different kinds of intellectual activity depending on our assignments. Their involvement in learning is in part determined by their perception of faculty members' interest and friendliness toward them, including the fairness and helpfulness of the testing and grading system and the teacher's communication about their work and their grades (Boice, 1996).

Astin (1996), summarizing hundreds of studies of college undergraduates, cites three "conditions of excellence" in student learning and personal development. The most important is the student's *involvement* (that is, "the amount of time and physical and psychological energy that the student invests in the learning process" [p. 124]). As he states, "Literally hundreds of studies of college undergraduates . . . have shown clearly that the greater the student's degree of involvement, the greater the learning and personal development" (p. 124). The other two conditions Astin cites are *high expectations* and *assessment and feedback.* A teacher's testing and grading system is crucial to all of these.

Chickering and Gamson (1987, pp. 3–7) summarize in seven "principles of good practice" what research suggests are the best teaching strategies for student learning.

Good practice in undergraduate education

1. Encourages student-faculty contact
2. Encourages cooperation among students
3. Encourages active learning
4. Gives prompt feedback
5. Emphasizes the time the student devotes to the task
6. Communicates high expectations
7. Respects diverse talents and ways of learning

How many of these principles of good practice in some way involve the grading system in your class, the tests and assignments on which that system is based, and your ways of communicating with students about their work and their grades?

Grading, then, is a powerful lever, capable of influencing the learning in your classroom. We suggest you make learning your primary goal and use grading in all its roles to enhance learning.

PRINCIPLE **10**
Be a Teacher First, a Gatekeeper Last

One function of the U.S. educational system, and especially its grading system, is to act as gatekeeper: to sort out those who aspire to advancement, allowing some students to move forward and keeping others in place. But in a just society, in a meritocracy, the sorting should happen only after everyone has had an equal chance to learn and should be based on what people have been able to learn.

School is the bridge between learning and gatekeeping. If we as teachers operate, explicitly or implicitly, as though our students were already sorted when they came to us—either by ability, talent, former learning, gender, race, or other factors—then we serve only the gatekeeping function. We must be gatekeepers at the end of the process, not at the beginning. Our entire effort, throughout the semester, should be pointed toward understanding our students, believing in them, figuring out what they need, and helping them to learn, no matter what their backgrounds.

PRINCIPLE 11
Encourage Learning-Centered Motivation

Grading is a powerful part of the motivational structure of the course. Student motivation is a key factor in student learning. Students are most affected by their engagement with you and with others and by the values of the campus community. Engaging and connecting with your students is a way to increase their motivation for learning. Further, you must battle against ingrained ideas that some of your students may hold: that they are powerless to affect what happens to them; that hard work will not pay off; that success is due to luck, and failure is due to circumstances beyond their control. Research suggests that these attitudes toward grades, more than the grades themselves, negatively affect students' motivation to learn (Milton, Pollio, and Eison, 1986).

PRINCIPLE 12
Emphasize Student Involvement

This principle summarizes all the others. As we mentioned earlier, student involvement is the bottom line for learning (Astin, 1985; Pascarella and Terenzini, 1991). Throughout this book we urge that, in every aspect of your teaching and grading, you seek meaningful student involvement—that is, the student's investment of time and energy in the academic enterprise.

These twelve suggestions do not eliminate all the problems with the grading system in classrooms and institutions. They do, however, provide a focus for faculty attention and energy—a focus that helps faculty construct classroom grading systems that are conducive to learning and that also, as the final chapters of this book explain, create information about student learning that can be used for departmental and general education assessment.

The twelve principles in this chapter underlie the more specific suggestions we make and the course-planning process through which we lead the reader in the next chapters. We discuss selecting assignments and exams that will both teach and test the learning you most care about (Chapter Three); helping and motivating students to learn what they need to know to do well on the assignments and exams (Chapter Four); establishing criteria and standards for grading (Chapter Five); calculating course grades (Chapter Six); communicating with students about their grades (Chapter Seven); making the grading process time-efficient (Chapter Eight); and using the grading process to improve teaching (Chapter Nine).

CHAPTER 3

Making Assignments Worth Grading

The way to save time, make every moment count, and integrate grading, learning, and motivation is to plan your grading from the first moment you begin planning the course and to consider not only how you will shape goals but how your students will. To do otherwise—to regard grading as an afterthought—is to create wasted time, dead-end efforts, and post-hoc rationalizations as students question their grades. The first step in course planning is to make sure that the assignments and tests assess the learning you and your students most want to achieve. Such planning makes the time you spend grading exams and assignments worthwhile.

To help ensure that your time is well spent and that your grading leads to learning, we present six suggestions we have found most helpful for ourselves and for the faculty in our workshops. The suggestions follow a course-planning sequence:

1. Begin by considering what you want your students to learn.

2. Select tests and assignments that both teach and test the learning you value most.

3. Construct a course outline that shows the nature and sequence of major tests and assignments.

4. Check that the tests and assignments fit your learning goals and are feasible in terms of workload.

5. Collaborate with your students to set and achieve goals.

6. Give students explicit directions for their assignments.

We now explore each of these suggestions in detail.

SUGGESTION 1
Consider What You Want Your Students to Learn

Effective grading practices begin when the teacher says to herself, By the end of the course, I want my students to be able to. . . . Concrete verbs such as *define, argue, solve,* and *create* are more helpful for course planning than vague verbs such as *know* or *understand* or passive verbs such as *be exposed to.* If you write, "I want students to think like economists," elaborate on what that means. How does an economist think? Which aspects of that thinking do you want to cultivate in students?

When asked what he wanted students to be able to do by the end of his Western Civilization course, here's how John Breihan, who teaches history at Loyola College in Maryland, responded. Using data gathered during a study of Breihan's classroom (Walvoord and Breihan, 1991), we'll follow more of Breihan's course planning, teaching, and grading practices in this and subsequent chapters.

At the end of Western Civilization [a 100–level general education course for first-year students], I want my students to be able to

- Describe basic historical events and people
- Argue as a historian does:
  Take a position on a debatable historical issue
  Use historical data as evidence for the position
  Raise and answer counterarguments

Here's an example from a math professor:

At the end of this math course, I want my students to be able to

- Solve [certain kinds of] mathematical problems
- Explain what they're doing as they solve a problem and why they're doing it

An instructor in a dental hygiene department responded this way:

At the end of the course, I want my students to

- Pass the state and federal board questions which deal with my area
- Demonstrate habits of critical thinking and problem solving
- Establish trust and cooperation with their patients

Here are examples from other teachers:

- A speech pathologist wrote that she wanted her students to "synthesize information from various sources to arrive at intervention tactics for the client."
- An economist wanted students to "use economic theory to explain government policies and their effects."
- A faculty member in design had the goal of helping students "analyze a design problem."
- A physicist was helping students "be able to state physical concepts in their own words and discuss what they don't know."
- Another physicist aspired to have students "exit with a sense of wonder."

Walvoord tried to describe *creativity* for a first-year composition essay:

> By the end of this course, I want my students to write a clear, coherent, well-organized and well-informed essay that gives the reader a sense of focus and that is also creative—that is, it does not merely state the obvious or sound cut-and-dried. Instead, the student shows creativity by making unusual connections, looking at something in a fresh way, noticing unusual relationships or aspects of the topic, pushing beyond surface observations, challenging what others take for granted, or taking a risk with a rhetorical technique, an unpopular idea, or a difficult topic.

Don't be afraid at this stage to write down goals you may not be able to measure exactly. Our favorite ineffable goal came from a faculty workshop participant in a swine management department. She established several specific objectives for her students such as "outline a financial plan for a swine operation." But at the end she wrote that she wanted her students to "appreciate the pig." She said, "I can't measure that, and I don't know how to test it, but it's important to me and my students, and I won't give it up!" We didn't think she should. Several of her workshop colleagues volunteered ideas (not all of them completely serious, we'll admit) about how she could measure her students' appreciation of the pig. Despite the hilarity, the point was serious: when you have goals that are ineffable but important, don't let the quest for measurable or behavioral objectives dissuade you from those goals. Do your best to pin down how you recognize those qualities in student work. You may not be able to measure or grade everything that you care about, but at this early planning stage, we urge you to include your most precious goals. The sources in Resource 3.1 will help with concepts and phrasing to describe various kinds of student learning.

Resource 3.1.

Sources to Describe Learning Goals and Objectives.

All Disciplines

Angelo and Cross, 1993. Based on responses from nearly three thousand faculty members, Chapter Two presents fifty-two possible learning goals and a worksheet for faculty to identify and rank their own goals.

Association of American Colleges, 1985. Competencies of educated persons.

Belenky, Clinchy, Goldberger, and Tarule, 1986. Stages of women's intellectual development.

Bloom, 1956. Taxonomy of educational objectives both intellectual and affective. (See also Tittle and others, 1993.)

Bowen, 1977. Analysis and classification of the outcomes of higher education.

Ennis, 1987. Aspects of critical thinking.

Facione, 1990. A panel of forty-six experts identifies characteristics of critical thinking.

Gardiner, 1994. Review of research lists key student competencies identified by business, government, and educational leaders.

Gardner, 1983. Proposes a theory of multiple intelligences; implies new types of learning goals for education.

Greenwood (ed.), 1994. In preparation for national assessment of college students' learning, authors identify competencies in citizenship, critical thinking, problem solving, speaking and listening, reading and writing. (See especially p. 73 ["Seven Dispositions/Abilities for Good Thinking"], p. 75 ["Some Basic Problem Types"], and pp. 94–97 [References].)

Harrow, 1972. Behavioral objectives for psychomotor skills.

Jacobi, Astin, and Ayala, 1987. Taxonomies of talent development.

Jones and others, 1995. Reports a study of the views of faculty, employers, and policy makers on essential skills.

Mentkowski and Strait, 1983. Learning objectives and assessment at Alverno College. (Also ask for updated materials on learning and assessment at Alverno.)

National Center for Education Statistics, 1995. Attempt to identify skills that college graduates should possess in writing, speaking, listening, and critical thinking.

National Standards Project, forthcoming. The U.S. Department of Education, other federal agencies, and foundations have made grants to major professional and scholarly organizations to develop voluntary national standards for K–12 students in different subjects (math, arts, civics and government, geography, history, science, English, foreign languages). There are separate standards for content and performance. The standards are quite controversial, but they do provide language to describe what students should be able to do, and that language can be useful at the college level.

Perry, 1970. Stages of the intellectual and moral development of Harvard males.

Powers and Enright, 1987. Reports a study of faculty views on skills needed for graduate study.

Rest and Narvaez (eds.), 1994. Articles on moral development in the professions.

Rock, 1991. Ways to measure and teach higher-order cognitive skills.

Tittle, Hecht, and Moore, 1993. Updates Bloom.

Individual Disciplines

Search the ERIC database, using as descriptors
- One or more of these subject headings:
  Competence
  Competency-Based Education
  Critical Thinking
  Education Outcomes
  Educational Assessment
  Educational Objectives
  Employment Qualifications
  Evaluation
  Evaluation Criteria
  Thinking Skills
- U.S.
- The level of education you want to include (such as higher education)
- The name of your discipline (For areas such as art, history, and health, which will be used in many contexts, add the word *education* [for example, *art education, health education*] or the word *instruction* [for example *history instruction, mathematics instruction*]. For English, use *college English* or *writing* [*composition*] or *literature.*)

Here are some references that emerged from such a search:

Science, Math, Engineering

American Association for the Advancement of Science, 1993
Lawson, Abraham, and Renner, 1989
Shavelson, 1991

Career and Technical

Felstehausen, 1995

Business

Sormunen, 1992

SUGGESTION **2**
Select Assignments and Tests That Measure What You Value Most

Because grading is perhaps one of the most labor-intensive things faculty do, why spend the time grading work that doesn't address your most important goals? Try to ensure that any assignments, tests, and exams that you give and grade will teach and test the knowledge and skills you most want students to learn.

Some research indicates that many faculty do not achieve a good fit between the learning they say they want and the tests and assignments they actually give:

> Faculty often state that they are seeking to develop students' abilities to analyze, synthesize, and think critically. However, research indicates that faculty do not follow their good intentions when they develop their courses. A formal review and analysis of course syllabi and exams revealed that college faculty do not in reality focus on these advanced skills but instead are far more concerned with students' abilities to acquire knowledge, comprehend basic concepts or ideas and terms, and apply this basic knowledge [National Center for Education Statistics, 1995, p. 167].

To ensure that your assignments and tests are assessing the learning you most care about, we suggest you use the sources listed in Resource 3.2, which includes a fuller treatment.

In this section we emphasize three main concepts that appear crucial to the validity and the motivational power of your tests and assignments:

1. *Choose assignments that are likely to elicit from your students the kind of learning you want to measure.* A combination of careful forethought, knowledge of your own students, and analysis of your students' work are the keys here. For example, the mathematician we mentioned who wanted his students to solve problems and explain the process realized that his existing testing and grading were putting too much emphasis on merely getting the right answers. So he added a requirement to some of his assignments and exams: students had to draw a vertical line down the center of a page, dividing it into two columns. In one column they solved the problem. In the opposite column they wrote in sentences, for each step, what they did and why they did it.

A psychologist with whom we worked wanted students to think critically. She was very proud of herself for giving essay tests—not just multiple-choice tests—in an introductory psychology course with a class of ninety students and no TA (teaching assistant). But when, in a workshop, she looked carefully at her grading processes and criteria, she saw that she was judging primarily mastery of facts,

Resource 3.2.

Sources About Assignment and Test Construction.

Adelman (ed.), 1989. Oriented to natural science and technology.

Anderson, Ball, Murphy, and Associates, 1975. Comprehensive encyclopedia, including technical aspects of test design.

Bloom, Hastings, and Madaus, 1971. On assessing the learning outcomes defined in Bloom, 1956.

Boud, Dunn, and Hegarty-Hazel, 1986. On laboratory skills.

Carey, 1994. General textbook on measurement and evaluation with sections on designing and using multiple choice, essay, and other types of assessment.

Cashin, 1987. Short summary on improving essay tests.

Clegg and Cashin, 1986. Short summary on improving multiple-choice tests.

Dressel, 1976. Includes sections on basic considerations and on evaluating student experience and educational progress.

Facione, 1990. Assessing and teaching critical thinking.

Feinberg, 1990. Strengths and weaknesses of multiple-choice tests.

Haladyna, 1994. On developing and validating multiple-choice tests.

Jacobs and Chase, 1992. Handbook for faculty on test construction, validity, and reliability; advice for various types of tests. Includes section on computer-assisted testing.

Linn, 1993. Standard reference. Covers theories and principles; construction, administration, and scoring; and applications.

Lowman, 1995 and 1996. General overview of testing and assignment-making, with special attention to motivation. (See in particular pp. 184–209 in the 1995 listing.)

McKeachie, 1994. Contains advice on testing.

Meyers, 1986. How to test critical thinking.

Milton, Pollio, and Eison, 1986. Especially good on relationship between testing and student motivation.

Owens and Clegg, 1984. Tips for writing tests.

Rock, 1991. How to test higher-order cognitive skills.

Scriven, 1991. Suggests replacing multiple choice with "multiple rating" formats, in which the student rates each member of a set. Claims this format avoids weaknesses of multiple-choice format.

Tobias, 1996. Based on previous studies of science departments, science teaching, and science students, recommends new practices for in-class exams in college-level science.

Weinstein, Goetz, and Alexander, 1988. Links testing to learning and study strategies.

Yelon and Duley, 1978. Assessing students' field experiences.

vocabulary, and basic concepts. She promptly instituted a multiple-choice test for that elementary knowledge, and she focused her valuable grading and responding time on a take-home essay that truly elicited synthesis and evaluation from the learners.

Pay attention to what you name your assignments and tests and what those names mean to your students. A sociologist was asking for a "term paper" from his students and getting encyclopedia-based reports that did not meet his goals for the assignment. In a workshop, when asked to define what he really wanted, he realized he wanted a review of the literature, so he began to call it that. Two positive results ensued. First, students no longer imported notions of the term paper as an encyclopedia-based pastiche of paraphrased material on a topic; they had never written a review of the literature before, so they knew they had to listen very carefully to his instructions about the assignment. Second, he was forced to clarify for them and for himself what he meant and to teach them how to write a review of the literature.

Pay attention also to how polished or finished an assignment must be in order to fulfill your goals. A political scientist has his students construct a set of questions for a major term paper, compile an annotated bibliography, then write the introduction—but he does not have students complete the whole paper. He says, "By the time they've done the annotated bibliography and the introduction, they've learned what I most want them to learn."

The most important point is that a test or an assignment is a valid measurement only if it elicits from your students the kinds of learning you want to measure.

2.   *Choose assignments that are interesting and challenging to your students.* The kinds of assignments and tests you give will influence students' motivation (Baird, 1987; Lowman, 1995, 1996). Consider creative kinds of assignments without being carried away by something "cute" that doesn't meet your needs. For example, an American historian asked students to write diary entries for a hypothetical Nebraska farm woman in the 1890s. He liked this assignment because it required that students know about economics, social class, transportation, gender roles, technology, family relations, religion, diet, and so on; yet it also gave students a chance to use their imaginations. He found that if he was explicit about his desire for them to use the diary to display the breadth of their historical knowledge, the assignment achieved his learning goals in an enjoyable way (see Appendix B for a list of types of assignments; see also Gibbs, Habeshaw, and Habeshaw, 1986).

3.   *Use peer collaboration.* Do not automatically consider that every test or assignment must be completed by the individual student in isolation; consider assignments and tests that students complete in groups. An obvious advantage is that if students com-

plete an assignment in groups of four, you have one-fourth as many pieces of work to grade; but collaborative assignments can also have strong pedagogical and motivational advantages. One advantage is the power of peer interaction. As Astin (1996) puts it, summarizing his comprehensive study of factors that influence college students' learning, "The strongest single source of influence on cognitive and affective development [in college] is the student's peer group. . . . [T]he study strongly suggests that the peer group is powerful because it has the capacity to *involve* the student more intensely in the educational experience" (p. 126). Assignments that get students involved with one another and with the teacher may draw on this powerful force. Further, when well managed, collaborative work can increase students' sense of their own control and power in the classroom (Perry, Menec, and Struthers, 1996).

The evidence for the potential of collaborative work to enhance student learning is so strong that a group of scholars, reviewing the literature on student learning and pedagogy, included cooperation among students as one of seven "principles of good practice" for undergraduate education (Chickering and Gamson, 1987). When poorly managed, however, collaborative assignments can decrease students' sense of control and increase their anxiety and anger. Careful planning and guidance of students is crucial to success.

Suggestions for designing and managing collaborative assignments can be found in the literature on collaborative learning or cooperative learning—increasingly, the two terms are used to distinguish two ways of managing group learning. Resource 3.3 offers some sources.

Resource 3.3.

Sources About Collaborative and Cooperative Learning.

Bosworth and Hamilton (eds.), 1994.

Cooper and others, 1990. Cooperative learning.

Goodsell and others (eds.), 1992. Sourcebook on collaborative learning.

Johnson and Johnson, 1996. Aimed at K–12 but adaptable for higher education. Addresses issues of assessing and using cooperative learning.

Johnson, Johnson, and Smith, 1991. Cooperative learning.

Matthews, 1996. Collaborative learning.

McKeachie, 1994. Chapter on peer learning, collaborative learning, and cooperative learning.

Millis and Cottell, 1997. Cooperative learning.

Slavin, 1995. Cooperative Learning.

Thinking Together, 1992. Videotape.

The most important principle to remember is that successful group assignments are those that can be better done by the group than by an individual student. You must build into the task the qualities that will make it more productive for students to work together than to work alone. If you do that, the group's motivation to work together, to solve group tensions, and to deal effectively with "free riders" (that is, nonparticipating students) will be strong.

SUGGESTION 3
Construct a Course Outline

Once you have decided the type of assignment or test you will give to students and its general features, the next step is to combine all your tests and assignments into a bare-bones course "skeleton" or outline so that you can see a broad profile of the course and can ask some important questions.

The course skeleton helps you see whether your assignments fit your course goals and whether they are manageable in terms of work load. The course skeleton helps you put together an "assignment-centered course." *Assignment* here can mean a test, an exam, a project—any student task that teaches and tests student learning. Research suggests that the assignment-centered course enhances students' higher order reasoning and critical thinking more effectively than the courses centered around text, lecture, and coverage (Kurfiss, 1988).

In the assignment-centered model, the teacher begins not by asking, What should I cover in this course? but What should my students learn to do? Coverage does not disappear under the assignment-centered model: basic facts, concepts, and procedures are still important; lectures may be used as a pedagogical device; textbooks may be assigned and read. However, the course planning process begins by focusing on the assignments, tests, and exams that will both teach and test what the teacher most wants students to know. The rest of the course is then structured to help students learn what they need to know if they are to do well on the tests and assignments. The course skeleton helps teachers achieve this initial focus on student learning.

To illustrate the difference between the assignment-centered model and the coverage-centered model, imagine a hypothetical teacher planning a Western Civilization course that is a general education requirement for first-year students. The hypothetical professor might first begin to think about the course when her department head says, "Jane, will you teach 'Western Civ' this fall?" She next checks (or composes) the catalogue description, which tells the content of the course: Western Civilization from

1500 to the end of the Cold War, emphasizing such-and-such themes. Now she plans the fifteen weeks, saying to herself, Let's see. I'd like to use Burke and Paine, Marx, Lafore, and *Heart of Darkness* in addition to the textbook. I'll cover 1500 to 1800 in six weeks and get through the French Revolution by midterm. Then in the second half of the course, I'll cover 1800 to the present. Her outline of the course might look like this:

Week	Topic
1	Renaissance and Reformation
2	Seventeenth-Century Crisis
3	Absolutism
4	Age of Reason
5	French Revolution
6	Burke, *Reflections,* and Paine, *Rights of Man*
7	MIDTERM
8	Industrial Revolution
9	Marx, *Communist Manifesto*
10	Imperialism
11	Conrad, *Heart of Darkness*
12	World War I
13	Lafore, *Long Fuse*
14	World War I, World War II, and the Cold War
15	FINAL

Note that in her conversation with herself, the subject of her sentences is *I*. The most common verb is *cover*. This teacher is already well launched on the coverage-centered model. Next, she will compose her syllabus. It will go something like this:

> Tues., Sept. 5: Social and religious background of the Renaissance and Reformation. Read ch. 1 and 2 in textbook.
>
> Thurs., Sept. 7: Economic and political background of the Renaissance and Reformation. Read ch. 3 in textbook; Machiavelli handout.

When students first see this syllabus, they are likely to assume that in class the teacher will tell them about the topics. They might also assume that they need not necessarily read the chapter before they come to class, because the teacher will lecture. Thus the traditional course-planning process and the syllabus that results from it can trap both the faculty member and the students into the coverage-centered model.

Assessment in this coverage-centered scheme is also problematic. Once the teacher has filled in the topics she has to cover, she is likely to say to herself, I'll use essay tests at midterm and final, with questions on lecture, textbook, and supplementary readings.

The midterm will cover 1500 to 1800. I'll have a comprehensive final, covering all the course material, but I'll weight it in favor of 1800 to the present. And I'll assign a term paper due near the end of the course. Students can choose which of the supplementary readings they'll cover in their term papers.

In this coverage-centered planning process, the tests and papers are added at the end, and their implied role is to test coverage.

When asked what she wants students to achieve at the end of the course, this faculty member is likely to say that she wants students not merely to describe events but also to analyze and construct arguments about historical issues. However, her exams and term paper are not likely to elicit coherent arguments with full evidence and answers to counterarguments. Essay exams may be merely what one teacher calls "fact dumps." Research indicates that many students experience school reading as a collection of discrete facts to be memorized and regurgitated on tests (Geisler, 1994). Further, some students have taken essay exams that were graded in this way: the teacher went through the student's answer, placing a check mark next to every fact or idea that "counted," and the student's score was the total of the check marks. The smart person's way of taking such a test is to dump as much information as possible as quickly as possible. Moreover, if the students see the exam question for the first time when they walk into the class and then have twenty minutes or fifty minutes to write a cogent argument, are they likely to produce a cogent, tightly argued, thoroughly logical essay?

There might also be problems in this class with the term paper. Students might submit cut-and-paste pastiches of library sources, following the "term paper" models they learned in other settings. Schwegler and Shamoon (1982) found that students they surveyed often described the term paper or research paper as a collection and combination of sources, not as an exploration, an analysis, or an argument. The term *term paper* may carry undesirable meanings for your students.

The true failure of the coverage-centered course is the set of assumptions it fosters about what school means:

- Sitting in lecture taking down what teachers say
- Studying lecture notes and the textbook the night before the test
- Regurgitating the right answers on the test

As part of a research project Walvoord and others conducted (Walvoord, McCarthy, and others, 1991), a student interviewed described to the interviewer her expectations on the first day of a

Western Civilization course: "I remember going in there thinking, O.K., this is just a basic history course, you know. It's not going to be a lot of work; you know what I mean. It's just going to be basically all lecture, and then I'm going to have to restate what he told me on an exam" (p. 99). Another student said, "I haven't done things like this before. In high school we took the answers straight from the book. I am not in the habit of developing arguments" (p. 102). The coverage-centered course may affirm these students' notions of the educational process.

In contrast, the assignment-centered model provides ways to address these problems. To see what an assignment-centered course might look like, let's examine Breihan's Western Civilization course skeleton (Exhibit 3.1). The information we present here comes from a course he taught and Walvoord observed. (The success for student learning was documented in Walvoord and Breihan, 1991.)

First, notice that there is no term paper. Instead, Breihan concentrated on three argumentative essays. He gave students the essay questions ahead of time so they could prepare, rather than write hastily to answer a question they had not seen before. He fashioned questions that would require them to synthesize what they had studied.

To keep them from merely copying sources, he asked them to draft an essay in class without notes. Then he responded to the drafts, and students revised their essays out of class and resubmitted them. For the first essay, revision was mandatory. For the second, it was optional. For the third (the final exam), it was not possible.

In his assignment-centered course skeleton, Breihan focused on a type of assignment that he believed had the best chance of eliciting from his students the careful arguments he most valued. He kept the paper load manageable. He structured the writing experiences so that students had the time and conditions necessary to produce coherent arguments. (The skeleton does not include minor assignments such as response to reading, map quizzes, and the like.)

We suggest that you begin your course planning in this same way. Your discipline may be quite different from history—you may have labs or clinics in addition to class. But the same principle applies: state what you want your students to learn, then list the major assignments and tests that will both teach and test that learning. You will want to describe the basic type of test or assignment and perhaps a few of the most salient characteristics. If you are planning multiple-choice exams, problem-solving exams, or short-answer exams, include a summary of the skills and knowledge that

Exhibit 3.1.   Skeleton for 100–Level Western Civilization Course.

I want my students to define and describe historical events.

Most of all, I want my students to use historical data to develop the elements of an argument:

- Taking a position
- Backing the position with evidence
- Answering counterarguments

1	9
2	10 Same, but on Industrial Revolution and Imperialism
3	11
4	12
5	13
6 Argumentative essay on Age of Reason, French Revolution	14
7	15 Same, but on World War I, World War II, and the Cold War
8	

Exhibit 3.2.   Skeleton for Senior Biology Course.

I want my students to use the scientific method to conduct original scientific research and to communicate their research orally and in writing to the scientific community.

1	9
2	10
3	11 Original scientific research project, presented in written and oral reports
4	12
5	13
6	14
7	15 Grant proposal
8	

the exam will test. List only the major exams and tests. At this early stage, you do not want to list the smaller classroom tasks that support the completion of your major assignments. In fact, it is possible to have a course skeleton that contains only one or two major assignments. For example, Exhibit 3.2 is the course skeleton for Anderson's senior-level biology course. There will be many smaller assignments, activities, tests, and quizzes along the way, but Anderson helps herself to concentrate on the essentials by making a skeleton that shows just the assignments and tests she cares about the most.

SUGGESTION 4
Check Tests and Assignments for Fit and Feasibility

As you examine your assignment-centered course skeleton, ask yourself two questions regarding fit and feasibility:

1. *Fit:* Do my tests and assignments fit the kind of learning I most want?

2. *Feasibility:* Is the workload I am planning for myself and my students reasonable, strategically placed, and sustainable?

Let's examine several course skeletons that were problematic. What do you see as the major problem with the course skeleton in Exhibit 3.3?

Laying out his course in this skeletal way helped the sociology professor realize that his tests and exams did not very well fit the learning he most wanted. Students were likely to study all night before the exams, using their texts and class notes, a procedure not likely to elicit thoughtful application of sociological perspectives to what they saw around them. The term paper was likely to appear to them as a library exercise, also unrelated.

The professor decided to change his assignments to fit more closely with what he wanted students to learn. He abandoned the term paper and the exams and instead asked his students, every other week, to write a journal in which they applied sociological analysis to something they had observed. However, the word *journal,* as he discovered the next semester, was a mistake: students interpreted the term too loosely and did not give him the rigorous sociological analysis he wanted. So he renamed the assignment *sociological analysis.* He explained that he wanted students to analyze some event or situation they observed in light of the sociological viewpoints they had been studying.

For example, suppose students had been studying the writings of French sociologist Émile Durkheim. A student attended his

Exhibit 3.3.   Problematic Skeleton for an Introductory Sociology Course.

Students: Primarily nonmajors fulfilling general education requirements.

I want my students to be able to apply sociological analysis to what they see around them.

1	9
2	10
3	11
4	12
5	13
6	14 Term paper
7	15 Final exam: essay and objective
8 Midterm exam: essay and objective	

Exhibit 3.3.   Problematic Skeleton for an Introductory Sociology Course.

cousin's bar mitzvah. For his analysis that week, the student might ask himself, What would Durkheim make of this? The professor stated three criteria for the analysis: (1) the student had to summarize accurately the sociological perspective—in this case, Durkheim's views; (2) the student had to include the kinds of specific details that sociologists observe (it did not suffice to say "the food was great"); and (3) the student had to link the theories and the observations in a reasonable and thoughtful way, applying Durkheim's perspective to the bar mitzvah.

These changes helped the sociology professor not only fit his assignments and tests to student learning but also spread the workload across the semester.

Exhibit 3.4 is another example of a course skeleton in trouble—this time because of workload. When asked about fit, this professor affirmed his current choice of the case method, saying, "I know there is some controversy in my field about whether the case method really does teach decision making, but it works as well as anything I know." The real problem was that, as this class grew to forty students, the professor said he was "going to die" if he couldn't get a handle on the paper load.

Colleagues in a workshop asked him, "Can the students write fewer cases?" He answered, "No, there are eight units in the course. I can't drop a unit because students need all of them, and they are all mandated by our business accrediting agency. And if they don't write on each unit, they don't learn it." Then colleagues asked, "Do students need to do a full five- to eight-page case study each time?" That question was the solution to the workload problem.

The business professor began to ponder whether, for some of the full case studies, especially early in the course, he could design shorter assignments that would help students learn what they needed. He had long recognized that there was a cohort of students in his class who wrote one mediocre case study after another. The papers were coming at him so fast, and there were so many of them, that he didn't have time to give these students the guidance they needed to improve, so next time they repeated their mistakes.

In particular, he noted that weaker students tended to stay too close to the chronological order of the case materials. Students were given sales figures, a history of the firm, interviews with employees and managers, descriptions of the firm's branches, copies of relevant legislation that governed the firm's operations, and so on, all in deliberately random order. Some students read through this case material, making suggestions along the way but never fully transcending its sequence.

A second but related problem was that students tended to recommend low-level "band-aid" solutions. They would say, "This

Exhibit 3.4.   Problematic Skeleton for Business Management Course.

I want my students to make business decisions, using the tools we have been studying.

1

2 Written case analysis

3

4 Written case analysis

5

6 Written case analysis

7

8 Written case analysis

9 Written case analysis

10

11 Written case analysis

12

13 Written case analysis

14

15 Written case analysis as final exam

person and that person need to talk to one another more often," or "The company should put more resources into its aluminum business," but they would not see the deeper underlying structural problems.

What could this professor do, in a one-page assignment in week two, to help students with these problems? The professor tried having students write down the single most important problem they saw in that week's case and then list three pieces of evidence from the case out of chronological order. However, he found that, so early in the semester, students could not yet identify the underlying problem. So he focused the first assignments on building-block skills. In the very first assignment, in week two, he asked students to analyze the life stage of the business (a topic they had covered in the textbook). Was the business in question an infant business? A mature business? They had studied the kinds of problems typically associated with these life stages, so he asked them to place the business in its appropriate stage and then ask whether it exhibited problems typical for that stage. In so doing, he propelled them out of a read-and-suggest mode and gave them a larger conceptual framework. He also facilitated their use of the language by which business professionals describe the basic, underlying problems of businesses. In the fourth week, he asked them for another short but more complex assignment, and he proceeded this way until in the eighth week they wrote their first full case analysis. The teacher reported that the cases were now better than before.

A biologist used the same principle in a different form. Weekly lab reports were killing him; yet, like the business teacher, he was reluctant to give up having his students write for each lab. He realized that some of his students were writing twelve mediocre lab reports; they never seemed to get the reports right, and he had to read and grade all those repetitively mediocre works. He finally asked himself, What do I want? and answered, I want students to learn to produce *a good* lab report—not twelve mediocre lab reports. So he decided to teach lab report writing more thoroughly and to use short, well-sequenced assignments to build students' skills. Instead of asking for a full lab report on each lab, he would require, on the first two labs, that students write just the first section, the Introduction. He would concentrate on helping students do that section well. Then, for the next two labs, he would ask for the Introduction and the Methods and Materials section, and so on through the parts of the scientific report. He not only cut his paper load that way but was able to give more focused instruction to help his students master one section at a time. By the end of the semester, they were writing complete reports that he judged to be substantially better than those he had received in earlier semesters.

A literature teacher used a similar principle of substituting shorter and less formal assignments for longer, more formal ones. She came up with the concept of the "start." On each major unit of the course, she asked her students to do a one- or two-page "start" for an essay of literary analysis. The "start" might be a thesis sentence that captured the main idea of the planned essay, and then an outline. If students did not feel comfortable outlining, the "start" could be a freewrite, a list of ideas, or a draft of the introductory paragraphs of the planned paper. These "starts" were treated as informal writing and were discussed in class. About two-thirds through the semester, the instructor asked students to choose their strongest "start" and begin working it into a polished paper of literary analysis. In this way, she kept them writing on every significant piece of literature, thus enhancing their learning, and she also worked intensively with them, over time, to help them shape good essay ideas. She gave limited ongoing response to their weekly work, partly in class and partly through written comments, but she only had to fully grade and mark one long, finished formal essay.

At the end of this chapter is an activity that asks you to sketch out an assignment-centered course skeleton. When you have completed your skeleton and asked your questions, you will have taken the key initial steps toward saving time in the grading process, integrating grading with learning and motivation, and enhancing students' learning with the assignment-centered approach.

SUGGESTION 5
Collaborate with Your Students to Set and Achieve Goals

So far, we've been imagining the planning you do before you meet any of your students, and we've acted as though your goals are the only ones in your classroom. There is another powerful set of goals at work in your classroom—your students' goals. Some faculty like to defer final establishment of the goals and syllabus until they meet with students once or twice, to let the students help set the goals of the course. But even if you take the liberty of establishing the goals without direct student input, you must find out about and relate to the goals your students have when they arrive. Ask them on the first day of class what they think the purpose of the class is and what they want to learn from it. Respond to their revelations. Through discussion, try to reach agreement and clear understanding about the goals of the course and the reasons for your major assignments and tests. Then ask students to write down their personal goals for learning in the course and some strategies by which they think they can accomplish those goals.

Ask them to recall the most successful course they've had in the past. What strategies worked for them there? Can they use or adapt those strategies for your class?

SUGGESTION 6
Make Assignment and Test Instructions Clear to Students

Once you have assignments and tests that assess what you most want your students to learn, it is time to ensure that your instructions will be clear to students. Students will complete the assignment they think you made, not the assignment you actually made. With sketchy or ambiguous instructions, you run the risk of having students draw on previous learning that may not be relevant or desirable in your situation. Students' propensity to do that was documented in an investigation in which Flower and her colleagues (Flower, 1990) gave first-year students a deliberately vague assignment to write a paper. Flower and her colleagues found that different students reading this vague assignment came up with quite different definitions of what their task was supposed to be. Some thought they should simply summarize the texts they had been assigned to read; some thought they should synthesize ideas around a controlling concept; others imagined something altogether different (see also Kantz, 1989; Walvoord and Sherman, 1991). How can we measure the learning we want to measure when students define the task so differently? With a careful and thorough assignment sheet, you can be more confident that an assignment is going to measure the knowledge and skills you want it to.

Anderson, the biologist whose course skeleton for the senior course on research we presented in Exhibit 3.2, developed a set of written instructions for her students as they worked on their original research papers (Exhibit 3.5). Anderson developed this assignment influenced by two conditions: first, her course did not have a lab attached, and there was no room for her students in the university's science lab; second, many of her students would, at graduation, be hired by laboratories in commercial firms and would test the characteristics of commercial products.

Anderson used the acronym AMPS—*A*udience, *M*ain point and purpose, *P*attern and procedures, and *S*tandards and criteria—to help her remember what needed to be included in an assignment sheet if students were to have the information they needed for solid writing decisions.

Another example of an effective assignment, from a different discipline and a different setup, is from Philip Way's Economics 101 class at the University of Cincinnati (Exhibit 3.6).

Exhibit 3.5.   Anderson's Assignment for Senior Biology Course.

In this assignment you will compare two commercially available products on the basis of at least four criteria to determine which is the "better" product as operationally defined.

You will *conduct* original science research and *compose* a twelve-hundred- to fifteen-hundred-word original scientific research report.

Audience: Write for your peers as junior colleagues in the scientific community.

Main point and purpose: For you to learn and demonstrate use of the scientific method for original scientific research. The skills you will develop in this project are those used by many Towson University graduates in their jobs at companies such as Noxell [local firm that hires Towson graduates].

Pattern and procedures: Please follow a scientific report form. Your final copy should be typed or word processed and should contain the following components:

- Title (twenty-five words or fewer, with appropriate descriptors)
- Abstract
- Introduction
- Methods and materials section
- Results section
- Conclusions and implications section
- Reference section (only if needed; not required)
- Minimum of three graphics with self-contained labels
- Preference tests (if used) with an *n* (sample size) of 20+
- Statistics appropriate to your expertise

[How to conduct the pilot, the experiment, and write the report. Includes deadlines for early proposal and draft.]

Standards and criteria: In completing this assignment, demonstrate that you can conduct scientific inquiry. Your written report should demonstrate that you have formulated a hypothesis, designed a good experiment, controlled variables, operationally defined terms, and interpreted data appropriately. In addition, you should demonstrate that you understand the scope and sequence of the scientific report format and the importance of quantification to scientific writing.

Exhibit 3.6.   Way's Assignment for Economics 101.

Due Date: November 30

Objective

The aim of this assignment is to teach you how to carry out economic research, much as you would if you were employed in an entry-level economist position. Essentially, you will learn how to use economic theory and empirical data to analyze a policy issue.

Your Role

You are an aide to Congresswoman Thompson, who has not taken an economics course since 1962. She must, therefore, delegate economic analyses to you. Whenever you perform economic analyses for Congresswoman Thompson, bear in mind that she is concerned with advocating policies that improve economic growth, efficiency, employment, price stability, and equity.

The Research Issue

Congress is considering amending the Fair Labor Standards Act of 1938 to raise the minimum wage to $4.75 per hour from its current level of $4.25 per hour. You are told to analyze the proposal using economic theory and data. You must decide whether Congresswoman Thompson should support or oppose the proposal and justify your position in a report addressed to her.

The Report

Your report should contain the following elements:

A. An executive summary that states your position and summarizes the main reasons for your conclusion.

B. A definition of the criteria you are using to assess the implications of the change in the minimum wage. You should also indicate the relative weighting (importance) of the criteria. (Hint: remember the congresswoman's concerns.)

C. A theoretical analysis that supports your position. Examine the likely impact of the increase in the minimum wage on the criteria you have selected in (B). You should analyze the effects in terms of a minimum of three different diagrams:

1. A production possibility frontier (perhaps to illustrate the effect on efficiency or growth).

2. A supply-and-demand diagram (perhaps to illustrate the impact on unemployment or prices or equity).

3. A production costs–supply diagram (perhaps to illustrate the effect on costs and prices or output).

Make sure you label your diagrams and explain the implications of your diagrams in terms of the assessment criteria.

D. An analysis of economic data that support your position. Quantitative and qualitative information concerning the effect of the increase in the minimum wage can be gathered from newspapers, magazines, reports by other economists, interviews, phone calls, and so on. A number of readings that may assist you in your research have been placed on reserve in the library. Make sure you summarize the evidence accurately, noting differences of opinion where they exist. Assess the reliability of the evidence. Reference your sources.

You should be succinct in your writing. Your paper should be two to three double-spaced typed pages plus diagrams. Style and grammar will be graded. You may find a style manual or the writing center helpful.

Note that the way in which you reach a position and the order in which you present the material need not be the same. I suggest that in order to form an opinion you (1) set criteria, (2) weight the criteria, (3) gather information, and (4) reach a conclusion.

Checklist

In order to ensure the quality of your work, it is suggested that you carefully proofread your paper and that you ask several of your classmates to review it as well in the light of the following list of hallmarks of a good paper:

1. A clear identification of the criteria used to justify your position.
2. A weighting scheme for the criteria.
3. A clear theoretical analysis of the impact of the increase in the minimum wage using three different diagrams.
4. A clear analysis of empirical data from primary or secondary sources.
5. A clear link between the theoretical and empirical analysis and the assessment criteria.
6. A clear stance on the minimum wage issue that is supported by the analysis.
7. Properly labeled and titled graphs.
8. Correct spelling and grammar.
9. Clear section headings.
10. Evidence of original thought; that is, your analysis is not simply a summary of others' opinions or analyses but rather your own evaluation of the proposals in light of the criteria and weighting scheme you have chosen.

[The assignment is accompanied by a grading sheet showing the criteria and standards for each grade level. We display the grading sheet in Appendix C.]

ACTIVITY _____

Earlier in this chapter we stated that grading begins with the very first moments of course planning. We suggested that you begin by reminding yourself what you most want students to learn and then that you adopt the assignment-centered course as a mode of planning.

Now, we invite you to

1. List specifically what you want students to be able to do at the end of your course.

2. Select types of major tests and assignments that will measure whether students can accomplish those objectives.

3. Compose a course skeleton, beginning with what you want your students to learn and then sequencing your major tests and assignments carefully. Remember that your course skeleton need not contain every assignment or test—just the major ones.

4. Ask yourself the following questions:

   a. *Fit:* Is there a good fit between the learning I want and the assignments I have chosen?

   b. *Feasibility:* Is this work load reasonable, strategically placed, and sustainable for me and for my students?

ACTIVITY _____

If you have followed our suggested course-planning process, you now have a course skeleton that begins with what you want your students to learn, and that includes a sequence of major assignments that teach and test those goals and that constitute a sustainable workload.

We invite you now to do the following:

1. Draft instructions for one of the major tests or assignments on your course skeleton. Use the AMPS acronym mentioned earlier to help you.

2. Check your draft with a colleague outside your discipline. Colleagues should put themselves in the place of the student and point out any places where they are confused or lack needed information.

CHAPTER 4

Fostering Motivation and Learning in the Grading Process

Teachers often ask, "How can I use the grading process to motivate my students properly and to help them learn?" This chapter addresses the heart of teaching, grading, and assessment: student learning is the product that counts. As teachers, we can facilitate learning, but we cannot make it happen alone. We must craft a motivational structure that serves learning. We must engage the learner.

If you followed the planning process in Chapter Three, you now have a course skeleton containing a statement of what you want students to learn and a sequence of assignments and tests that can both teach and test that learning. The next task in shaping the assignment-centered course is to fill in the muscles and tissue of the skeleton—to decide how to conduct the course on a daily basis. Research suggests that what you do on a daily basis in the classroom will strongly affect student learning (Pascarella and Terenzini, 1991).

One important principle is to aim for student involvement (Astin, 1985; Pascarella and Terenzini, 1991). As Astin states (1985, pp. 133–151), "The theory . . . students learn by becoming involved . . . seems to explain most of the empirical knowledge gained over the years about environmental influences on student development. . . . What I mean by involvement is neither mysterious nor esoteric. Quite simply, student involvement refers to the amount of physical and psychological energy that the student devotes to the academic experience." If you aim at levels of learning beyond short-term recall of information, your teaching and grading processes will be most effective if students become actively involved in the learning process. That means that students must write, talk, solve problems—they must practice the skills you want them to learn and use the knowledge you want them to apply. This chapter offers suggestions about how to get your students actively involved in learning.

Motivation is an important key to active learning and student involvement. Resource 4.1 offers sources about student motivation.

Teachers often maintain, and research affirms, that students differ in their motivation. For example, Milton, Pollio, and Eison (1986, p. 144), on the basis of questionnaire surveys of more than forty-three hundred students at institutions across the country, categorized students as "grade-oriented" or "learning-oriented." Each group endorsed different kinds of statements:

Endorsements from Grade-Oriented Students

"I think that without regularly scheduled exams I would not learn and remember very much."

"I do not find studying at home to be interesting or pleasant."

"I will withdraw from an interesting class rather than risk a poor grade."

"I get irritated by students who ask questions that go beyond what we need to know for exams."

Endorsements from Learning-Oriented Students

"I find the process of learning new material fun."

"I enjoy classes in which the instructor attempts to relate material to concerns beyond the classroom."

"I discuss interesting material that I've learned in class with my friends and family."

"I try to make time for outside reading despite the demands of my coursework."

Other categorizations of students focus on how students would differently answer the following questions:

"Do I control what happens to me, or am I helpless?"

"If I work hard and well, will my effort pay off?"

"Why do I fail? Why do I succeed?"

Theories of learned helplessness (Abramson, Seligman, and Teasdale, 1978), self-efficacy (Bandura, 1986; Schunk, 1985), and attribution (Weiner, 1986) address these issues. They suggest that some of our students see themselves as helpless, do not believe that their efforts will pay off, attribute success to luck, and blame failure on forces outside their control. Other students feel they

Resource 4.1.
Sources About Student Motivation.

Davis and Murrell, 1993. Synthesizes research on motivation and proposes three foundations for student responsibility.

Forsyth and McMillan, 1991. Theories of motivation suggest three approaches to enhancing college student learning: (1) reshaping students' overall achievement orientation; (2) creating the expectation of success; and (3) increasing the value of academic outcomes by helping students develop personal goals and identify means of achieving them.

McMillan and Forsyth, 1991. Presents a model to explain college students' motivation. Urges attention to students' needs and expectations for success.

Milton, Pollio, and Eison, 1986. Classifies students as grade-oriented or learning-oriented. Presents results of a national study of attitudes toward grades by students, parents, faculty, and others.

Perry, Menec, and Struthers, 1996. Most human motivation is complex, blending intrinsic and extrinsic factors.

have control over what happens to them, that their effort will pay off, that their successes are due to their own ability or hard work, and that their failures could be remedied by studying harder or more effectively.

These findings keep teachers, on bad days, from dismissing all their students as hopeless grademongers. The research helps identify the components of motivation and urges teachers to define what they mean when they say that their students are not motivated.

But if teachers regard motivation as a fixed aspect of students' characters, then the classification of students in this fashion becomes dangerous. Research suggests that student motivation can change. In her workshops and classes, Walvoord has asked both students and faculty to recall a course in which initial lack of motivation and interest turned to fascination, involvement, and hard work. Almost everyone can recall at least one incident. A teacher, then, will not want to accept a student's initial signs of poor motivation as a reason for giving up on that student; on the contrary, a teacher could take up the challenge. As a sociologist we interviewed said about his general education students at an open-admissions two-year college, "You always get the students who are interested right from the start, but the ones I really like, the ones that get my adrenalin going, are the ones who are slouching in the back, thinking, 'What a jerky course this is.' Then you show them what sociologists do, and how much fun it is, and sometimes, wow. They *get* it."

The question then is, What can teachers do to achieve the best possible motivation from students in their courses? The words commonly attributed to E. M. Forster come to mind: "Only connect." Students pick up motivational cues from those around them (Davis and Murrell, 1994). Student-faculty contact and student-student contact have been repeatedly shown to be powerful factors in student involvement (Pascarella and Terenzini, 1991). Boice (1996) offers very practical, research-based suggestions for how teachers can connect in meaningful ways with their students—even simple actions such as arriving five minutes early to class to talk informally with students, maintaining eye contact while lecturing, leaning forward toward the student, and so on. The sources on collaborative learning in Resource 3.3 (Chapter Three) also offer helpful suggestions. Parker Palmer's work (1983, 1987, 1990, 1993) offers a thoughtful and provocative vision of the community of learners. As he states (1987, p. 24): "Knowing and learning are communal acts. They require many eyes and ears, many observations and experiences. They require a continual cycle of discussion, disagreement, and consensus over what has been seen and what it all means."

The literature suggests, too, that you may be able to influence students' experiences of learned helplessness, self-efficacy, and attribution. For example, in all your talk to students, reinforce that you believe they can succeed. Lay out for them the specific steps needed for success; let them taste success early and sequentially; help them see how their own actions can lead to learning. Statements such as "Look around you; half of you will be gone by the end of the semester," and "This test will separate the sheep from the goats" may be intended by the teacher to motivate students, but some will immediately assume they are the ones who cannot make it and will be inclined to give up. Even when a student cannot pass your course, and you must advise him or her to drop it or must hand out an *F* grade, you can still affirm your belief in the student's ability to learn, and you can help get the attribution right: "It's too late to save this semester, but I know you can learn this if you work hard and use good study strategies. I hope you'll try again." In sum, keep reinforcing in your classroom the kind of thinking that says, "I want to learn, I can learn, I can control outcomes, my efforts can pay off, and if I don't do well, I can do better."

Having now established the basis of learning and motivation, we are ready to move forward with the course-planning process. As you try to flesh out your course skeleton, we have two suggestions for you to consider as you involve students in the learning process and as you plan classroom activities: (1) teach what you are grading and (2) rethink the use of class time.

Teach What You Are Grading

We faculty sometimes pride ourselves on not "teaching to the test." But if the test is right—if it really tests the central learning goals of the course—then we should teach to it. In fact, it seems criminal not to. Why would we test and grade students on skills and subject matter we haven't taught them? At the same time, we don't want to teach to the test too narrowly. Deborah De Zure, director of the Faculty Center for Institutional Excellence at Eastern Michigan University, put it nicely in a conversation with Walvoord: "Teach not to the test but to the criteria by which you will evaluate the test."

The sociologist we met in a previous chapter changed his class assignment from a term paper to a review of the literature. One of his criteria for the review was that students should not produce an annotated bibliography in prose form; instead, they should construct an interpretive frame for the review. He began to think how he would teach them to provide such a frame. When asking himself which frames are common, he came up with three:

1. *"Stand on my shoulders":* the writer sees the field as a steady progression in which each person's work builds on previous work.

2. *"Major shift":* the writer sees the field as having gone in one direction until a major new discovery, theory, or paradigm shift sent the field in a different direction.

3. *"Warring camps":* the writer sees the field as characterized by warring camps adhering to diverse theories or modes of research.

Next, he asked himself, How does the writer of a review decide which frame is most appropriate? Examining his own writing processes, he realized he looked in the literature for certain indicators: did the author view his or her work as contradictory to others? As an extension? Did the author refer to shifts in the field? He also realized that he used certain techniques, such as listing the findings of each author in sequence and examining the list to see which pattern or combination of patterns applied.

Now that he had the frames, along with clues about how he chose an appropriate frame, the sociologist could teach these frames to his students. He could have them

- Read reviews of the literature and, individually or in groups, identify the frames

- Read articles and underline information that would help students build an interpretive frame, then compare each other's underlined passages

- Read abstracts of articles and decide which frame the group of articles suggested
- Draft their reviews, have peers identify and evaluate the interpretive frame the student writer had used, and then let the writer revise to make the frame more clear and appropriate

After using some combination of such strategies, the sociologist would collect and grade reviews of the literature from his students, and his grades would demonstrate whether students had learned what he taught: a process and a set of skills for analyzing the literature in the field and writing a review of the literature. At the same time, he would have involved the students actively in learning, guided them, used the power of peer collaboration, and provided a structure that was likely to motivate students toward learning.

Here is how an art historian, Barbara Filo, was better able to teach what she was grading after a workshop Walvoord led at Whitworth College, a small, religiously affiliated liberal arts college in Spokane, Washington.

How I Taught What I Was Grading
Barbara Filo, Whitworth College

My syllabi for Art History I and II included an assignment requiring students to visit a gallery, observe the work displayed there, and write a two-page review of the art work. Accompanying each syllabus was a two-page list of vocabulary terms defining the visual elements and the principles of design. Those terms were further explained with a slide lecture. The actual assignment from an earlier syllabus asked students to "attend two on-campus art exhibits. Write a review of each, using visual art vocabulary, describing the exhibit and your reaction to it."

The purpose of this assignment was primarily to get students actually to visit an art gallery or museum twice during the term. For many students these visits were their first experience inside an art gallery or museum. Second, the review paper assignment was an attempt to inspire students' thoughtful reaction to the art works, in a written form.

But the entire experience, both the art gallery visit and the review papers, was a mixed bag. Some students had a positive experience both in their visual reaction and written response, but for most students the experience had little effect on their understanding or appreciation of art. Even with the vocabulary handout, unless I was present to guide the exhibit tour, the typical students seemed to lack the skill to really "see" what was before their eyes.

After participating in a faculty workshop, I was inspired to improve this particular assignment because I felt it was perhaps the most important assignment in Art History I and II. After all, long after students leave my class they continue to have the opportunity to view art. I wanted them to know how to intelligently interpret and critique what they see. I knew this type of assignment could make a long-lasting impression on the ways they view and think about art if it could become a valid experience now, in the college classroom.

I searched many sources looking for ideas on how to view art and write critiques. *A Short Guide to Writing About Art* by Barnet (1989) [5th ed. 1997], *Writing About Art* by Sayre (1989), and *Living with Art* by Gilbert and McCarter (1988) [3rd ed. 1992] proved most helpful. Now, along with my review assignment, I guide students' learning process by giving them this sheet on how to view works of art:

Handout to Students for Art Assignment[1]

The goal of an artist is to create an interaction between the work and the observer. Fine art is created for the educated observer; therefore it is most important for the observer to become a critical thinker.

Here is a list you can use as a guide for the critical observation of works of art. It may also be used as a guide to writing reviews of art works.

1. *Familiarity:* Is the work connected to other works you have seen, or is it something totally unlike anything you've ever seen?

2. *Artist:* Who is the artist? Have you seen other works by the artist? What do you know about the artist? (Read artist's biography if possible.) Does knowledge of the artist's personal history influence your impressions of the work?

3. *Style:* Does the work fall into a particular art history style? Can you recognize characteristics, whether in content or form, that show an influence of or a reaction to a particular style?

4. *Historical context:* Note the original date and location of the art piece and the events—historical, political, social, scientific, geographical, cultural, and so on—taking place at the time of the creation.

5. *Form:* Describe the appearance of the work and the materials and medium used.

6. *Visual elements:* Look for the most emphasized elements: line, shape, color, value, light, space, texture, time and motion, and so on.

7. *Composition:* Notice the principles of design used in the arrangement of the visual elements: unity, variety, balance, emphasis, proportion, rhythm.

8. *Content:* Describe the iconography, subject matter, and symbolism. Is the subject matter recognizable?

9. *Personal response:* How does the work make you feel—happy, sad, angry, excited, frightened, detached, inspired, depressed,

---

1. Adapted from Gilbert and McCarter, 1988 and Gilbert, 1992.

uplifted, repulsed, disgusted, shocked? Are there any personal memories or associations evoked? What do you think the artist felt about the work during its creation? Do you feel any relationship with the artist?

10. *Experience:* Would you buy this work so you could view it every day? Have you gained an appreciation for the work, whether or not you like it?

The results of this guide, which I go over in class, have been most satisfying. Students now have in hand a personal guide for viewing art. Without exception, on the reviews, students write more than they did before. They are far more descriptive. The second review is typically better than the first. Many students are excited, responding that they never knew so much could be derived from a single piece of art.

At the start of each course, I always remind students that my intent is not to insist or expect they will "like" the art they see but that my hope is for them to become educated, intelligent viewers of art who can come to an appreciation for the art they see. This assignment seems to help me and the students reach that goal [Adapted from Hunt, 1992, pp. 54–56].

Anderson, the biology professor, also teaches what she tests. One of her assigned papers is on "recent use of scanning electron microscopy in _____." (Students fill in the blank with their own areas of interest: entomology, sports medicine, paleontology, and so on.) Upper-level biology majors have to synthesize a paper from primary research articles. To teach the researching and synthesizing skills this assignment demands, Anderson has students submit interim assignments throughout the term paper process:

Write two paragraphs answering these questions: What is a term paper? How have you written term papers in the past? How is the term paper for this course different? How is it similar? How do you plan to write your term paper in this course (include a time line, with dates)?

Write 20 questions about your topic. Star the one or two you think are most interesting as the basis for your term paper. Be ready to share your questions for peer response in class. Remember—your term paper must address a specific question, not just collect random facts about a topic.

In one sentence explain your working definition of "recent" in your term paper title.

Complete these sentences: "Plagiarism is . . ." "In order to avoid plagiarism, I will . . ."

Talk for 20 minutes about your question with someone who knows more about it than you do, and make notes on what you learn. You can use these notes for your paper [This activity gets students away from total reliance on print material and helps them achieve synthesis rather than paraphrasing.]

Breihan, the historian we met earlier, wanted the thirty students in his first-year general education Western Civilization course to argue about historical issues. He was convinced that the argumentative essay was the most efficient format in which to assess students' skills of historical argumentation (Exhibit 3.1). He decided that the first essay he assigned, dealing with the years 1500 to 1800, would offer students several questions to choose from. Here are two examples:

1. An essay question in which they had to recommend a type of government for a hypothetical country whose characteristics, outlined in the question, resembled those of seventeenth- and eighteenth-century European countries in class structure, economic condition, patterns of commerce, anxiety about the danger of anarchy or bloody revolution, and so on. Breihan asked his students, "If you were adviser to the ruler of this hypothetical country, based on your study of European countries from 1500 to 1800, which type of government would you recommend to this ruler?"

2. An essay question in which students had to decide whether Edmond Burke and Thomas Paine would judge that Louis XIV of France was a "good" king for his time or not.

Breihan's next job was to figure out which knowledge and skills these argumentative essays would require of students. Exhibit 4.1 is his list.

From such a list, Breihan then must ask himself, How can I best help students learn these things? The research literature on how students learn higher-order reasoning suggests that, rather than lecturing as a primary model of instruction, Breihan should use interactive class discussion, debate, writing, and other strategies to involve his students in learning and practicing argumentation. Resource 4.2 offers sources that suggest how a class may be made interactive.

Resource 4.2.

Sources for Interactive Teaching and Learning.

Bean, 1996. Integrating writing, critical thinking, and active learning.

Bonwell and Eison, 1991. Strategies for active learning.

Brown and Ellison, 1995. Single chapter overview, with specific examples of faculty using active learning.

Halpern and Associates, 1994. Part one contains six articles on instructional strategies that promote active learning.

Meyers and Jones, 1993. Strategies for active learning.

Exhibit 4.1.   Breihan's Analysis of History Skills Required for Argumentative Essay.

1. Reading accurately (including an accurate sense of chronological narrative).

   Students must be able to report accurately on what they have read. They must know, for example, that events in 1645 could not have caused events in 1641.

2. Realizing that published works have authors.

   This includes paying attention to authors' personalities, possible biases, and attempts to organize material for the reader. Students should know who wrote their textbooks and be aware of the major section and chapter headings in them.

3. Perceiving and using standard analytical categories.

   These include political, social, economic, religious, and cultural factors often cited in explaining past events.

4. Perceiving historical theses.

   Students must be able to see that historians *argue* about the past. They debate, for example, whether or not absolutism was beneficial to the majority of the French subjects of Louis XIV.

5. Using written sources as evidence.

   Facts only become *evidence* when brought forward in relation to a thesis. Both primary sources (contemporary eyewitness) and secondary sources may be used to state or defend a historical thesis.

6. Stating and defending a historical thesis.

   Accurate and specific examples and evidence are key to this; secondary-source authors may be used as models. This can be done in two stages:

   1. Defending a thesis selected by the instructor
   2. Choosing one's own thesis

7. Defending a historical thesis against counterarguments.

   Agreeing with one secondary-source author is not enough; students need to say why they rejected carefully argued opposing views. Again, accurate and specific examples and evidence are key.

You may be thinking to yourself, It's all fine and good to be interactive in class, but how can Breihan cover 1500 through 1800 and also take time for in-class interaction? Students cannot frame cogent arguments if they don't know the basic facts, vocabulary, and concepts. Also, students often don't read the material ahead of time, or they don't read it carefully enough for intelligent discussion. If students haven't read Thomas Paine's work carefully, how can they discuss it? If they haven't grasped the basic principles, how can they be asked in class to show how the principles can be applied to problems?

The answer to these dilemmas is that Breihan must think carefully about structuring both coverage of basic facts and vocabulary and argumentation skills. He must plan which activities he wants students to do in their study time and which he wants to do in class. And he must solve the class-preparation problem—he must find a way to have his students read carefully before they come to class.

Rethink the Use of In-Class Time

Breihan figured out how to get his students to read the assigned material outside of class. We call this the *first-exposure* part of learning, when the student first encounters new information, concepts, vocabulary, and procedures. Students may gain first exposure through observation, lecture, reading, visual media, or other modes. After establishing the first-exposure part, Breihan used the in-class time for the hard part of instruction—having students actively analyze and argue, based on the assigned reading. We call this broadly the *processing* part of learning, where students synthesize, analyze, compare, define, argue, or solve problems based on the material to which they have been exposed. Breihan now lectures in class only about half the time; in the other half he engages students in activities designed to have them learn and practice argumentation and the skills that lead to argumentation.

The key to using class time for the processing part is to actively establish the first-exposure part: to get all or nearly all students to read the assignment in their own study time before class. Breihan did that by asking students, as preparation for every class, to write a short piece based on the readings. The writings counted in the final course grade; thus he sent a message to students that these writings were important to him and to their learning. He had about thirty students in a class, and often had two sections of Western Civilization at a time, so he did not add these writing assignments lightly. But the daily assignments did not cost him much time outside the class, because he found that *the class itself can be the teacher's way of responding to the student's preparatory work.* Teachers must get past the notion that the class preparation—writing, drawing, math problems, and so on—must be extensively marked with comments by the teacher in his or her own time outside of class. Some student work can be marked by the teacher outside of class; but these preparatory writings need not be. They are preparation for class and can be handled in the class. The student's preparatory first-exposure work becomes the basis of class. The result is a built-in assessment—the teacher becomes familiar, minute by minute, with what students are thinking and learning, where they need more help, whether concepts are getting through. This is classroom assessment as Angelo and Cross describe it (Angelo, 1991a; Angelo and Cross, 1993). Such assessment shows the teacher where the students have arrived on their own, and it provides the basis for classroom interaction in which the teacher helps students move beyond what they could achieve on their own.

By the time Breihan's class was over, the student's understanding had progressed beyond the point shown by the preparatory writing. So the students' preparatory work was now out of date. At home, after class, Breihan simply skimmed the students' work rapidly and gave each paper a number of points. Walvoord marks her students' work "pass" or "no credit." Anderson, in a class of 125, asks students to keep their daily writings in a portfolio and then, at midterm, to revise and type their two best writings and hand them in, along with the original versions of the other assignments and a tally of how many assignments are included. Anderson bases the portfolio grade on the quality of the two revisions and the presence of the other unrevised original writings.

Though different methods must be employed for large classes, the principle is the same—the teacher must rethink the use of class time and study time and devote as much class time (or lab time or clinic time) as possible to process-oriented teaching. Resource 4.3 offers sources for making large classes interactive.

Table 4.1 compares the use of teacher time and student study time in lecture-based teaching and in interactive teaching. In the lecture-based model, the teacher spends much of the class time lecturing first-exposure material the students have not met before. Then the students are expected on their own time to do the processing part—analyzing and synthesizing the material, using it to solve problems, and so on. The class time is used to hand the students' products to the teacher or sometimes to administer in-class exams. The teacher then must spend large amounts of private time responding to students' attempts at sophisticated thinking, again without face-to-face interaction.

Resource 4.3.
Sources for Making Large Classes Interactive.

Bonwell and Eison, 1991. Summary of research about learning in large classes and suggestions for making them interactive. (See pp. 14–19.)

Gibbs and Jenkins (eds.), 1992. Teaching large classes in higher education: how to maintain quality with reduced resources. Theoretical issues, case studies, and institutional support for change.

Tobias, 1994. Reports how a chemistry professor improved students' pass rate in large classes.

Walvoord and Williams, 1995. Video for faculty shows how five faculty from various disciplines are making large classes interactive.

Weimer (ed.), 1987. Collection of essays on teaching large classes.

Electronic discussion group to share ideas about large classes. To join, send the following e-mail message [SUBSCRIBE LCIG-L first name last name] to [LISTSERV@UGA.CC.UGA.EDU].

The assignment-based model we propose, on the other hand, asks students to be responsible for their first-exposure learning outside of class. Then, in class, the teacher can work on the processing part. Because class interaction gives students constructive feedback on their preparatory assignments, the teacher does not have to dedicate hours of outside-class time writing comments on those assignments.

How does class proceed in the interactive model? Exhibit 4.2 contains transcripts of two classes. Both classes are on the same topic—whether Louis XIV of France was a good king for his time or not. The readings Breihan chose were a collection of primary sources

Table 4.1. **Teacher Time and Student Study Time in Lecture-Based Versus Interactive Teaching.**

	Lecture-based teaching	Interactive teaching
Class time	First exposure (student first hears or observes facts, ideas, processes not encountered before)	Process (student applies, analyzes, argues, solves problems using first-exposure material)
Student study time	Process	First exposure

Exhibit 4.2.   Two Versions of a History Class Session.

Lecture-centered way:
Many students do not read the assignment before class. Thus the teacher is forced into lecturing first-exposure material.

Breihan's interactive way: Students do first-exposure on their own time before class. Class is used for critique, argument, and collaborative work based on students' prior reading and writing.

Students enter class and take their seats.

Students enter class with written answers to the following questions:

1. What is the issue at stake in the selections you read for today?
2. Bishop Bossuet: who was he, when did he write? How can his material be used as evidence?

[For each of the other authors students read, same questions are repeated as for question 2.]

Teacher: The topic for today is Louis XIV of France: whether he was a "good" king for his time or not. First, do you have any questions on the readings?
Students: [*silence*]
Teacher: [*begins lecture*]

Students lay a copy of their written work on the teacher's desk and take a copy of it to their seats to work with.
Teacher: Mr. Freiburg, do you have the issue at stake today?
Freiburg: Sorry, I was sick last night and didn't get the reading done. I'll be ready next time.
Teacher: Okay, hope you're feeling better. Ms. Washington, do you have it?
Washington: Yes.
Teacher: Would you put it on the board, please?
Washington [*writes on the board*]: The issue at stake is whether Louis XIV was a good king for his time.
Teacher: Everybody clear on the issue?
Class: [*nods and murmurs in agreement*]
Teacher: [*reads the next question on the assignment*] Bishop Bossuet: who was he? When did he write? Mr. Ackerman?
Ackerman: He was a tutor in Louis's court.
Teacher: Right. So what is his position on the issue at stake? [*silence; teacher waits*]

Continues lecture

Ruiz: Well, he thinks Louis was a good king.

Breihan: Yes, but you've only *summarized* what he said. How can this material be used *as evidence?*

Ruiz: [*silent*]

Breihan: Anyone?

Robinson: He owed his job to Louis, so he probably *had* to say good things.

Breihan: So he may be biased. Excellent. But is the evidence then totally useless?

Hammond: Well, he was there in the court, so it's eyewitness evidence.

Teacher: Yes! So his writings are good evidence in some ways and not so good in other ways. This is what I mean when I say that, in your essays, you have to evaluate the historical material *as evidence.*

Now let's ask what evidence the bishop himself uses to back up his position. [*students reply*] Now let's take the next writer. Saint Simon: who was he? When did he write? [*continues in this vein; teacher eventually sets up a quasi-debate*] Ms. Lanahan, would you be Saint Simon? [*Lanahan nods*] What did Saint Simon say about Louis improving the army?

[*Lanahan explains*]

Teacher: Mr. Belanco, would you be the bishop? [*Belanco nods*] How would the bishop have responded to Saint Simon?

[*The two students answer one another; other students join in.*]

about whether or not Louis was a good king. The right-hand column of our transcript is a condensed version derived from Breihan's classes that Walvoord observed—classes conducted in the interactive, process-oriented way we have described. The left-hand column is a hypothetical class on the same topic, following the lecture-based model.

You will see from the transcript that, after a number of exchanges in which students answer Breihan's questions in a teacher-student form of dialogue, Breihan gets them talking to each other by giving them roles. ("Will you be the bishop?")

At the end of the class Breihan reminds students that a later class period will be a debate about Louis. Half the class will defend Louis as a good king for his era; half will argue Louis was not a good king. Breihan reminds students that they must bring written debate notes to class and must be prepared to argue either side. He will assign them to sides at the beginning of the next class. He reminds them that after the debate, there will be only ten more days until their argumentative essays are due, and the material on Louis will be needed for those essays. He refers them to the criteria for those essays, which are part of the assignment already given to them. He helps his students to see that he is "teaching to the criteria." Thus he helps to motivate their preparation and participation in class.

Breihan did not institute interactive strategies just for the sake of interactivity. The exercise in Exhibit 4.2 and the debate that followed it were carefully sequenced as part of a plan to build necessary information, vocabulary, and skills sequentially across the semester. (Exhibit 4.3 contains his plan for building knowledge and skills in the weeks before the first essay exam.) By such a use of class time, Breihan helped his students to learn the argumentative skills, the vocabulary, and the factual knowledge they would need to write high-quality argumentative essays that met his criteria and standards for their learning. He helped them not by lecturing over their passive heads but by getting them involved in judging evidence, constructing arguments, and answering counterarguments.

Teachers sometimes fear that if they teach interactively, they will not be able to keep the class on task. For that reason, we have chosen Breihan's class, where the interactive discussion is highly structured. The students are given roles to play. The teacher guides the class by carefully planned activities with specific goals linked to learning and to assessment. In some contexts, the teacher may want a more loosely structured discussion, but our example illustrates that interaction in the classroom can be highly structured and focused.

Exhibit 4.3.   Breihan's Plan for Teaching Argumentation in a Western Civilization Course.

Exercises	Skills
Stage 1: Showing How a Single Reading Can Be Used As Evidence	
Author's Purpose and Summary: Week 1 What do you know about the textbook author? What can you guess? When was the text written? Published? List its subheadings and summarize a chapter.	Recognize that history is written by people who reflect their cultural biases. Pay attention to author's subheads. Summarize.
Narrative of the English Civil War Write a one-paragraph narrative incorporating eight terms provided by Breihan.	Summarize events accurately.
Analysis of Anarchic Episodes: Week 2 From eyewitness accounts of seventeenth-century riots, find evidence of the following factors: economic, political, social, religious, and so on.	Become familiar with various analytical categories and use them to categorize evidence.
Primary Sources on Louis XIV: Week 3 What is the issue at stake in this collection of documents? Who was the author of each document? When did the author live? How can the author's material be used as evidence on the position at stake? [Questions are repeated for each source.]	Understand how "primary source" material can be used as evidence by stating connection between eyewitness material and opinions on the historical issue.
Secondary Sources on Louis XIV: Week 4 What is the issue at stake? Who is the author? When did the author write? What is the author's position on the issue? How does he or she back it up?	Understand what a "secondary source" is. Use secondary sources as models for shaping historical arguments. Understand how arguments are backed by evidence.

Exercises	Skills
Stage 2: Contributing to an Argument on a Assigned Historical Opinion	
Louis XIV Debate Worksheet Prepare notes in support of your assigned position on whether or not Louis was "good" king for his era, plus arguments for the opposing opinion.	Understand that history is argument about the past. Collect evidence for a position. Take notes that allow easy access to evidence during debate.
Second Chance on Louis XIV Debate Write two points that were not discussed in the class debate. For extra credit, say why you did not say them in the debate.	Learn skills and points not used in the debate.
Stage 3: Choosing One's Own Position on a Historical Issue and Briefly Defending It with Evidence	
Best Solution to Anarchy Essay: Week 5 In a one-paragraph essay, state which solution to the problem of seventeenth-century anarchy—French or English—you personally find more realistic and attractive. Try to explain why you feel the way you do, and back your feelings with evidence.	Choose one's own position. Address the relevant issue. Support the position with evidence.
Stage 4: Choosing One's Own Position and Defending It in a Full Essay, Including Counterarguments and Answers to Counterarguments	
Essay 1: Week 7 Select from among three essay topics: 1. For a hypothetical country (whose characteristics are described) suggest an optimal style of government, based on governments studied in class. 2. Whose theories about the French Revolution—Burke's or Paine's—were more "valid"? 3. From class readings by Burke and Paine, infer their views, pro and con, of Louis XIV's reign.	Use several techniques for historical argument: analyzing the problem, stating your position, supporting your position with evidence, and answering counterarguments.

How does this principle work for a very different discipline? A physics teacher used most of his class time to demonstrate how to solve physics problems. There were some questions from students while he did this, but not many. The teacher frequently asked students, "Are you getting it?" "Are there any questions?" But they were so busy trying to get everything down, and it was coming at them so fast, that they didn't know what to ask. In the classroom, they might have thought they understood, but when they got home and tried to do the homework problems he assigned, they frequently found that they didn't understand after all. Then, at 2 A.M., when they were on their own, they needed their professor.

Colleagues suggested to this physicist that he should adopt Breihan's solution: provide guide sheets and other aids so that students could read the physics book before they came to class. But this teacher replied, "The students I get can't read a physics book on their own, even with a study guide, and really figure it out. They have to see somebody walk through the problem, explaining it." So he had himself videotaped explaining concepts and demonstrating how to solve the problems. Students were required to see the videotapes before class (they were on reserve in the media library). Then in class, in groups of three, they did their homework problems.

Three positive results ensued. One was that students taught each other; that saved the professor's time. Second, if an entire group was confused or stuck, they raised their hands, and the professor could come right over and help them. Third, once the professor had made the tape of a problem demonstration, he never had to spend time preparing the demonstration again. Think of the hours that ordinary physics teachers spend preparing and delivering a demonstration lecture in physics this semester, then again next semester, and the next, and the next. Think of the time saved if the lecture is delivered once and then used again and again without further time investment from the professor. It's possible in some fields to purchase lectures or demonstrations on tape or CD-ROM or to find them on the Web. What the students lost through this format was the capability for any interaction with the professor during the initial demonstration. What they gained was the ability to play and replay the tape at their own speed, in their own time; then, when the time came to apply the demonstration to their own problem solving, they could solicit the professor's guidance.

What about large classes? Breaking a class into interactive, self-directing groups, as the physics teacher did, is a strategy that can work even for large classes. Even if the chairs are bolted to the floor in rows, students can talk in pairs. Many teachers, therefore, use intermittent small-group interaction to break up the class hour.

Plan the actions of these small groups carefully so they enhance rather than waste the learning time.

A second strategy for large classes is to have small groups meet outside of class. The traditional recitation or lab is one type of small group; but do not assume that recitation and lab sections, just because they are small, are necessarily interactive. Teaching assistants who are leading recitation sections may be relying on lecture or may not be fully utilizing the possibilities of interactive learning. They may be using much of their time administering and reviewing quizzes or problems—an activity that may or may not provide interactive learning that is well integrated with the rest of the course. To address these problems, psychologist Tony Grasha, Distinguished Teaching Professor at the University of Cincinnati, asks the two hundred students in his introductory psychology class to meet outside class in small groups to perform specific, structured tasks that are fully integrated into his class sessions. Students conduct observations and gather data, discuss a particular topic, or complete a writing assignment. Each group has, as leader, one or two junior and senior undergraduate psychology majors who have taken the class previously and who are earning credit for a practicum in teaching psychology. Grasha meets weekly with his student facilitators. (See Walvoord and Williams, 1995, for more details.)

Technology can create spaces outside class for student interaction. Biologist Carl Huether, also of the University of Cincinnati, invites students in his large introductory biology course to form small groups that conduct e-mail discussions about several biological articles that Huether has chosen. In several rounds, students in each small group respond to the articles and to each others' responses. Again, the key is thorough planning and clear instructions.

Labs are intended for students to apply principles they learn in lecture or, sometimes, to discover principles inductively through experimentation. Science faculty often complain that students are not prepared for labs and that they do not apply to their lab work the principles they learned in the class. One group of scientists discussing these issues in a workshop decided to address such problems by making the lab more like the class and the class more like the lab and also by making better use of students' study time. They suggested, for example, that even in large classes, the instructor could stop the lecture periodically to ask students to complete a few questions or talk with a neighbor or sketch out a lab procedure that would prepare them for the lab to come. They suggested that the instructor collect a "ticket" from each student before the student was allowed to begin the lab. The "ticket" is a short statement of basic principles the student must have gained in reading or in the large lecture class, such as "We are using *E. coli* in the lab today because . . ." or "The purpose of today's lab is to. . . ." The ticket may also ask students to explain in their own words a principle that lies behind the lab they are about to complete.

We're suggesting, then, that as part of your course planning you carefully examine how you are using available times and spaces for learning. Ask yourself, What do students think are the purposes of the lab, the class, and their own study time? What are my purposes? How can each time and space best be used?

ACTIVITY

If you have been following our course-planning process, you now have a course skeleton and the draft of instructions to students for your first major assignment.

Now we invite you to complete the following steps:

1. For the first assignment (or any other), list what your students will need to learn in order to be successful.

2. List in-class and out-of-class activities or small assignments that might help students learn those materials and skills.

3. Consider one instance in your own teaching where you are doing first exposure in your classroom. Discuss with colleagues how you might move that first exposure to student study time and thus free class time for more interactive teaching.

4. If you teach in a discipline that has labs, clinics, or similar scheduled sessions, ask yourself, What is the relationship between the class and the lab or clinic? Is the class supposed to prepare students for the interaction of the lab or clinic? Does it do this effectively? Why or why not? How might I improve?

5. Plan a schedule of in-class time (plus lab or clinic time) and study-time activities for the first few weeks of your class.

CHAPTER 5

Establishing Criteria and Standards for Grading

"Establishing Clear Criteria and Standards for Grading" is one of the most popular faculty development workshop titles in all the institutions where we have worked. Having clear criteria and standards can

- Save time in the grading process
- Allow you to make that process consistent and fair
- Help you explain to students what you expect
- Show you what to teach
- Identify essential relationships between discipline information and processes
- Help students participate in their own learning, because they know what they are aiming for
- Help students evaluate their own and each other's work
- Save you from having to explain your criteria to students after they have handed in their work, as a way of justifying the grades they are contesting
- Help student peers give each other constructive feedback on plans and drafts
- Help team teachers or teaching assistants grade student papers consistently
- Help teachers of sequenced courses communicate with each other about standards and criteria
- Form the basis for departmental or institutional assessment

Because establishing criteria and standards is so crucial—and because it takes some space to explain—we devote a separate chapter to it, though in practice it is inexorably linked to the clarity of your instructions and to the ways in which you teach to the task.

Consider this case in point: for three semesters, Anderson asked first-year students in Biology 101 to answer this test question: "In a coherent paragraph, compare and contrast prokaryotic and eukaryotic cells in four ways." Each semester, a large number of students did poorly on this fifteen-point question designed to measure vocabulary usage, concept mastery, and information integration. So Anderson ordered a better movie on the cell than she had been using and beefed up her lecture coverage, but still there was no significant improvement. Then an indignant student in lab—armed with a pen and a textbook—demanded to know why he only got half credit when all four of his answers were right.

Then it dawned on Anderson: she had let the atrocious "it-has-a-nucleus" topic sentences, the *membrain* misspellings, and the scrambled prose of poor answers hide the truth. The students didn't need more biology—they needed to know how to compare and contrast, which was exactly what Anderson required. Anderson assumed students understood that the answers to her questions comprised eight components: four comparisons and four contrasts. She had been so busy grading the seventy-five–plus papers that she hadn't been analyzing. The grading process was all wrong. Anderson saw that she should have constructed explicit criteria for grading rather than rely on her global judgment simply to award overall points.

Anderson recognized that she needed to state her criteria much more explicitly for her students and to intervene in the learning process much sooner. So she kept the better movie, dumped the extra lecture material she had added, and stated exactly what she expected in a comparison-contrast paragraph. Then she selected several sample student compare-contrast writings, read them in class (without identifying the student writers by name), and graded them orally, making her new and clearly constructed criteria extremely explicit. Finally, she made students practice. She asked them to compare and contrast plant and animal cells in three ways as a "ticket" to a lab. Collected at the door of the lab, these writings functioned as tickets normally do—students had to have one in order to enter. And student test scores did indeed improve.

Checklists, key questions, worksheets, peer response sheets, drafting conferences between student and teacher, and whole-class instruction on criteria such as Anderson gave are all ways to make grading criteria more explicit. They are diverse and unique and may work very well in classrooms when teachers are making criteria and standards explicit just for themselves or their students.

In this chapter we present a particularly careful and thorough method for stating criteria—a method that will bring rigor to a classroom and will allow grading to be used, if desired, as the basis for departmental, programmatic, or institutional assessment. The method establishes a common format for stating criteria, while leaving the criteria themselves for the teacher to establish.

The method is called Primary Trait Analysis (PTA) (Lloyd-Jones, 1977). It creates a scoring rubric that can be used to assess any student performance or portfolio of student performances—written, oral, clinical, artistic, and so on. PTA is assignment-specific; that is, the criteria are different for each assignment or test. PTA could be used to establish criteria for an external exam as well as for classroom work. In fact, PTA was developed to score essays on the National Assessment of Educational Progress—a national exam administered periodically over several decades to thousands of U.S. students at several levels. But as we apply it here, PTA is a way of explicitly stating the teacher's criteria, and it is used in the classroom to make grading criteria very clear and specific.

As we show in the last chapters of the book, PTA works for departmental or institutional assessment because it provides a common format for stating various teachers' criteria and standards. PTA, because it is very explicit, allows criteria to be made public and understandable to outside audiences. Here, however, we show how teachers can use PTA inside their classrooms to make criteria and standards clear to themselves and their students and to guide classroom teaching and learning.

Characteristics of Primary Trait Analysis

It is helpful, in understanding PTA, to place it along two continua:

1. The continuum from unstated criteria ("It feels like a *B*") to highly explicit criteria (Primary Trait Analysis)

2. The continuum from norm-referenced scoring (grading on a curve) to criterion-referenced scoring (PTA)

PTA is both highly explicit and criterion-referenced. To construct a PTA scale, the teacher (1) identifies the factors or traits that will count for the scoring (such as "thesis," "materials and methods," "use of color," "eye contact with client," and so on); (2) builds a scale for scoring the student's performance on that trait; and (3) evaluates the student's performance against those criteria.

A Sample PTA Scale

As we saw in Exhibit 3.5, Anderson asked her students in an upper-level biology course to design and carry out an original scientific experiment comparing two commercially available products and to present the comparison in scientific report format.

Anderson used PTA to assess student work on that assignment. She began by choosing ten traits she wanted to measure:

1. Title
2. Introduction
3. Scientific format demands
4. Methods and materials section
5. Nonexperimental information
6. Experimental design
7. Operational definitions
8. Control of variables
9. Collection of data and communication of results
10. Interpretation of data: conclusions and implications

Depending on her purposes, Anderson could have decided to measure only one or two traits, or more than ten.

Anderson's second step was to build a two- to five-point scale for each trait, describing each performance level. For example, Exhibit 5.1 is Anderson's scale for one of her traits, the "methods and materials section." She used a five-level scale, with five as the highest score. It is possible to use four, three, or two levels, depending on your purposes. A two-level scale is essentially a pass-fail or yes-no decision and can be used where you need only that level of judgment.

Anderson constructed a similar scale for each of the other nine traits she had identified. Her complete PTA scale is in Appendix C.

How to Construct a PTA Scale

Exhibit 5.2 summarizes the steps for constructing a PTA scale.

To begin her PTA scale for the scientific experiment assignment, Anderson selected a sample of former student papers, across a range of quality. (You don't have to have former papers, but they can be useful. If you don't have them, then try to imagine what students' papers might contain.)

Next, Anderson asked herself, What are the factors or primary traits that I want to measure? The *traits* are the factors that will

Exhibit 5.1.   Portion of a PTA Scale.

Assignment: Design and conduct an original scientific experiment and write a report using scientific format. (See assignment sheet in Exhibit 3.5.)

Trait: Methods and Materials Section

Level 5   Contains appropriate, quantifiable, concisely organized information that allows the experiment to be replicated. All information in the report can be related back to this section. Identifies sources of data. Sequences information appropriately. No wordiness.

Level 4   As above, but contains unnecessary information or wordiness.

Level 3   Experiment could be replicated from the information given. All information in the report can be related back to this section. However, fails to identify some data sources or has problematic sequencing.

Level 2   Marginally replicable. Parts of basic design must be inferred. Procedures not quantitatively described. Some information in Results or Conclusions sections cannot be anticipated by reading this section.

Level 1   Describes experiment so poorly it cannot be replicated.

[See entire scale in Appendix C.]

Exhibit 5.2.   Steps for Constructing a PTA Scale.

If possible, work from examples of past student performances, grading checklists, descriptions of criteria, comments on assignments or tests—anything that has helped you in the past to articulate criteria for students' performances.

1. Choose a test or assignment that tests what you want to evaluate. Make clear your objectives for the assignment.

2. Identify the criteria or "traits" that will count in the evaluation. These are nouns or noun phrases, such as "thesis," "eye contact with client," "use of color," or "control of variables."

3. For each trait construct a two- to five-point scale. These are descriptive statements. For example, "A '5' thesis is limited enough to treat within the scope of the essay and is clear to the reader; it enters the dialogue of the discipline as reflected in the student's sources, and it does so at a level that shows synthesis and original thought; it neither exactly repeats any of the student's sources nor states the obvious."

4. Try out the scale with a sample of student work or review with colleagues and revise.

count for grading or scoring the student's work. A glance at Anderson's ten traits presented earlier will show that traits are expressed as nouns or noun phrases.

Traits may already be stated in your assignment sheets, grading checklists, peer response sheets, or other material. If you cannot immediately come up with a list of the traits, then begin by describing an *A* paper or a *C* paper. The traits may emerge within your descriptions.

To develop traits, it also helps to talk with a colleague. If you have students' earlier work, let a colleague outside your discipline read a few examples. Then try to tell that colleague exactly why you gave that paper a *B* or a *C*. Anderson, a biology teacher, found it perplexing but very helpful to explain these things to Walvoord, an English teacher. For example, when Walvoord complimented one student's research report for beginning with such an "effective quotation," Anderson had to find the words to explain concretely what makes a good opening for a science report and why a good opening does not contain a quotation. Once you have your traits, construct a scale for each trait, as Anderson did for the Materials and Methods section.

Collaboration continues to be helpful as you construct the scales. For example, once Anderson's scale was drafted, Walvoord and Anderson separately scored several of Anderson's student papers. The discrepancies in their scoring led to further revision. Such a cycle can be repeated as many times as necessary until the scale and the agreement between graders meet your particular needs.

Scoring with a PTA Scale

Having explained how to construct a PTA scale, we move to the next topic, which is how to score student work using a scale. Anderson's "title" trait, for her students' scientific reports in biology, provides a quick and easy example (Exhibit 5.3).

Try using the PTA scale to rate each of following titles. They were written by Anderson's students before she developed her PTA scale. All titles contain fewer than twenty-five words, as the assignment sheet stated. Please use whole scores, not halves.

A   A Comparison of Prell and Suave Shampoo

B   The Battle of the Suds: Budweiser and Weiderman Beer

C   Would You Eat Machine-Made or Homemade Cookies?

D   A Comparison of Arizona and Snapple Ice Tea for pH, Residue, Light Absorbancy, and Taste

E   Research to Determine the Better Paper Towel

F   A Comparison of Amway Laundry Detergent and Tide Laundry Detergent for characteristics of Stain Removal, Fading, Freshness, and Cloth Strength

Let's see how you did. Here are Anderson's scores:

A   3   Prell and Suave identify the brand names. The word *comparison* vaguely hints at design and function but without specificity.

B   2   Only the brand names are explicit, and the title is almost misleading.

C   1   Perhaps it is modeled after a Speech 101 title that worked, but it doesn't fit this upper-level biology assignment.

D   5   The design is clearly specified, and the writer includes all the key words that will accurately classify this report in permuterm indexes or electronic databases.

E   2   As perfunctory as "Book Report on *Silas Marner.*"

F   4   Very good, but wordy.

Exhibit 5.3.   Anderson's PTA Score for Title of Scientific Report.

Trait: Title

Level 5   Is appropriate in tone and structure to a science journal

Contains all necessary descriptors for placement in a scientific data base

Contains necessary brand names

Identifies functions of experimentation

Allows reader to anticipate design

Level 4   Is appropriate in tone and structure to science journal

Contains most descriptors

May lack brand names

Identifies function of experimentation

Suggests design

Level 3   Identifies function and brand name but does not allow reader to anticipate design

Level 2   Identifies function or brand name, but not both

Lacks design information or is misleading

Level 1   Is patterned after another discipline or missing

After trying this scoring, you might recommend changes to the scale. Perhaps, after trying to score title F, you would recommend that the words *is concise* be added to Level 5 and *meets all criteria for 5 but may be wordy* be added to Level 4. After trying to score title C, you may suggest that the scale specify whether modeling after another discipline forces a score of 1 regardless of whether the writer identifies brand names or includes other features.

PTA scales tend to be revised as you use them, and they should be. The benefit of doing a PTA scale lies as much in the hard thinking it forces the teacher to do, and in the influences it exerts on teaching and learning, as in the final scale that emerges.

Why Take the Time to Do PTA?

How much time does it take to do a PTA scale? That depends on whether you are only measuring one or two traits or ten, as Anderson did. It also makes a difference whether you have previous assignment sheets or written grading criteria. Faculty members working from previous grading checklists have produced a draft of a four-trait or even an eight-trait PTA scale in under an hour. Some faculty may need up to ten hours, spread over time.

Why should you spend the time? When Anderson was constructing her scale, she was teaching a twelve–hour load, working for her doctorate at an institution fifty miles from her home, and was a single mother with two teenagers and a baby.

She did it because she wanted to

- Make grading more consistent and fair.
- Save time in the grading process. Once she was very clear about what she was looking for and had the PTA scoring rubric, she could move quickly through the students' work.
- Diagnose her students' strengths and weaknesses very specifically in order to teach more effectively.
- Track changes in her students' performance over several semesters so she could see how changes in her teaching affected student performance (see Anderson and Walvoord, 1991).

Here are some reasons why other faculty in our experience have found it worthwhile to do PTA:

- To help teaching assistants (TAs) grade papers consistently
- To reach agreement with colleagues on criteria for common exams, for multiple sections, or for sequenced courses

- To introduce greater distinctions into one's grading (For example, a psychologist had written a set of loosely stated criteria, but she found herself giving *A*'s to papers she felt did not deserve an *A*. Somehow, she had not captured in her loose list the full range of criteria she wanted to use to make distinctions. A primary trait analysis, with its greater specificity, helped her tease out for herself what those criteria were and then to distinguish the truly excellent papers from the others.)

- As data for departmental and general education assessment (see our final chapters)

PTA and Grades

It is important to realize that Primary Trait Analysis is not necessarily the same as grading, though grades can be derived from PTAs. Anderson had several reasons for using PTA, not all of which were linked to grading. For example, she could track whether her students improved from one semester to the next on a trait such as "experimental design." A paper might get a low grade but score highly on that trait. In this case the teacher's attention would be focused on the design score, not the grade. When a PTA scale is used for other purposes, it may act as a clarifying exercise to inform grading in a general way, making the teacher more clear about criteria. In this case, grading can continue to be done holistically, without actually scoring each student's paper on each trait of the PTA scale.

But let's look at how Anderson's PTA scale might translate into grades. Her current PTA scale awards a separate score on each of the ten traits. The PTA scale at this point could be used in several ways:

Option One: The teacher may build a grading scale that is less complex than the primary trait scale, but based on it. An example is Dorothy Solé's PTA-based scale for Spanish journals (Exhibit 5.4). Solé combines several traits—such as comprehensibility, grammatical correctness, risk-taking, and variety of sentence structure and form—into a single four–point scale.

A somewhat more complex example that combines all traits into a single scale anchored to grades is provided by John Breihan, the history faculty member we have been following. Exhibit 5.5 is the scale he uses to evaluate students' argumentative essays in Western Civilization. He constructed the scale by examining actual student papers. The eleven statements describe the kinds of papers

Exhibit 5.4.   Solé's PTA Scale Used to Determine Portion of Grade.

Class: Beginner's Spanish
Assignment: Journals

In addition to this scale, part of the grade is based on the number of entries and their length.

Note that several traits (comprehensibility, usage, risk taking, and variety of subject and form) are combined into a single scale.

4   The content of the journal is comprehensible. Although there are errors, verb tenses, sentence structure, and vocabulary are correctly used. The author has taken some chances, employing sentence structures or expressing thoughts that are on the edge of what we have been studying. The entries are varied in subject and form.

3   There is some use of appropriate verb tenses and correct Spanish structure and vocabulary, but incorrect usage or vocabulary interferes with the reader's comprehension.

2   The reader finds many of the entries difficult to understand, or many entries are simplistic or repetitious.

1   The majority of the entries are incomprehensible.

Breihan normally receives. Notice the primary traits that are embedded with the eleven statements: *thesis, evidence, counterargument, grammatical correctness.* Breihan indicates approximate grade equivalents along the left hand side of his sheet. When he responds to a student's draft or finished essay, he circles one of the eleven statements, writes a grade on top of the paper, and also makes marginal comments designed to illustrate and expand upon the information offered by the eleven statements.

Option Two: The teacher may employ the PTA scale. Solé and Breihan did not choose this option, but a number of teachers use a full scale with primary traits separately identified. This latter option offers the ability to rank traits separately from others. The scale is highly diagnostic and specific. When a PTA scale contains separated traits, the traits have to be weighted according to their importance. The maximum number of points students can gain on each item is different, depending on the importance the teacher attaches to the item. The total points for all the items combined can then be translated directly into a grade. For example, in grading students' scientific reports, Anderson might have awarded a maximum of five points for title but a maximum of twenty-five points for experimental design.

Option Three: PTA scores can be used to establish only a portion of the grade. For example, Anderson might have used students' PTA

Exhibit 5.5.   Breihan's Grading Scale for Argumentative Essays in Western Civilization Course.

The scale describes the common *types* of paper but may not exactly describe yours; my mark on the scale denotes roughly where your essay falls. More precise information can be derived from comments and conferences with the instructor.

[Breihan would offer written comments on the paper, in addition to his mark on this scale.]

Grade

1. The paper is dishonest.

F   2. The paper completely ignores the questions set.

3. The paper is incomprehensible due to errors in language or usage.

4. The paper contains very serious factual errors.

D   5. The paper simply lists, narrates, or describes historical data and includes several factual errors.

6. The paper correctly lists, narrates, or describes historical data but makes little or no attempt to frame an argument or thesis.

7. The paper states an argument or thesis, but the argument or thesis does not address the question set.

C   8. The paper states an argument or thesis, but supporting subtheses and factual evidence are

     Missing

     Incorrect or anachronistic

     Irrelevant

     Not sufficiently specific

     All or partly obscured by errors in language or usage

9. The paper states an argument on the appropriate topic, clearly supported by relevant subtheses and specific factual evidence, but counterarguments and counterexamples are not mentioned or answered.

10. The paper contains an argument, relevant subtheses, and specific evidence; counterarguments and counterexamples are mentioned by not adequately answered:

B   Factual evidence is incorrect, missing, or not specific.

     Linking subtheses are either unclear or missing.

     Counterarguments and counterexamples not clearly stated; employs "straw man" argument.

11. The paper adequately states and defends an argument and answers all counterarguments and counterexamples suggested by

A   Lectures

     Reading assignments (specific arguments and authors are mentioned by name)

     Common sense

scores to establish 80 percent of the grade, letting the other 20 percent depend upon issues such as whether the student had used the appropriate number of graphics, had followed the word limit, had met deadlines for draft submission, and had edited the final copy for grammar, punctuation, and spelling. Dorothy Solé's scale (Exhibit 5.4) determines only a portion of the grade given to student journals in a beginning Spanish class. The other portion is based on length and number of entries.

Option Four: Students can be asked to comply with certain requirements before using the PTA scale. This is a kind of gateway approach: students must meet certain requirements even to get into the ballpark where the PTA scale will be used. Student work that does not meet the gateway criteria is simply returned to the student with a failing grade or instructions to revise and resubmit. In this scenario, if a student turns in a final scientific report that does not meet the teacher's announced standard for typing, labeling of graphs, grammar, punctuation, or other aspects, the teacher responds by handing it back either with an *F* grade or with instructions to revise and resubmit for grading. Such a report does not made it into the ballpark, so it doesn't even get to the point of applying a PTA scale.

Exhibit 5.6 is a sheet that Walvoord used to explain to her students a gateway policy of grammar, punctuation, and spelling. Note that Walvoord did not apply this policy to drafts, in-class writing, or informal writing but only to finished, formal work. Walvoord reminded her students that the writing lab would help them with these criteria, and she handed out a sheet showing writing lab hours and location. She reminded her students about her gateway policy frequently, both orally and in writing. She let her department head know that she was implementing this policy. She offered students an opportunity to bring typed drafts of the paper to her up to twenty-four hours before the paper was due, and she helped students proofread the paper for the gateway criteria.

The result is that virtually all the final papers Walvoord received made it through the gate. Walvoord used the policy with first-year students in a selective private college; you will certainly want to set the criteria at different levels for different groups of students. The idea is not to hand out a lot of *F* grades but to teach students that, to function in the outside world, they will have to master Edited Standard Written English (ESWE), or their work will be tossed aside before the reader has even dealt with the writer's ideas. Walvoord wants to teach students the care required to bring a paper to a polished use of ESWE and to develop habits of attention and time management that will allow students to meet those criteria.

Exhibit 5.6.   Handout Used to Explain Walvoord's Gateway Criteria.

Policy for Use of Edited Standard Written English

Suppose a group of people were living on an island, all using the same language, until one day the island broke in two, separated by impassable water. In one hundred years, with no contact, would the people on both halves still use the same language forms? No. Human language is always changing. Language on each half of the island would evolve with different forms and rules. Neither would be better in any absolute sense—just different. Similarly, in the United States, language variations have developed among people separated by culture, socioeconomic status, or geography.

However, the language of the ruling class commonly comes to be regarded as standard. In the United States, the "standard" is the language of the white middle and upper classes. Forms of English developed by people of color and by people who have been poor or geographically isolated (as in Appalachia) are sometimes said to be "bad" or "incorrect" English, but such forms are only different, not bad. Each form of English has its own rules. People who say "she working" are not speaking "bad" English; they are using a different set of rules for forming the present tense.

One of the tasks of a good education is to make students aware of these facts about language. Another task of education, however, is to prepare students to function effectively in the world where readers generally expect writers to use Edited Standard Written English (ESWE). Thus, in this class, you must use ESWE. Here is the standard I will apply:

On finished, final, formal papers (not on drafts, in-class writings, or writing that I specifically label as informal), you must have no more than an average of two departures from ESWE per page, in any combination of the following areas:

- End-of-sentence punctuation (avoid run-on sentences, comma splices, fragments, or misuse of semicolon). Occasionally you may use a fragment or comma splice for a special effect. Label it in the margin.
- Verb forms (use ESWE rules for adding -*ed* and -*s,* for using helping verbs, and so on).
- Verb tense (avoid confusing shifts in verb tenses).
- Agreement of subject and verb.
- Pronoun form (use ESWE rules to choose between *I* and *me, she* and *her, who* and *whom,* and so on).
- Agreement of pronoun with antecedent (the antecedent is the word the pronoun refers to).
- Use of apostrophe *s* and the suffix -*es.*
- Use of quotation marks for all quoted words.
- Spelling (a typo counts as a misspelling).
- Proper sentence sense (no words omitted, scrambled, or incomprehensible).

Note that the policy applies only to finished, final, formal writing, *not* to drafts, in-class writing, or writing that I specifically label as informal.

In sum, PTA need not be the same as the grade, but can be used to derive the grade. The ways of doing so are as varied as teachers' ingenuity: simplifying the PTA scale into a single scale or a specifically grade-anchored scale; using a disaggregated set of traits weighted according to their importance; using a PTA scale for only a portion of the grade; and applying gateway criteria that students must meet before the PTA scale is applied to their work.

Frequent Questions in Developing PTA Scales

In working with faculty as they built primary trait scales, we have found some common questions.

At What Level of Generality Should I State the Traits?

Everyone we have known who composed a PTA scale has struggled with this issue. Let's take Anderson's biology scale as an example (Exhibit 5.1). Her "materials and methods" trait incorporates other traits: how replicable and quantifiable the data are, whether information is properly sequenced, and so on. Some of those might become separate traits, but there's no absolute rule about this; you can state traits at whatever level meets your needs. As your scale develops you may not only disaggregate traits but also combine them.

Typically, traits continue to be revised over time. For example, when Anderson composed her scale, she chose "nonexperimental variables" and "control of variables" as separate traits. Subsequent experience showed her that, as her students became more proficient at controlling variables (the more inclusive skill), their ability to recognize nonexperimental variables also improved. She might, if it were worthwhile to take the time, now fold the two together.

Which Forms of Language Should I Use?

In both Breihan's and Anderson's scales, the traits are stated as nouns or noun phrases. We think this rule should be broken only if you've thought carefully about it and made a conscious decision to change it for good reasons. Here are traits taken from two faculty members' drafts of PTA scales. They are not stated as nouns:

From an English course

Trait: Make inferences that are supported by specific information presented in the paper.

From a statistics course

Trait: Obtain a random sample of members of the population.

Trait: Obtain measures of the variables of interest from the members of the sample group in an appropriate manner.

None of these traits is cast as a noun or noun phrase. When traits become commands, descriptions of actions, or descriptions of levels of performance, the character of the scale changes, and confusion may result. We'd suggest changing the traits just mentioned to nouns:

English revision: Inferences

Statistics revision: Random sample (or sampling)

Statistics revision: Measurement of variables

The traits are nouns, but the scales within each trait are descriptions of student work. Scoring is done by matching student work to the description within various levels. For example, in a draft scale for a computer spreadsheet project, under the trait "spreadsheet accuracy," the teacher took over some of the language from the assignment sheet: "Spreadsheet must provide. . . ." It's better to leave out *must.* You are describing rather than giving orders. A draft of a scale for essays in French reads, "Student has made an attempt to follow correct French verb forms and syntax." It would be better to describe the verbs and syntax that will appear in the paper; whether the student made an attempt or not is a matter of conjecture.

How Many Levels Should the Scale Contain?

It depends on your purpose. You could have a two-level scale, which is a pass-fail scale. We have illustrated five levels, but three or four or six are certainly possible. How many distinctions do you need to make? How many can you make, given your present insight and the language you can find to describe what you want? Teachers often begin with two or three distinctions and then gradually find ways to distinguish additional levels.

What Are the Relations Among Levels in a Scale?

There are two basic relations among levels in a scale, and they are not mutually exclusive but often found in combination. The first relation is additive-subtractive. For example, a 5 is described as doing something better or more than a 4, or a 2 is described as doing something less well than a 3.

Here is an example of an additive scale from biologists Lesta Cooper-Freytag and Beverly Knauper of Raymond Walters College of the University of Cincinnati. This is the scale for the trait "Conclusion of a lab report." Note how, after level 5 is fully described, levels 4, 3, and so on are described as doing less of the same things.

Trait: Conclusion of the Lab Report

5 Report is arranged in a logical, coherent manner.
  Restates the hypothesis
  Explains how data supports or refutes the hypothesis
  Integrates information from lecture, test, and so on in the explanation of the data
  Recognizes and explains results that are unexpected or due to experimental error
  Applies scientific terminology (reflecting an understanding of scientific principles involved in the experiment)
  States acceptance or rejection of the hypothesis
4 Report meets first three criteria for 5 and meets any two of the remaining four criteria.
3 Report meets first three criteria for 5 and meets one of the remaining four criteria.
2 Meets any three of the seven criteria.
1 Meets two or fewer criteria.

The example begins with a 5 and then subtracts. A draft from a historian does it the opposite way: beginning with a lower-level description and then adding

4 Fulfills all the requirements for a 3 and excels in at least one of them.

Many primary trait scales, we've found, build on the additive-subtractive principle. However, a second type of relationship among levels is that the levels represent different qualities. Here is a draft from sociologist Grace Auyang of Raymond Walters College of the University of Cincinnati, for an assignment where students must respond to sociological articles:

Trait: Approach to the Problem Described in the Article

5 Student synthesizes the problem.
4 Student analyzes the problem.
3 Student explains the problem.
2 Student describes the problem.
1 Student merely identifies the problem or does not address the problem.

The teacher provides further descriptions of what she means by the terms *identify, synthesize,* and so on, but our point here is to show in skeletal form that the scale is not additive or subtractive—each level represents a different skill.

How Should I Handle Concepts Such as Adequate
and Appropriate?

You can use such terms as long as they are specific enough for your needs. If you want to explain your criteria to students, ask yourself (and them) whether they know what *appropriate* means or whether you need to specify. If you are preparing the PTA scale for use by an outsider, ask whether that person is sufficiently familiar with your discipline to know what you mean.

Let us look at the use of *appropriate, correct,* and similar terms in an example. Here is the draft of Bill Marsh's PTA scale for a statistics assignment at Raymond Walters College of the University of Cincinnati, in which students conduct a statistical study. They construct a null hypothesis, select a random sample, collect data, and draw conclusions. We have highlighted words such as *good, correct,* and so on.

Trait: Hypothesis Construction

3   *Correct* statement of problem with accompanying null and alternative hypothesis. *Good* choice of alpha level.
2   *Correct* statement of problem but does not include alternative hypothesis or alpha level.
1   Statement of problem is vague or missing, or hypothesis is *incorrect.*

Trait: Random Sample of Population

3   Population is *correctly* defined, and *correct* procedures are utilized in selecting a random sample from the population. The size of the sample is *appropriate* for the availability of the data.
2   The sample obtained is *adequate,* but it is evident a more thorough approach was possible.
1   Sample is nonrandom: it is biased and *inappropriate* to be used in the study.

Trait: Measurement of Variables

3   *Appropriate* test instrument (if necessary) is used *correctly.* Data is *properly* recorded and easy to understand.
2   At least one of the qualities listed above is missing.
1   It is unclear how the data were obtained, or the measures are not clear and evident to the understanding.

In this discipline (statistics) there are commonly accepted procedures on which professionals generally agree. The words *correct, appropriate,* and so on refer to these procedures. In some cases—such as point 3 under "Measurement of Variables"—it would probably take half a statistics textbook to explain what an "appropriate" instrument would be for each of the topics students might choose. Whether and to what extent the teacher would revise the scale to explain these terms would depend on the audience and purpose.

A different slant on words such as *correct* and *appropriate* is presented by a historian, Jim Cebula of Raymond Walters College of the University of Cincinnati, who in this PTA scale draft is trying to describe what he calls Elegance of Argument for history essays:

Trait: Elegance of Argument

5   Original and clearly stated thesis; persuasive, well-organized, imaginative use of source material.

4   Clearly stated thesis, good use of sources, well-organized.

3   Facts straight with a reasonable explanation of the subject under consideration.

2   Poorly stated thesis, inadequate survey of available sources, poor organization.

1   No awareness of argument or complexity.

In this scale, there are words of quality such as *good, well,* and *poor.* Depending on audience and purpose, the faculty member might want to define these. There are also words that describe characteristics such as *original, persuasive,* and *imaginative.* Again, depending on audience and purpose, the teacher may want to try to pin down at least some of the characteristics by which she or he decides that a student's work is original or imaginative.

When teachers are trying to construct PTA scales, words such as we've examined here will crop up continually. Decisions about such terms must be based on use. Is this teacher simply trying to articulate her criteria for herself and her students? If so, whatever level of specificity is needed for her own and her students' understanding will be enough. If PTA scales are being used for departmental or institutional assessment, some terms might need further definition, depending on how much agreement there is among the external readers about what *correct* in statistics or *original* in history means. A committee would want to establish guidelines about such matters when it requests the materials.

When dealing with such issues, don't forget the power of examples. Here's part of a primary trait scale draft by Ruth Benander, of Raymond Walters College of the University of Cincinnati, for First-Year Composition. Her assignment calls for students to read several different essays on a single topic and then to write an essay that synthesizes the readings. Here is her scale for the trait "Synthesis of Ideas":

Trait: Synthesis of Ideas

4   Presents a perspective that synthesizes the main ideas of several readings. This perspective creates an informative way to view the several main ideas of the readings in a way that

gives more meaning to the readings as a whole rather than if the main ideas were presented individually.

Example: Urban and rural violence may differ in frequency but not in the intensity with which they affect the lives of the people involved.

3   Presents a perspective that synthesizes the main ideas of several readings. This perspective may be very general.

Example: Violence is everywhere and affects us all.

At least two different readings are presented, though they may not be clearly related to each other under the umbrella of the synthesizing idea.

The two different readings chosen may demonstrate similar rather than different views of the perspective that synthesizes them.

2   The main idea of one reading is presented as the dominant perspective of the paper.

Example: The article "Gangster Wake-Up Call" deals with gang violence.

The main points of the reading are used to support the main ideas of the reading. (The paper will look more like a summary of the article than a synthesis of ideas.)

No alternative views are presented.

1   There is no clear main idea to the paper.

A reading may be discussed, but the main idea is not related to any other ideas.

Such examples are one way to clarify broad or vague concepts within a PTA scale. Another way is to focus on describing those physical, observable, or even, if possible, quantifiable aspects that led you to decide what is creative or appropriate to the conventions of the discipline. For example, an education department was struggling with how to reach consensus on evaluating students' senior portfolios. The portfolios contained three kinds of material: lesson plans, observations of individual students or of classrooms, and essays in which the seniors considered theoretical or practical issues in teaching and learning.

One of the things the professors all valued, as a trait for the portfolios, is what they called reflective practice. It means that the student teacher habitually reflects on and theorizes about his or her teaching experience rather than merely following unexamined practices or recording events.

To try to describe reflective practice more concretely, they took some portfolios they all agreed were outstanding in reflective practice and some they agreed were poor in that quality. Then they said, "There must have been some physical, observable characteristics in these written artifacts that led us to conclude that this portfolio shows a reflective practitioner and this one does not. What were they?" Carefully examining the students' texts, the faculty saw that the students who scored high on reflective practice shared these characteristics:

- They routinely stated why they themselves, or students with whom they were working, exhibited certain behaviors.
- They explained reasons and outcomes in terms of theoretical statements or hypotheses about teaching, usually expressed in the present tense.
- They routinely recorded questions and dilemmas.
- They recorded and described patterns in their own or in others' behavior.
- They reported having done reflective thinking. ("All that week, I thought about why Randy's behavior had surprised me so much.")
- They exhibited a musing, questioning tone.
- They noted missing information needed to draw conclusions from data or experience.
- They hypothesized as to causes, connections, or outcomes.

Detailed descriptions of the physical characteristics of the student's work, then, can help you be specific about qualities such as reflective practice.

What Kinds of Student Performances Can Be Scored by PTAs?

Almost any type of student performance involving higher-order thinking, creativity, or integration of skills can be examined effectively with a PTA. For example, PTAs can be constructed for oral presentations. Here are some traits used to evaluate oral reports in Mia Moore Barker's Food and Nutrition course at Indiana University of Pennsylvania:

> Organization
> Content
>   Problem statement
>   Accuracy
>   Depth
>   Logic of conclusions
> Applications
> Use of research
> Visuals accompanying the presentation
> Voice and demeanor

What about performances that are neither oral nor written but consist of actions in a particular setting? Let's turn to a grading checklist by Judith Bloomer of the Department of Occupational Therapy and Evelyn Lutz, of the Department of Nursing at Xavier College in Cincinnati. (The full scale is in Appendix C.)

Work-Related Performance

Traits
- Comprehension
- Problem identification and solution
- Organization
- Acceptance of responsibility
- Initiative or motivation
- Creativity
- Task completion
- Attendance

Work-Related Interactions with Others

Traits
- Collaboration
- Participation
- Attitude
- Independence
- Communication
- Responsiveness

(For other examples of PTA scales that evaluate students' actions, see Lawrence Fredendall's scale by which employers rate student intern teams in Appendix C.)

Our point in giving these examples is that oral, clinical, artistic, and other kinds of student performances can be assessed by PTA scales just as well as written work.

What If the Scale Leads Me to a Score That Does Not Feel Right?

Suppose, for example, that you find yourself giving high scores to student work you find competent but somehow lacking in the originality, creativity, or risk taking you want for *A* work. Often the problem is that you haven't included in the scale all the traits you are using. Look again at the student work that makes you uneasy. Compare it with samples that score above and below it. Ask yourself, What is missing in my scale? What is most important? Try to capture that in the scale. If you want originality, define and describe it as best you can and make it part of the scale. If you don't want to give an *A* to any work that doesn't have originality, then weight your scale accordingly.

How About Involving Students in Constructing Standards and Criteria?

We know faculty who like to involve their students in establishing criteria for student work. For example, a physicist whose students give oral reports on a physics project asks the students to brainstorm a list of the qualities that make an effective oral presentation from their point of view. Students typically offer items such as "speaker talks clearly and can be heard by everyone," "has good eye contact," "uses charts and graphs that are clear and correctly labeled," "explains the experiment in a well-organized way," and so on. These can then be incorporated by the instructor when building the PTA scale. For example, some traits suggested by these sample student comments might include "delivery," "charts and graphs," and "organization." In composing the scale under "delivery," the students' comments suggest that a high score might include speaking clearly, being heard by everyone, maintaining consistent eye contact with all areas of the room, and so on.

Can PTA Be Used with Multiple-Choice Tests?

What about situations where the teacher is using multiple choice tests? Are PTA scales useful there? Yes, they can be very useful, for the same reason we cited earlier: they force the teacher to state very explicitly what skills and knowledge she expects and to communicate those expectations to students.

To construct a PTA scale on the basis of a multiple-choice test, first describe the various levels of knowledge and skill that the questions address. For example, Exhibit 5.7 is a scale on which Patricia Schlecht, of the Nursing Department at Raymond Walters College of the University of Cincinnati, has categorized the multiple-choice questions she gives her students on a test. The levels are determined by two factors: (1) whether the question requires a high level of thinking, using Bloom's *Taxonomy of Educational Objectives* (1956) and (2) whether the textbook or Schlecht's lectures have given students the answer directly. Questions that may appear, by Bloom's *Taxonomy*, to require critical thinking may in fact only ask the student to repeat material given in the textbook or in lecture.

After classifying your multiple-choice tests according to the levels of skill and sophistication they require, you can then construct a PTA scale. For example, the top score on the PTA scale would be earned by the students who correctly completed all of the multiple-choice questions that tested the higher-level skills.

The sample PTA scale elements that follow force the teacher to specify the level of learning each multiple-choice question requires

Exhibit 5.7.   Using PTA Scores with Multiple-Choice Test Questions.

Level A	*Higher critical thinking:* Questions would fall in the *analysis*, *synthesis*, or *evaluation* levels of Bloom's taxonomy. Course materials give needed background to answer the questions. There is no directly visible connection between the course material and the test question.
Level B	*Lower critical thinking:* Questions would fall in the *application* level of Bloom's taxonomy. Course materials give needed background to answer the questions. There is a directly visible connection between course material and the test questions.
Level C	Questions would fall in the *knowledge* and *comprehension* levels of Bloom's taxonomy. Material is directly from the course presentation, with some changes in wording and phraseology.

and may lead the teacher to see how to improve the exam so that it more clearly reflects the course's learning goals.

5   Correct answers on all or all but one of questions 4, 7, 12, 13, 16, 19, 20, and 24.

4   Correct answers on all or all but one of questions 5, 6, 10, 14, 18, and 22.

Can PTA Scales Be Used for Portfolios?

We have discussed how faculty developed PTA scales for portfolios or collections of students' work. The basic process is the same. You decide which traits of the portfolio you will evaluate, then build a scale for each trait.

Evaluators of portfolios frequently want to see growth over time. Growth can be handled as a trait like any other. A high score on growth might be defined as a substantial difference between early and late work in certain qualities such as level of reasoning, creativity, and the like.

Another issue that arises in portfolios is whether you are judging them on the highest level present or on the percentage of the total that is of high quality, or both. But again, those decisions can be stated in your scale. In the previous example of the education department, faculty members believed that reflective practice should be habitual, so they reserved the highest score for those portfolios where reflection was common and typical, not sporadic. If they wanted consistency among graders, they might specify the number of separate works in the portfolio that had to have at least one passage that was reflective by their definition.

Table 5.1. Portion of PTA-Based Grid for Scoring Portfolios.

Trait: Use of *Warrants* in an Argument

		Minimal or no use	Moderate use	Extensive use
	1	1	1	2
Number of essays	2	1	2	3
	3 or more	2	3	4

Adapted from Schultz and Laine, 1986, p. 80.

Schultz and Laine (1986) present an ingenious way of combining the trait itself and its frequency in a portfolio. They constructed a PTA grid for scoring students' use of supporting statements they call *warrants* in argumentative essays. The grid awards points for the trait itself and for the number of portfolio essays in which the trait appears. Table 5.1 is a portion of their grid for scoring one trait in student portfolios. Obviously, other traits could be similarly scored. Resource 5.1 lists helpful sources for assessing student portfolios.

How Can PTA Be Used with Team Teachers and TA Graders?

Gisela Escoe, Philip Way, and their graduate assistant Jack Julian, who teach economics at the University of Cincinnati, use PTA to help gain consistency among TA graders in large microeconomics and macroeconomics classes. Exhibit 5.8 is an example of the short assignments that Escoe and Way frequently assign to their students throughout the course. After introductory sessions in which Escoe, Way, and the TAs go over the PTA scale and score sample papers,

---

Resource 5.1.

Sources for Assessing Student Portfolios.

Black, Daiker, Sommers, and Stygall (eds.), 1994. A collection of essays about portfolio assessment.

Hamp-Lyons and Condon, 1993. Two faculty committed to portfolio assessment nonetheless question some of its assumptions.

Exhibit 5.8.   Assignment and PTA Scale for Way's Microeconomics Course.

Assignment 3: Market Structure (5 percent of grade)

Questions and Instruction

1. Choose an industry that we have not discussed in class or in homework problems. Decide whether it approximates perfect competition, monopoly, oligopoly, or monopolistic competition.

2. Explain why your chosen industry has the market structure you identified in (1). Refer to the characteristics that distinguish the four types of market structure.

3. Suppose that you wish to be a producer in the industry that you have chosen. Is it likely that you would be able to make economic profits in the long run? Explain why or why not with reference to the theory of long-run equilibrium in the type of market that you identified in (1).

4. Does your chosen industry maximize social welfare? Explain in terms of a diagram.

This exercise is to be completed independently. Please type your solutions. Do not write more than one page. Your assignment should be handed in on Tuesday, November 29.

Grading Criteria

You will be graded on a scale from 5 to 0 according to the following criteria:

5   You specify the market structure correctly and identify sufficient characteristics that make it distinctive (without identifying any incorrect characteristics). You correctly determine whether profits can be earned in the long run, and you adequately explain why. You correctly state whether the industry maximizes social welfare, and you illustrate your response with an appropriately drawn diagram.

4   As in (5), except that you err in one way.

3   As in (5), except that you err in two ways.

2   As in (5), except that you err in three ways.

1   As in (5), except that you err in four ways.

0   As in (5), except that you err in five ways, or you fail to follow instructions.

the TAs grade all the papers. TAs are encouraged to bring to the faculty any papers about which they are unsure.

Let's see how Escoe, for example, handles the communication with her students. Escoe is very candid with her students about the fact that TAs grade the papers. She shows students the PTA scale right along with the assignment, as you can see in Exhibit 5.8. Escoe tells students that if they think the TA's grade is not appropriate, they may submit the paper and the TA's grade to her, with a written explanation of the student's views. She promises she will never lower a grade in that situation but only raise it if deserved. This makes submitting papers a no-risk act for students, which is what she wants. About 5 percent of the students submit their papers to her. In a class of three hundred, that's fifteen students—a number she feels she can manage. Student complaints also can alert Escoe to TAs whose grading may be frequently contested.

How do you arrive at the scale in the first place, when you are working with TAs or colleagues in a team teaching situation? One way is to have one person compose a scale that everyone uses. This method might be common when a single faculty member is working with TAs who are new or inexperienced.

However, in a team-taught course, or in a situation where TAs participate as colleagues in establishing criteria and standards, your goal is to establish a collaborative way of arriving at a PTA scale. You want to maximize participation while not wasting time. We suggest the following procedure:

1.   As the course goals are established, basic assignments set in place, and learning activities planned, the group should map out the main criteria and standards by which the most important assignments and exams will be evaluated and by which students will receive ongoing feedback on their progress.

2.   Working from the basic outlines established in those discussions, the group meets to establish the PTA scale to be used for each major assignment and test. First, discuss who needs to know the criteria and standards, and in which format. This step helps the group decide how complex the scale needs to be and which form it will take for various audiences.

3.   For each assignment or test in turn, establish a list of the traits. If you have sample papers, you might begin by talking about which grade you would give them and why. This discussion will reveal traits. For example, suppose someone says, "I'd give this paper a *B* because it has a clear problem statement, and it analyzes the problem well, but the solutions do not take into account all the

important factors." At least three traits are embedded in that statement: (1) the problem statement, (2) analysis of the problem, and (3) solution. Someone should be listing these traits on a board or newsprint pad. Do not try to assign weights to the traits at this point (though for later use you might want to jot down information that emerges about the relative importance of traits). If the group disagrees, try to pinpoint the traits that are at issue and to reach consensus.

You will have traits stated at various levels of generality. For example, in this situation, the "solution" might be a trait with the factors considered as part of the description of the solution, but "factors considered in the solution" might also be a separate trait with its own scale. At this stage, take down peoples' insights about which traits are overlapping or subordinate, but do not try to make decisions about aggregating or separating traits in the large group because it will take too long and lead to confusion.

As discussion proceeds, it may emerge that the assignment or even the entire course plan needs to be changed or explained more clearly. If you have time, let that happen. One of the most useful outcomes of discussions about standards and criteria is the opportunity to rethink course goals, course structure, and the nature of tests and assignments.

4.   The group should decide how many levels the scale needs at the start. We suggest three to five levels.

5.   Now we suggest that one or two people take this brainstormed list and draft a PTA scale. They return with the draft, and the entire group offers suggestions for changes in the scale, which the writers then incorporate. Repeat this cycle until everyone is comfortable with the scale or until everyone is too tired to object. If you cannot reach consensus on all the traits, consider the possibility that common traits on which people do agree may be used by everyone and give individuals the freedom to construct their own scales around other traits.

6.   As soon as you have sample student papers, let the group score papers using the scale. Have individuals score papers independently at first, then meet to compare scores, discuss discrepancies, and change the scales as needed.

7.   You will want to hold periodic discussions in which sample papers are scored, discrepancies discussed, and the scale and assignments changed as needed.

This procedure assumes everyone's participation. If there are too many people for this "town meeting" approach, a committee may do the same thing.

ACTIVITY

If you have been following our course-planning procedures, you now have a course skeleton and a draft of at least one assignment. Now we invite you to do the following:

1. Construct a list of primary traits for one of your assignments or tests. You may simply choose two or three traits that seem most important, or you may try to construct a list of all the traits you want to use for grading. (Remember that some aspects that count in the grade, such as having the paper typed, editing for standard English, or avoiding numerical errors may be handled as "gateway" characteristics separate from the PTA scale.)

2. Construct a PTA scoring scale for at least one of your traits. You may use a two-, three-, four-, or five-level scale, depending on how many levels you can or want to construct.

3. Score one or several papers on this scale and revise the scale as needed.

4. Revise your draft of assignment instructions to students to reflect clearly your criteria and standards. (Remember that you may include the PTA scale itself, a simplified version of it, or other language that makes criteria and standards clear.)

CHAPTER 6

Calculating Course Grades

A model for calculating course grades is not just a mathematical formula; it is an expression of your values and goals, because different models will express different relationships among types of student performance and will have different effects on how students perceive the reward system in the course. Your model for weighting various components is also a communication to your students about what you think is most important and about where you want them to put their effort.

Grading Models

It is worthwhile to consider the three models presented in the following pages and to choose thoughtfully among them. For each model we present an example and a description. Models differ in their accommodation to students' development after a weak beginning and in whether they allow students to substitute high performance in one area for a low performance in another. At the end of the chapter we discuss issues such as extra credit, contract learning, and curving.

Model 1: Weighted Letter Grades

Example

Tests average letter grade counts 40 percent of course grade
Field project letter grade counts 30 percent of course grade
Final exam letter grade counts 20 percent of course grade
Class participation grade counts 10 percent of course grade

Characteristics

    A. The underlying pedagogical assumption is that several kinds of performances are distinct from one another, and that they are differentially valued in calculating the final evaluation.

    B. Student performances in various categories are kept separate: for example, tests are separate from the field project. This tends to erase or minimize variances of performance within a single category. A student who has scored high *F* average on tests has *F* as 40 percent of his or her grade; a student who has scored a low *F* average on tests also has *F* as 40 percent of his or her grade.

    C. Different kinds of excellence are differently valued. For example, if class participation counts as only 10 percent of the grade, and a field research project counts as 40 percent, the very best class participator can only slightly influence his or her overall grade by stellar performance in class participation. However, the very best field project researcher can much more heavily influence his or her final grade.

    D. The teacher may apply various values and criteria in deciding how heavily to count each type of work. There may be a developmental progression, for example, where the teacher gives a low weight to early tests and a higher weight to later tests or to the final exam. However, the system itself does not necessarily imply a developmental progression. The system, with its emphasis on the average grade in each category, implies that all tests, however they are placed in the semester, will be averaged to provide 40 percent of the grade.

Model 2: Accumulated Points

Example

Tests	0–40 points
Field Project	0–30 points
Final Exam	0–20 points
Class participation	0–10 points
Course grade determined by accumulated points	92–100 points = A
	85–91 points = B
	76–84 points = C
	69–75 points = D
	68 points or below = F

Characteristics

A. The underlying pedagogical assumption is that, to some extent at least, good or poor performance in one area can be offset by work in other areas. For example, take these two students in light of the point system just presented:

	Student 1	Student 2
Tests (possible 40 points)	25 points	15 points
Field project (possible 30)	25 points	25 points
Exam (possible 20)	15 points	15 points
Class participation (possible 10)	5 points	5 points
Total	70 points	60 points

Both students did poorly on the tests. If points had been translated into grades, both would have received an "F" test grade. They did equally well on all other categories. In the weighted letter grades system, they would have received the same course grade. However, in the accumulated points system, the fact that Student 1 got more points on the tests than Student 2 allowed Student 1 to accumulate enough points to pass the course, whereas Student 2 failed the course.

B. The faculty member can strengthen the substitution quality of this model by offering total points that equal significantly more than the number required for an *A* course grade. In the example above, the total number of points in all categories is 100. Suppose the teacher had offered a total of 120 points, but still counted 92–100 as an *A*. Such an action would enhance the substitution quality of this model: a student who earned maximum points in one area could greatly offset poor performance in another area.

C. This model is developmental in the sense that a poor performance early in the course is not necessarily crippling if the student earns enough points. The points earned count toward the final accumulated total.

D. The system also allows students to some extent to decide where to put their effort. Just as students who make a poor start may be working very hard at the end, others may accumulate enough points for their desired grade in your course by the thirteenth week and then put their energy into other courses. This may affect class preparation or participation at the end of the course.

Model 3: Definitional System

Example

To get a particular course grade, you must meet or exceed the standards for each category of work. The following table illustrates a course where there are two distinct categories of work: graded work and pass-fail work.

Course grade	Graded work	Pass-fail work
A	A average	Pass for 90 percent or more of assignments
B	B average	Pass for 83 percent or more of assignments
C	C average	Pass for 75 percent or more of assignments
D	D average	Pass for 65 percent or more of assignments

If a student gets an *A* average on her graded work but earns a pass for only 65 percent of the pass-fail work, she receives a *D* for her course grade, because *D* is the highest level at which she meets or exceeds the standards for both graded and pass-fail work.

Characteristics

A. The underlying pedagogical assumption is that different categories of work are each important, and the teacher does not want to allow one to compensate for the other in any way. For example, Walvoord uses this system in a literature class where students are required to bring to class, nearly every day, writing assignments based on their readings. Walvoord uses these writing assignments as the basis of class discussion, much as Breihan the historian does. Walvoord does not grade these assignments, other than pass-fail. However, being prepared for class most of the time is a non-negotiable and very important value to Walvoord. Thus her definition of an *A* student is one who not only does well on tests and exams but who also is prepared for class at least 90 percent of the time. If a student is habitually unprepared for class, in Walvoord's system, no brilliance on tests and papers can raise that student to an *A* grade, because the student has not conformed to Walvoord's definition of an *A* student. On the other hand, Walvoord also does not want to let students' class participation raise their grade beyond what they are able to achieve in their formal tests and papers.

B. The definitional system is possible also when you give grades, rather than pass-fail to every category. For example, a science teacher may want to require that for an *A* grade in the course, the student score at least an *A*-minus average on the tests and exams, and at least *B*-minus average on the lab reports:

Course grade	Tests and exams	Lab reports
A	A average	B average
B	B average	C average
C	C average	D average
D	D average	D average

Again, there are two distinct categories of work, and the teacher values both. Performance in one is in no way a substitute for performance in another.

C. A definitional grading system must be carefully and thoroughly explained to students because it is not as common as the other models. Put your policy clearly in writing in the syllabus and on the assignment sheets, and explain it several times in class. Students will tend to assume that you will combine or average their grades in the various categories. It may appear to them that you are awarding them the grade determined by their lowest performance. Students may complain that they were knocked down to the lowest grade. Walvoord patiently explains, in answer, that they were not knocked down to their lowest grade; the system is not conceived that way. What they did was to fail to meet her definition of the higher grade. A basketball player must both drop the ball into the basket and follow the dribbling and traveling rules. If any of these conditions is not met, the basket doesn't count.

Penalties and Extra Credit

The teacher may modify any of these grading systems with penalties and extra credit.

A penalty occurs when, for example, the teacher lowers the grade a certain amount for infractions such as handing in late work, failing to edit carefully for grammar and punctuation, being overreliant on sources, failing to cite sources, or outright plagiarism.

Extra credit is most obviously applicable to the accumulated points system, but it can also work with any of the other systems.

You can simply allow extra credit to raise the exam average by 10 percent or so, or factor in the extra credit assignment as 20 percent of the tests grade. And so on.

Characteristics

A. Penalties place a premium on punishment for infractions. This calls the students' attention to the seriousness of the infraction. It is perhaps best used for matters about which the teacher feels strongly, or which the teacher knows will carry a heavy penalty in the outside world.

B. Being docked often inspires the pugilistic instincts of human beings, and students are likely to contest such penalties. Alternately, the penalties may be demoralizing to the students. Such a system should be used with care. The teacher should make extra efforts to convey that, though the work is being penalized, the teacher still respects the student, appreciates what she has achieved, and believes she can do better in the future.

C. Additions such as extra credit are useful in situations where the teacher wants to let the students compensate for failures in one area by extra work in another area. In this sense, extra credit, used with any model, can enhance opportunities for the student to substitute work in one area for work in another.

Establishing Ceilings and Floors

In any of these systems, it is possible to establish ceilings or floors. For example, you can say that extra credit can only raise the grade by one letter, or, in the definitional system, you can say that the student will be awarded only one grade below his or her test grades, no matter how little of the pass-fail work she or he has done. Such strategies help to blunt or extend some of the qualities of a grading system.

Developmental Versus Unit-Based Approaches

Within any of the systems mentioned earlier, you can work from a developmental approach or a unit-based approach. In the developmental approach, the student's work at the end of the course is assumed to demonstrate the stage she or he has reached and is counted much more heavily than earlier work, leaving lots of room for early failures and slow starts. In such a system, for example, a cumulative final exam or project may count very heavily or may even be the only official grade, with earlier work given unofficial grades or not graded at all.

The drawback to this system is that students may slack off in the earlier weeks, believing they can gain the golden ring at the end by a final spurt of energy. Another consideration is that some students will be uncomfortable or unhappy because so much weight is placed on final work. They want a more solid fix on how they are doing early in the course. Also, students may want credit for high-quality early work.

The unit-based approach considers that the course is composed of discrete units, each of which counts. Thus the grade on the first unit test may be as heavily weighted or almost as heavily weighted as the grade on the final unit, because all units are seen to be important in and of themselves. This approach minimizes the developmental aspect—the notion that the student grows in his or her ability and that early failures are less important than final achievement.

A middle ground is to count all tests and assignments heavily but to allow the student to drop his or her lowest grade. Another middle ground is to count the final work somewhat more heavily than earlier work. Also, you can hold back a "fudge factor" of 10 percent or so that you can award to students whose work shows major improvement over the semester. Or you may simply announce in the syllabus and orally to the class that you reserve the right to raise a grade when the student's work shows great improvement over the course of the semester.

Contract Grading and Contract Learning

The term *contract grading* has now largely been replaced by *contract learning*—an expanded concept, differently framed. Contract learning is not so much a system for encouraging students to choose among various levels of teacher-determined work; rather, it is a way of negotiating with the students, of drawing them into the learning process. (Knowles, 1986 is a good starting place for more help on contract learning.)

Characteristics

A. Contract learning attempts to maximize student choice and student responsibility.

B.   Contract learning allows tailoring of work to individual students' needs, learning styles, backgrounds, and goals. Students often have a voice in establishing learning goals and other aspects of the course.

C.   Contract learning makes explicit the contractlike aspects of any grading system, and it substantially extends and changes the traditional contract. In one sense, all grading systems are contracts. In the traditional system, the teacher establishes the learning goals and the categories of performance. The students assume that if they meet the criteria for a *B* they will get a *B*. In contract learning, the student is invited to help establish the learning goals, standards, and criteria.

D.   The "contract" in contract learning may have a psychological effect of making the student feel more obligated to do the work to which she or he aspired. Especially in systems where the teacher actually discusses with each student what she or he hopes to earn and what work will be done at what level, the personal nature of the contract may be a high motivator for the student.

E.   Contract learning may take more teacher time; it certainly will change the traditional dynamic of the classroom.

Choosing a Grading System

We have tried to convey here three basic models and some permutations. You should choose the model that best fits your own style, goals, and values, and then adapt it as you judge best. In the final section of this chapter we discuss how to determine the distribution of students' grades within a class. Should you grade on a curve? Will your department head frown on your giving too many *A* or *F* grades?

To Curve or Not to Curve

Grading on a curve means that a certain percentage of students receive each grade—for example, 10 percent get *As* and so on. Grading on a curve, we believe, introduces dynamics that may be harmful to learning:

1.   The notion that grades, and the learning they supposedly represent, are a limited commodity dispensed by the teacher according to a statistical formula

2. Competition among students for a limited number of high grades—competition that encourages students to keep the other person from learning, lest that other person take one of the precious and limited high grades

3. The notion that learning is a demographic characteristic that will show a statistical distribution in a sample population

4. The notion that each class is a sample population

5. A teacher's role that focuses on awarding a limited number of grades by a formula, rather than a role that includes rewarding all learning with the grade it deserves

6. The possibility that standards for a grade will be lowered to enable a certain percentage of students to receive that grade

Instead of these dynamics, we recommend communicating to your class that learning often happens most richly from collaboration within a community of learners. You want learners to help each other (in legitimate ways), to contribute their best ideas to class discussion, and to work effectively in groups and teams, as they often will have to do in their future lives. You want them to believe that they and their classmates can be rewarded for outstanding effort and achievement. You want to be free to help and encourage all of them to their highest possible levels of achievement. Further, we recommend setting standards for student work that represent your best judgment of what they need to know and of what they can achieve with their best effort and your best teaching.

Faculty sometimes tell us that they fear a political problem with the policy we recommend. When teachers teach well, coach students through the learning process, motivate them strongly, and facilitate learning in highly successful ways, students will learn more. So shouldn't they get higher grades? But if they get higher grades, will the professor's department head or dean or colleagues disapprove? Tough question. Unfortunately, we have no perfect answers.

One suggestion, though, is that, before you assume that you cannot follow our recommendations about grading, you should find out exactly what the constraint on your grading is. Which forces motivate the person (department head, dean, colleagues) whom you think is imposing the constraint? Have a frank talk with that person. Ask if there is an expectation about the distribution of grades. If the person responds in the affirmative, then probe politely but firmly to find out why the person wants your grades to fall within a certain distribution. Do not exaggerate the constraint. We have heard faculty talk as though they were being forced to grade on a curve, when in fact the only real constraint was that they not give too many *A* grades or too many *F* grades. Once you understand the worries that are influencing your department head or dean and the real constraints that are operating, perhaps you can work out a solution that meets both your and your department head's needs and enhances student learning and motivation.

Do not assume, or let others assume, that a challenging course that makes high but achievable demands on students will inevitably result in high attrition rates or low student satisfaction. The literature strongly suggests that the greatest motivation comes from a challenge that is neither so easy as to be boring nor so difficult as to seem impossible to achieve (Forsyth and McMillan, 1991). And, as we heard Baltimore psychologist Susan Robison once aptly say in a workshop, "Self-esteem comes from doing hard things well."

Once you understand the constraints clearly, you might consider one approach or a combination of several. One response to the criticism that your grades are too high is to raise your standards. You do not limit the number of *A* grades by a statistical formula but rather by setting the standards sufficiently high that, even with your brilliant teaching, getting an *A* takes special effort and talent. Raising the standards for an *A* may be all that is required. In many situations, it doesn't matter to the department head or dean how many *B* grades you give; after all, *B* is the national average grade. Teachers we know who follow this pattern save the *A* grade for truly outstanding work that, realistically, not many students can achieve, but the teacher's careful, interactive guidance and instruction create a setting in which many students who work hard get *B* grades.

If the constraint limits the number of *D* and *F* grades you can give, try working especially hard with students who are having a hard time; try to understand what will motivate and help them, rather than lower your standards. But also understand that the meaning of a grade is socially determined. You have to teach and grade within the grading system as it is currently interpreted in the society that you and your students inhabit, and you have to teach and grade the students you have now, not the ones you wish you had, or the ones you had in 1975, or the ones you had when you were a TA at Berkeley. Check with colleagues who are teaching the same class as you are. Would the students who receive *D* or *F* in your class get higher grades in all your colleagues' classes? If so, you are running a different currency system than the one in which you live. It's as if you tried to float confederate dollars in Nebraska or if you tried to insist that a dollar should have the same value now that it did in 1975. Grade inflation is a major national problem, but it can only be addressed on a national level, not by individuals working alone.

A final way to meet criticism of your grade distribution is to offer to show the critic your assignments, tests, criteria, and standards for each grade and samples of student work at each level. If your critics are not willing to look at your students' work, your offer may put them on the defensive and silence them. If they are willing to look at your students' work, then you have initiated a dialogue about standards that may benefit you and the department. You might be able to turn this dialogue from a criticism of your grading systems to a policy discussion within the department.

In any case, even if you foresee no problems, we advise that you discuss with your department head your grading criteria, standards, and practices, especially in your first five years at a new school or with a new department head. You need not ask his or her permission for decisions that should rightly be in your control, but you can approach him or her in a spirit of consultation and information. After all, this person is in charge of recommending you for promotion or tenure and may have to answer students who complain about your grading practices. When those things happen, you want the department head to have a copy of your syllabus in the file and to remember your having stopped in to discuss your syllabus, course plans, and grading practices.

ACTIVITY

1. Jot down the most important things you want your course grading system to accomplish, for yourself and for your students. You might use the following outline or devise one of your own:

   A. In this course, I want to allow good work in one area to compensate for poor work in another area.

   _____ Yes (consider the Accumulated Points Model)

   _____ No (consider the Definitional Model)

   _____ To some extent (consider the Weighted Averages Model)

   B. The work in this course is

   _____ Developmental: what the student has achieved by the end is far more important than early failures or slow starts (consider developmental approaches to your chosen model)

   _____ Unit-based: each unit is important; units are not highly cumulative; there is no final exam or project that measures students' total achievement (consider unit-based approaches to your chosen model)

C. My students are most powerfully motivated by a grading system that (you may check more than one)

_____ Gives early, firm grades and rewards strong work no matter where it appears in the semester (consider unit-based approach)

_____ Allows early failure and slow starts (consider developmental approach)

_____ Allows a great deal of individual flexibility, student choice, and student participation in establishing expectations (consider contract learning)

2. Construct a grading system for your course. Discuss it with colleagues and students. Modify as needed.

CHAPTER 7

Communicating with Students About Their Grades

A grade is not just an evaluation; it is also a communication, embedded within other verbal and nonverbal communications: your syllabus, explanation of the grading system, explanation of the criteria and standards for the grade, oral discussions in class about grading, conferences with students about their grades, and the entire semester's conversation between you and your students, with all its nuances of gesture, tone, and stance. This chapter concentrates on the communication that takes place around grades. Resource 7.1 suggests resources for establishing healthy communication with your students.

Suggestions for Effective Communication

In the following pages we offer you suggestions that can guide effective communication about grading and can contribute to a healthy level of trust and motivation in your classroom.

Assume Students Want to Learn

Like all human beings, students have many kinds of motivation. We all at times want to get by with the least possible work and bother. We all at times want to blame someone else for our shortcomings. But we and our students are also motivated by curiosity, interest, and a desire to be well educated, to understand complex subjects, to do difficult things well. So in your communications with students about grades, avoid the assumption that students are

---

Resource 7.1.

Sources for Establishing Good Student-Faculty Communication in the Classroom.

Boice, 1996. Based on empirical observation of teachers, offers principles for faculty success, including specific suggestions about how to establish good communication in the classroom. See especially Boice's first principle. Don't be put off by the book's obtuse title.

Palmer, 1983, 1987. These are by far the most philosophical of the works cited on this page. Palmer offers a broad view of the meaning of community in the academy.

Paulsen and Feldman, 1995. Reviews the literature and offers suggestions about communicating with students. (See the section titled "Listening to the Voice of Students," pp. 53–66, which focuses on collecting helpful written and oral student evaluations.)

"grademongers." Listen carefully, appeal to their highest motivations, and respect them as people who want to learn—perhaps in confused and limited ways, perhaps with mixed motivations—but who want to learn. This attitude of listening and respect undergirds all the other suggestions in this chapter.

Embed Grading in a Course That Sets High Expectations and Helps Students Meet Them

Grades become a motivating part of the learning process when the teacher has set high expectations and then helps students meet those expectations (Chickering and Gamson, 1987; Kurfiss, 1988). Grades should emerge as part of the learning process within a well-designed, assignment-centered course in which goals are clear, tests and assignments help students reach those goals, student work is evaluated by clear criteria known ahead of time, teaching is interactive, and students receive ongoing feedback about their work.

Use the Syllabus to Show Students How Tests and Assignments Serve Course Goals

The teacher may have worked out a well-organized course but then may fail to communicate that logic to students. One way to communicate is through your syllabus. List what you expect students to be able to learn. Then show, in writing, how the assignments and exams help them to learn and demonstrate their learning. Show how in-class and out-of-class activities help them meet your expectations.

For example, a syllabus that Walvoord constructed for a course titled "The Outsider in Modern American Fiction" read on its front page "What You Can Learn in this Course" and included the following points:

- Familiarity with a body of well-known modern fiction
- The ability to analyze fiction orally and in writing using the tools of the discipline
- Particularly, the ability to analyze the role of the "outsider" in fiction
- Enjoyment of reading fiction as a life-long habit

Then, in a section labeled "How the Course Will Help You Learn These Things," a few paragraphs explained how the course was organized around the learning goals.

Part of the schedule part of the syllabus is presented in Exhibit 7.1. Each unit of the course was printed in boldface, followed by the goals for that particular unit, all of which related to the general course goals. Under the unit title and goals was the daily schedule of events for the weeks within that unit, including preparation for class and a description of in-class activities. To show how tests, assignments, and course work addressed the goals, Walvoord frequently used phrases such as *in order to* or *to help you learn . . .* and then the description of what students were to do.

Inquire, Reinforce, and Remind Students About Course Goals

The syllabus only lays the groundwork for communicating to your students the goals and structure of your course and the role of your assignments and tests in meeting those goals. Here are some other suggestions:

- Ask students their goals at the beginning of the course. (Angelo and Cross, 1993, suggest how to plan and use short, informal, ungraded questions in the classroom.)
- At midterm, ask them to write how they are doing in meeting their goals.
- When they hand in an assignment or test, ask them to write an introductory paragraph that answers the question, Why are we doing this assignment?
- In class, every week or two, review the basic structure of the course. Ask, "What are the three units of this course again?" Or "Why are we doing this assignment?"

Exhibit 7.1.   Portion of Syllabus for Walvoord's Literature Course.

Unit 2: First-Person Accounts by "Outsiders"

Goals of Unit 2

- To become familiar with some major American fiction that is written as a first-person account by an "outsider"
- To analyze this fiction orally and in writing, using the tools of literary analysis, particularly focusing on symbolism, plot, and allegory
- To analyze orally and in writing the role of the "outsider" in this fiction
- To enjoy reading, discussing, and writing

Day	Preparation	In-Class
Tue 3/3	Read Prologue and Chapters 1–7 of Ellison's *Invisible Man* (2 hours). To help you analyze plot, symbol, and allegory, write the following (1 hour): 1. How would your reaction to the story be different if the prologue had been omitted? Why does Ellison choose to arrange his plot by telling the ending first? 2. How is the boxing match an allegory? 3. What does the briefcase symbolize to the young man? To you as the reader? Bring your writing to class for discussion. Hand in, pass-fail.	1. Manuel López: report on Tuskegee Institute. (5 min.) 2. Ruth Harrison: What is lobotomy? (1 min.) 3. Clear up basic questions about the novel. 4. Discuss plot, allegory, symbolism. 5. In-class freewrite: discuss your reactions to the novel so far. Share. (5 min.) 6. Discussion: what do you think will happen next in the novel? Why?

Discuss the Roles of Grades

In Chapter Two we outlined four roles that grades play:

1. Evaluation
2. Communication
3. Motivation
4. Organization

It pays to ask students what they think grades do and to discuss with them the most useful roles for grading in your classroom. Difficulty between teachers and their students over grades may arise from three additional roles that students often assign to grades but that teachers often resist:

1. Reward for effort
2. Ticket to upward mobility
3. A purchased item that has been paid for

It does little good to deny or ignore these last three roles. Students' experience is that grades do function in these ways. We suggest, therefore, that teachers and students should communicate about the roles they envision for grading.

A related issue is the criteria for the grade. A clear statement in the syllabus and on assignment sheets should let students know what role, if any, effort and progress will play in your grading and why it plays that role.

Discuss Fairness

Difficulty may arise around the complex notion of fairness. You need to know what your students think fairness means; you need to talk with them about how to achieve fairness for everyone (including you) in your classroom. One way to do this might be to ask students, toward the beginning of the course, to describe a class they've had in the past where they thought the grading system was fair and helped them learn well, and then describe a class in which the grading system was unfair and interfered with their learning. You will learn a lot this way about your students' definition of fairness and about how they envision grades contributing to their learning.

Explain What Each Grade Represents

The fairness issue can often be effectively addressed and student learning can be guided by clear explanations of what the grades represent. Look back at Breihan's grading sheet for his history essays (Exhibit 5.5) and the PTA scales in Chapter Five and in Appendix C. We recommend that such information be given to students before they start work on their tests or assignments. Teachers who use such lists of standards and criteria report, and we ourselves have experienced, that such explanations help to motivate students, to show them our expectations, to link their grades to demonstrated learning, and to convey that we have graded their work fairly; that is, we have graded it consistently according to clear criteria that are known ahead of time and that are the same for everyone.

A grading sheet such as Breihan's also cuts down on the number of students who will ask you why they didn't get a higher grade. When students do come with those questions, the grading sheet provides a basis for the discussion. The grading sheet also provides a basis for discussion if the student appeals your grade to your department head or to a grievance committee. If your standards and criteria are clear, and if you can show that you applied them, you are on solid ground.

Speak to the Learner, Not the Error

When we, as teachers, are sitting alone with the student's work in front of us, it's easy to imagine that our primary relationship is with the product, particularly with the errors in the product. We may imagine that our chief responsibility is not to let any errors pass our desk unmarked. In reality, the most important relationship is between us and the learner. The grade is a communication, and it must communicate to a person who can use it for learning. Our chief responsibility is to help this learner move forward. So think to yourself, What does this learner need from me at this time? Then shape your comments accordingly.

One common trap for teachers is to focus on justifying the grade. When justifying the grade, teachers tend to focus on describing how the paper is bad: it's poorly organized, it lacks evidence, it uses the wrong equation, and so on. The underlying message is, Here's why this paper did not get a higher grade. Please don't come to my office to ask me why you didn't get an *A*. But when we keep in mind our aim to teach, we tend to focus on what the student has achieved and what might yet be achieved.

For example, the following is a comment that Breihan made on a student essay draft in his history course on Western Civilization (see Exhibit 3.1). In this case, the student received back from the teacher the grading sheet with a circle around the statement that best described the paper draft. In addition, Breihan gave the student the handwritten piece of scratch paper on which Breihan had attempted to outline the draft as he read. If the outlining process broke down, there was clear evidence to the student that the teacher could not follow the organization of the essay. In addition to those two items, Breihan also typed on his computer this comment to the student's draft. (The assignment had asked students, based on their study of sixteenth- and seventeenth-century European governments, to recommend a form of government that would avoid anarchy and bloody revolution for a hypothetical country called "Loyoliana.")

Mr. Carter:

This essay puts forward a very clear thesis that a "strong government" is needed to end anarchy. After reviewing several alternatives, you end by saying that a mixed government on the English model would work best for Loyoliana.

What is missing here is argument and evidence in favor of the thesis that you state so clearly. Why would this system work so well? Have you any specific evidence? What about the arguments of Paine, Bossuet, etc.? What about the fact that the Hanoverian kings were not strong? That England had no written constitution?

In revising this, you should try to provide more evidence for your arguments and try to answer these counterarguments.

Notice that Breihan takes the time to reflect on and respond to what the student said. It is almost like a professional article, where one begins by summarizing what other writers on the subject have said. Breihan's comment communicates his respect for the student as a person with a position on an issue, rather than primarily a maker of errors. The comment acknowledges what has been achieved. Then Breihan suggests what the student can do to improve the essay.

Save Your Comments for the Teachable Moment

A teacher's response to early stages of an assignment often reaches the student in a more teachable moment than comments on a final paper. For example, Breihan's draft comment tries to direct the student's revision, and students are highly motivated to use his comments because they can still do something about that particular paper.

When you're responding to work in progress, it's easier to nurture students' growth. You're trying to praise the student for progress made, indicate what yet needs to be done, and give advice to the student about how to do those things. Quite naturally, you invite the student to come to you or to the TA for further help as needed. By contrast, when you're responding to finished work you can easily slip into the autopsy mode of describing why the paper is bad. You find yourself trying to justify the grade and to keep students' grade complaints out of your office. Many teachers with whom we have worked, and we ourselves, limit the number of formal assignments and tests so that we have time to give early response and full guidance to proposals, thesis sentences, outlines, freewrites, dummy graphs, procedural steps, or drafts.

Sometimes, however, response to the final, finished work can be motivating and applicable to the student. For example, Anderson holds individual conferences with the seniors in her class, using her PTA scale to go over their completed scientific research reports in detail—a process she believes is valuable to them because it forms a bridge to the work settings they will shortly enter as newly-hired scientists, perhaps conducting similar kinds of experimentation.

In addition to knowing when to respond in order to nurture growth in teachable moments, you need to know how to respond. You may respond with a written or e-mailed comment, an audio-taped comment that you hand to the student, or with a face-to-face discussion. Teachers often believe that face-to-face comments will take too much time, and perhaps they will. But Walvoord and other teachers we know handle a draft of a five- to ten-page paper in a ten- to fifteen-minute student conference, which is about as much time as Walvoord would take at home to write comments on the paper. Sometimes she holds no formal classes in that week but instead uses all scheduled class time, plus additional times, to meet with students individually or in small groups to review their work. Walvoord passes around in class or places on the course's electronic bulletin board an appointment sheet that lists all her available conference times, in ten- to fifteen-minute slots. Students sign up for a time. The sign-up sheet is then posted on Walvoord's office door or on the course's electronic bulletin board. Walvoord's policy is to tell students that if they do not come to their appointment on time, with the requisite draft, they will forfeit the right to turn in the revised paper, which results in an *F* paper. (Of course, in case of illness or accident, new arrangements will be made.)

During the week of conferences, Walvoord sits in her office seeing students in ten- to fifteen-minute slots (saving herself a ten-minute break every hour or so). Each student arrives with a typed rough draft, so Walvoord can read it more quickly (typos are okay). She looks at the draft for the first time and asks the student, "Where are you, and what do you think you need help with?" Students often have quite an accurate idea of where they are. If so, the conference may be short. If Sara, for example, knows what she needs to do, Walvoord can just reinforce her and send her on her way. If Tim does not know where he is, Walvoord has a chance to read the paper and reflect where the major problems lie. She doesn't comment on everything but identifies the problems that need immediate attention and gets the student working on them.

Make clear to your students, in writing, orally in class, and again in the conference, that this is not a conference where their papers will be fixed or where you will say everything there is to say. Rather, you are dipping in at a particular point in the growth of the paper to offer a few suggestions about where the student needs to go.

Hold back a few unpublished appointment times, so that if a student needs more time or needs to come back, you can schedule that appointment. If there is a major problem, such as suspected plagiarism, and you don't want to handle it on the spot, it's perfectly okay to tell the student that you need more time to read and think about the paper and then to reschedule a later appointment.

An alternative but potentially more time-consuming approach is to have students meet with you in groups of four or five. In the group meeting, which lasts an hour or a class period, students read their work and receive each other's response in addition to yours.

Some teachers have students respond to one another's work in small groups without the teacher present. The success of this method depends on four factors:

1. You must provide clear, written criteria and clear instructions for student response.

2. You need to be available for support if students need you. Some of them will want your response no matter what the group says. Walvoord offers to meet individually during her office hours with anyone who wants her response, but only after the group has responded. She warns students that when they come for her response, her first question to them will be, "What did your group say about the draft?" Then she can tell them she thinks the group gave them good advice, or she can provide what the group did not.

3. Students ought to reflect to each other what they see in each other's work. For example, instead of saying whether the organization is good or not, students can be asked to outline each other's papers. If the reader cannot outline the paper, the writer gets the point. For example, Exhibit 7.2 is a guide that Walvoord uses for students in a first-year composition class to respond to one another's work.

4. Students need a chance to reflect on group process. For example, at the end of the group meeting, each person in the group might thank the classmate who gave them the most help. That strategy tends to make very clear to the group that explicit criticism is often counted as the most helpful feedback by the writer.

Intervening in early stages also helps you control plagiarism and other disasters. If you ask to see a proposal, outline, or draft of a student's paper, it is much harder for that student to purchase or

Exhibit 7.2.   Walvoord's Guidelines for Group Response to Drafts.

1. Before handing out copies of the draft, the author should read aloud the first sentence of the paper. The group should then tell the author what the sentence leads them to think is the main point of the paper and what main points the author will make.

2. Then the author should hand out copies of the draft to each group member.

3. The author should read the paper aloud.

4. There should be 2 to 3 minutes of silence to allow group members to digest the paper and gather their thoughts.

5. Group members should then, in turn, voice their reactions to these questions:
   - State the main point of the paper in a single sentence. Who do you think is the audience for the paper? What is the paper's purpose?
   - What are the major subpoints for the paper? (In other words, outline it.)
   - Which aspects did you like best about the paper?
   - Were there any points at which you were confused about the subject or focus of the paper or its sections?
   - Consider each section of the paper in turn: is each developed with enough detail, evidence, and information?
   - Is there material you think the author should add?
   - Are the opening and concluding paragraphs accurate guides to the paper's theme and focus?
   - Considering the paper paragraph by paragraph, what seems most vivid, clear, and memorable? Where does the language seem especially effective? Where is it awkward or unclear?
   - What would an opponent of the author's position say? Has the author accurately represented and responded to the most telling points of the opponent?

6. The writer should follow these guidelines:
   - Do not argue with the readers, and do not explain what you meant. You are gathering data about audience response, so simply gather it. If a particular response seems not useful, you are free to ignore it in revising your paper. But for you to spend the group's time arguing and explaining is wasteful, and it can result in the group's getting focused on understanding what you meant, rather than on reacting to what you wrote.
   - It is usually productive for you to remain silent, taking careful notes about what is said by readers. In addition, you may want to
     - Ask a reader to clarify or expand on a statement, so you understand it thoroughly.
     - Ask readers to respond to an idea you have for improvement of some aspect of the paper they're unhappy with.
     - Repeat back to the group what you think they're saying, just to make sure communication is accurate.

copy someone else's work at the last minute. It's also much easier for you to head off a student's innocent misuse of sources. You can often avoid having the student put hours of work into a flawed product. You help the student work on the project in a timely way rather than procrastinate until the night before it's due. All these steps help avoid the unexpected disasters and failures that make students angry, lead to grievances, and interfere with learning.

Communicate Priorities

When a student receives a draft on which the teacher has marked heavily in the margins and also written at the end that the draft is not well organized, needs better evidence, or some other large-scale concern, the student is receiving a contradictory message. Since students often revise by trying the fix the paper locally, they are tempted to ignore or underemphasize the final, global comment and instead revise by trying to fix the first passage the teacher has marked, then the second passage, and so on. They never fully deal with the global comment, which would require more reading, or restructuring of the entire piece—in other words, which would render many of the marginal comments irrelevant. Our own study (Walvoord and Breihan, 1991) and those of others (Sommers, 1982) suggest that when a paper is in deep trouble with its conceptualization, organization, evidence, and similar global matters, teachers should only communicate those concerns and not confuse the learner with superficial issues. Make clear to students, however, that issues such as phrasing, computation, labeling of graphics, grammar, and so on are crucially important and must be addressed at their proper time, even though at the moment you are not focusing on them.

Avoid Surprises

The only kind of surprises you want for students when they receive a final paper or course grade is a positive surprise, when they did better than they had dared hope. But you don't want them shocked by a low grade they did not foresee. If the criteria and standards are carefully spelled out, and if you have coached the process, students often can avoid spectacular crashes or at least can see them coming.

Grades and Student Evaluations

Faculty sometimes believe that student evaluations will be higher if the teacher makes the course easy or gives undeserved high grades and, conversely, that if the teacher is rigorous, student evaluations

---

Resource 7.2.

Sources About Student Evaluations.

Cashin, 1988, 1995. Short summaries of the research. According to 1995
    source, 1988 summary is still reliable.
Centra, 1993. Summary of the research (see Chapter Three).
Feldman, 1996. Summary of the research.

---

will be low. The bottom line is this: setting high expectations and helping students meet them, while also making sure that you are clear, well-organized, fair, accessible, friendly, and enthusiastic, seems the best way to enhance student learning and to get high student evaluations.

Research suggests that a teacher cannot buy high student evaluations just by making the course easy (see Resource 7.2). Based on nationally normed student evaluation forms that have been administered in institutions over the years, researchers found there was no significant correlation between the overall satisfaction of students on the global question (which asks for the students' overall evaluation of the teacher) and the difficulty of the course as students perceive it. The results suggest that making a course difficult need not necessarily lower your student evaluations. Table 7.1 presents a summary of the research.

There is a positive correlation between the grade students report that they expect and their global evaluation of the teacher. There are several hypotheses to explain this correlation:

1. If the teacher gives high grades, students evaluate the teacher highly.

2. If the teacher is good, students learn more, get higher grades, and like their teacher.

3. There are underlying qualities in students that cause them to learn well, get high grades, and like their teacher. The student evaluation questions are really measuring these underlying qualities.

The second two hypotheses, says Cashin (1988, 1995) are more likely, given other research. Thus, just giving unmerited high grades will probably not cause your student evaluations to rise.

This is all good news, it seems to us. Students are human; sometimes, like the rest of us, they just want to get by with as little effort as possible. However, we believe these data suggest that a teacher can trust that students also very much want to learn. They do not want to be given unearned grades; they are capable of

Table 7.1. Factors Related to Students' Global Evaluations of Instructors.

Variable	Is there a significant correlation with "global questions"* according to the national research literature?
Class size	Weak correlation. Smaller classes tend to receive higher ratings.
Time of day of the class	No correlation.
Level of the course	Weak correlation. Higher-level courses, especially graduate courses, tend to receive higher ratings.
Academic field of the course	Yes; humanities and arts courses are generally ranked higher than math and science courses.
Teacher's age or teaching experience	No correlation.
Teacher's rank	Weak correlation: faculty tend to get higher ratings than graduate assistants.
Teacher's research productivity	No correlation.
Student's age, gender, level, GPA, personality	No correlation.
Course taken in major field or as elective	Weak positive correlation.
Workload and difficulty of the course	Weak correlation. Students give higher ratings in difficult courses where they have to work hard.
Grade that the student reports expecting to get	Weak positive correlation.

*Global questions ask for an overall rating, such as "I would take this course again," or "Among all the courses I have taken at this university, this course ranks among the ___ top 10 percent ___ top 25 percent . . . " and so on.

Note: Compiled from Cashin, 1988; Centra, 1993; and Feldman, 1996.

respecting a demanding teacher and of working hard for their grades. They can appreciate a well-structured course where the teacher sets high expectations and then, in a clear, friendly, and well-organized way, helps students to meet those expectations.

ACTIVITY

1. Review the suggestions in this chapter, jotting down several ideas you can use in your own course.
2. Work out the details of one of your ideas.
3. Review your plans with a colleague and with students. Revise as needed.

CHAPTER 8

Making Grading More Time-Efficient

One of the basic principles explained in Chapter Two was to reconsider your use of time. Throughout the book, we have been presenting suggestions for how to use in-class time and out-of-class time and how to distribute your time among giving, guiding, and grading assignments. This chapter forms part of that larger picture. In it, we discuss how you can do a good job of grading while also keeping your grading time to a minimum and making sure that every minute you spend grading pays off handsomely in terms of student learning and useful assessment.

Strategies for Time-Effective Grading

To achieve these goals, we suggest you consider these strategies, around which our chapter is organized:

1. Separate commenting from grading, and use them singly or in combination according to your purpose.
2. Do not give to all students what only some need.
3. Use only as many grade levels as you need.
4. Frame comments to your students' use.
5. Do not waste time on careless student work.
6. Use what the student knows.
7. Ask students to organize their work for your efficiency.
8. Delegate the work.
9. Use technology to save time and enhance results.

We describe each of these briefly and then offer some examples of teachers who use various combinations of the principles to keep their grading time to a minimum and make every minute count.

STRATEGY 1
Separate Commenting from Grading

One action that will enormously affect your grading time is to think very carefully about which combination of comments and grades will be most time-saving and effective for learning. Grades need not be given to every piece of student work—only if you or your students need that type of assessment. Comments need not necessarily accompany grades—only if learning results.

With each piece of student work, ask yourself the following questions:

- Why am I assigning a grade to this?
- Will the benefits be worth my time?
- Could I do something else instead?
  - Merely offer credit for having done the work?
  - Offer comments but no grade?
  - Fold this work into a larger work?
  - Include this work in a portfolio?
- Do all my students need a grade?

Here are some examples. If you ask students to submit a prospectus, thesis sentence, sketch, graphs, data, outline, proposal, draft, or other work that is preliminary to a larger work, the preliminary material may not need to be separately graded because it later becomes part of the grade of the larger or more polished piece. For example, as students prepare essays, an English teacher asks them to bring tentative thesis sentences to class on transparencies. They write their names on the very bottom of the transparencies so the teacher can display the transparencies on the screen without showing the name but can later give credit to the student for having done the assignment. In class, she pulls transparencies at random from the pile and reviews as many of them as she can right there in the class, displaying them anonymously on the screen, discussing them and making suggestions for improvement. Five minutes before the end of the class, she sits down at her desk in the front of the room, takes out her gradebook, and makes a check next to the name of each student who has handed in a transparency. Then she hands all transparencies back to the students so they can take them home and use them as they further develop their essays. She tells her students, "If I did not get to your transparency in the class discussion, and you still need response, see me after class." A few students do so, and she either responds on the spot or makes an appointment. But most students, even those whose theses were not discussed in the class, have the feedback they need. They typically respond with comments such as, "Oh, yeah, mine was like that second one you showed. Too broad. I know what to do." The teacher does not need to grade these theses. Notice that she does not even take them home. Yet she has been able to give very helpful feedback to her students, and on end-of-semester evaluations, they frequently mention its value.

Here's another example: portfolios are frequent in fields such as art, architecture, and design, but other faculty can use them also. For example, one chemistry faculty member who teaches a large lecture class asks students to write frequent short assignments but does not grade each one. Instead, he responds to them in two ways: (1) he uses them as the basis for class discussion, asking students to read them with a neighbor or to bring them on transparencies to discuss with the class as a whole; (2) he then has students keep the assignments in a folder. At midterm and at the end of the semester, he has students hand in all their short assignments in a portfolio. The student makes a table of contents so the teacher can see that all assignments are present. The student also chooses two assignments, revises and types them, and includes them as the first two items in the portfolio. The teacher bases the portfolio grade on two factors: the percentage of total assignments present in the portfolio and the quality of the two revised and typed assignments.

In the examples we have given, students have not complained about not receiving grades for the informal writing. However, if yours do, you need to rethink what you are doing. We do not advocate doing anything that makes students feel their teacher has not paid appropriate attention to their work. One important action on your part is to explain fully and often why you are handling student work in the way you are, what you think grades are for, and why you are or are not giving grades or comments on a particular assignment. Relate ungraded work clearly to work that will be graded. Help students see how the ungraded work will be useful to them.

STRATEGY 2
Do Not Give to All Students What Only Some Need

We advise asking yourself, Do all my students need grades? Perhaps most of your students do not need a grade on a particular assignment, but a few students feel very anxious if they get any paper back without a grade. But must you grade every paper to meet the needs of a few? That issue bothered Walvoord greatly until she hit upon a solution. In class, she said with a grin, "Hey, I'm a teacher, I'm paid to grade student work, I've given thousands of grades in my career, and I can grade *anything!* If you want an unofficial grade on any piece of informal writing, or on a draft, just write 'please grade' at the top, or come and ask me, and I'll tell you unofficially what the grade would be." That solution worked. Students who needed to know a grade got their needs met. The grades were unofficial, so Walvoord did not have to figure out how to determine final course grades for students who got more grades than others. She did keep a record of unofficial grades she had given to her students and checked to be sure they were consistent with grades or comments she later made on their work.

You can also shape comments to student needs. If you think that, because of class discussion or some other reason, some of your students may not need as full a comment from you as other students do, ask them to write at the top of their papers, as they submit them, whether they need further comment.

STRATEGY 3
Use Only As Many Grade Levels As You Need

The traditional grading system, with pluses and minuses, is a thirteen-level system. If you decide you should grade a particular assignment, ask yourself, Do I need a thirteen-level system, or would fewer levels accomplish the purpose? The fewer the levels, the faster you can grade.

What can you use instead of a thirteen-level system?

- Use a six-level system (*A* through *F*) without pluses and minuses
- Use a four-level system ([1] check [2] check-plus [3] check-minus [4] no check)
- Use a three-level system ([1] outstanding [2] competent [3] unacceptable)
- Use a two-level system (pass-fail or credit–no credit)

The basic rule is to use the lowest number of grading levels consonant with your purpose and with student learning. It is easy to assume that, because at the end of the course you must assign grades in a thirteen-level system, every grade along the way must be calibrated on the same system.

Two systems that release you from having to grade everything on a thirteen-point scale are the accumulated points system and the definitional system we explained in Chapter Six.

The next sections contain suggestions for offering comments.

STRATEGY 4
Frame Comments to Your Students' Use

The basic principle of commenting is that your comments are part of a communication between you and your student, and the comment only succeeds if it produces the desired learning on the student's part. Research suggests that your comments will be understood within the context of the individual classroom, your ongoing conversation with the students during the semester, and students' preconceptions about the roles of comments. Particularly, students are likely to fix upon a goal of doing what the teacher wants, when you might rather have them strive to develop independent judgment (Ferris, 1995; Sperling and Freedman, 1987; Yagelski, 1995). Your goal, then, is to ensure accurate and effective communication with students while using your time to the best advantage.

The first question to ask yourself is, Have I chosen a teachable moment to make this comment? Especially, you will want to question the usefulness of making extensive comments on students' finished, graded work when no further revision is possible. A true anecdote illustrates. Walvoord recently overheard two students: one said to her friend, "What did you get on the paper?" The friend replied, "Eh, I only got a *B*. I was really disappointed." She was probably a good student who had expected a good grade. She went on to say, "He wrote all over the paper! He wrote a book! I didn't even read it." Imagine the faculty member, sitting there on a Sunday afternoon when he could have been out walking in the woods, earnestly writing comments all over the paper, trying to explain in great detail why this student got a *B*, perhaps knowing she'd be disappointed—and what happens? She doesn't even read his comments.

We think one moral of this story is this: *only put your time into comments that reach students in a teachable moment.* Don't throw away your work on an unteachable moment. When that student saw the *B* it was psychologically all over for her. There was nothing more she could do. The professor had to take enough time to grade the paper fairly; his mistake was to think that he also had to write all over it. Often, a teachable moment is when there is still something the student can do to improve the grade on a live assignment. Comments on drafts or on works in progress are likely to be more worthwhile than extensive comments on final work. The exception might be when subsequent work will be sufficiently similar that the students believe they can readily use in the next assignment whatever you say on this one. But don't overestimate their ability to see the carryover. Some semester, ask them what use they made of your comments. We suggest that you ask for your own classes, What are the teachable moments? Try to gather real information about how your students use your comments. Commenting is so time-consuming, it is worthwhile to examine it carefully, making sure that every moment is paying off.

In addition to knowing when to make comments, it's helpful to know what kinds of comments, and how extensive, are useful. Do not automatically assume you must comment on everything you can think of, offering both marginal and end comments. Nancy Sommers (1982), interviewing students after they had received back their papers with teacher comments, found that a number of things might go wrong when the teacher combines local-level suggestions about grammar and punctuation with more global suggestions about content and organization. First, the student might be misled by a large number of grammar and punctuation comments into spending disproportionate energy on those aspects and ignoring the larger issues of content and structure. Also, extensive local-level comments may encourage students in the view that it is the teacher's job to mark everything that is wrong, and their job to change what the teacher wants changed. The work is no longer theirs but the teacher's. Extensive comments may encourage a revision process by which a student merely goes through the paper line by line fixing whatever the teacher has marked without internalizing the principles that could guide revision in the student's future work. Finally, when revising the work their teacher has extensively marked, students may be reluctant to make any changes in *unmarked* text, thereby circumventing the growth and discovery that might otherwise take place in the student's thinking (see Walvoord and Breihan, 1991). So the time you spend marking local problems in the margins of the student's paper may backfire.

If the student's paper is flawed in its conception, evidence, structure, or line of reasoning, it may be best to say only that. Concentrate the learner's attention on the crucial thing that must be addressed first. You may warn about lower-level problems to be addressed later, but you need not mark each one. For example, unfocused drafts often need take only a little of your time. You might only need to say, "I can't discern this paper's main point. Try writing in a single sentence, 'What I really want to say is . . .' then plan the paper to support that main point. If you need help, I'd be happy to discuss it with you."

When commenting on global issues, you will want to use marginal comments or specific examples to illustrate what you mean.

For example, "Your thesis is clear, but support for your claims is thin: I have marked a few examples in the margins. Your support is strongest in the third paragraph on page 3; my marginal comments try to show you why that paragraph is strong."

This brings up a related, potentially time-saving question: do you need to comment on everything or only on some aspects of the assignment? If the assignment serves a limited purpose, then perhaps you need comment only on that issue. When your tennis teacher wants to spend a lesson on your backhand stroke, she may comment only on that, leaving your wretched serve or your erratic net play for a later lesson. In a geography class of two hundred students, a professor gives students raw data on a chart and asks them to draw conclusions from it. In grading and responding to that assignment, he concerns himself only with the quality of their inferences from the data, and his comments address only that issue. If you limit the concerns you will address for a particular assignment, you need to tell students that clearly and early on the assignment sheet.

So far, we have assumed that your comments will be written (or sent by e-mail). It may seem anomalous in a chapter on saving time to suggest that you shift from written comments to verbal, face-to-face comments. However, as we explained in Chapter Seven, face-to-face comments may accomplish more effective communication in the same amount of time it would take to write comments on the paper. But the secret is to restrict your comments to the aspects that are appropriate to the writer at that point in the process.

Breihan, the historian, provides an example of thoughtful deliberation about which kinds of grades and comments to give at which points for which purposes. We've seen how he uses class time to give response to informal writings that then get only a credit–no credit mark or a certain number of points, with few if any written comments. But now let's look at how Breihan handles grading and commenting on the formal, graded argumentative essays. First, his comments are most thorough on drafts. He requires all students to hand in drafts of their first essay of the semester, he responds, and then students revise. That's heavily time-consuming, and he can't afford to do it for the second and third essays. On the second, he makes revision voluntary, so fewer students choose it, and on the third, it's the final exam, so they write it in class. But Breihan uses draft response for the first essay, when students have the most to gain by a learning experience. How can he afford the time to do this? He uses time previously spent writing all over the finished essays. He spends more time on draft response than on response to the final paper because drafts

Exhibit 8.1.   Breihan's Responses to History Students' Essays.

Response to Draft	*Response to Final Essay*
■ Grading checklist with relevant item marked	■ Grading checklist with relevant item marked
■ Up to 1 typed page of comments, plus marginal comments	■ 1- to 2-sentence comment
■ Oral conference (first essay only)	

present teachable moments. We saw earlier his comment on a student's draft for an essay. Breihan also wrote marginal comments on that paper, primarily to back up and illustrate his end comment. Further, he used the checklist you saw in Exhibit 5.5. Exhibit 8.1 summarizes Breihan's responses.

Obviously, Breihan invested a lot of work on the drafts and offered a very thorough response. That's because it was a teachable moment; students revised the drafts for their final grades. But at the point of the final grade, Breihan spent only enough time to ensure that the grade was fair. He typically would scribble a sentence or two on the paper, such as, "Much better on evidence." He made another check on the checklist to represent the new status of the paper. He wrote a grade at the top of the paper. Period. Students who wanted more explanation were warmly welcomed to see him, and a few did. In this way, Breihan said, "I got myself out of the business of justifying the grade and into the business of coaching the student's progress."

Breihan's method changes the traditional distribution of teacher time for grading and guiding students' work. In the old method, the teacher gave the assignment and answered questions about it but otherwise spent very little time guiding the process, and then spent most of his or her time writing comments all over the final version, describing the faults of the *product*—it's poorly organized, unfocused, too general, lacks support, and so on. Such comments often do not help students know where their *processes* went wrong for that paper, much less what they can do to make the next one more successful. Breihan's method places emphasis on teaching and guiding during the process. The final grading then takes less time. Figure 8.1 is a diagram of time distribution of teacher time for giving an assignment, guiding the process, and grading it.

One special question to consider is the extent to which you want to comment on small, recurring details in student work. In written work, this means grammar, punctuation, and spelling; in

Figure 8.1.   Distribution of Teacher Time.

Emphasis on Grading

G i v i n g \ Guiding \   G   R   A   D   I   N   G
· · · · · · · · — — — — — — — — — — — —

Emphasis on Guiding

G i v i n g \ G   U   I   D   I   N   G   \ Grading
· · · · · · · — — — — — — — — — — — — — — — — —

other media, it may mean technical aspects, arithmetic, and the like. When problems in these areas are numerous, it is tempting to mark each one—for example, to circle all the grammar, punctuation, and spelling errors. In special situations, and in language classes, you may want to do that. But for the faculty member in geology or philosophy or business, marking all the grammar and punctuation is probably a waste of time.

Consider a few different scenarios. One is that you have required well-edited work, and the student knows the rules but simply has not carefully proofread or checked her work. One thing you want to teach is proofreading skills. Another thing you want to teach is the importance of spending time on checking the details of one's work. If you mark all the errors, you are teaching neither of these things. You are doing half the work for the student. It is better to say, "There are many spelling and grammar errors in this paper. Please find and fix them. I have marked a sample paragraph. If you need help, call the writing center at extension 3583."

A second scenario is that you have required well-edited work, and the student's errors are due to lack of knowledge about the rules. Now you need to determine whether you can teach the rules in the available time. Some rules can be taught quickly and cleanly in a marginal comment. ("Periods and commas almost always belong inside the quotation marks.") But most rules of grammar and punctuation run deep into the roots of the language, and it takes special expertise to teach them. For the sociology teacher to scribble *fragment* and *run-on* at various points on the paper probably will not greatly help an eighteen–year-old or a fifty-eight–year-old student who has not already learned the rules about written English sentence construction. That student, whether speaking English as a native or a second language, needs a series of sessions at the writing center or a self-guiding book or computer program that will take him or her systematically through the complex grammatical issues involved. Perhaps your best comment is to recommend that course of action.

A third scenario is that you did not or need not require well-edited work. Here are three kinds of work on which you may not want yourself or your student to spend much time worrying about grammar, punctuation, and spelling: (1) informal exercises such as Breihan uses daily in his classroom (Exhibit 4.3); (2) in-class work where students are in haste and have no dictionaries or time to proofread; (3) drafts of work that will eventually be polished.

A faculty member in architecture applies a similar philosophy to students' graphic work. He urges his students, in early stages of a project, to just get ideas down without worrying about details or technique.

Some disciplines, such as languages and athletics, routinely create times and places where students are urged to build fluency and confidence, to speak or run or play fluidly even though they will make errors. In these cases the teacher or coach does not pick at the errors but urges learners to just play or just talk. In your classroom, ask whether it might be appropriate to create such occasions to build fluency and confidence.

STRATEGY 5

Do Not Waste Time on Careless Student Work

This suggestion is not contrary to the one preceding. This one concerns the time you spend responding to work where you have asked for care, on any dimension, and have instead received careless work. Can you figure out how to get that work off your desk quickly? Or not to let the work get on your desk in the first place? And to teach the student what she or he needs to learn?

One literature faculty member, for example, asked students to complete a checklist and attach it to the top of their papers. On it, the student had to check off a number of items:

_____ I read the short story at least twice.

_____ I revised this paper at least once.

_____ I spent at least five hours on this paper.

_____ I started work on this paper at least three days ago.

_____ I have tried hard to do my best work on this paper.

_____ I proofread the paper at least twice for grammar and punctuation.

_____ I asked at least one other person to proofread the paper.

_____ I ran the paper through a spelling check.

"If you can't check off on these items," the teacher said, "I don't even want to see your paper." Of course, students might check the items without actually doing them, but at least the checklist taught students something about their teacher's expectations, and she believed that it enhanced the quality of the work she got and saved her from having to spend time on hasty or superficial work.

STRATEGY 6
Use What the Student Knows

Faculty members could often save time if they tapped what students know about their own work. Why spend time writing comments about a paper's focus when the student, if asked, would respond, "Oh, I knew that paper wasn't well focused"? How can you tap this information? Some teachers we know ask students to preface work they hand in with a half-page evaluation of the work. The student need not say what grade she thinks the work should get but tells what she thinks are its strongest and weakest points and what advice she would give herself for further improvement. Often the teacher only needs to write, "I agree." For oral or performance situations, you might take a few moments for the student to "debrief"—to tell you or the class what she or he thought about the presentation ("I thought I might have picked up the pace a little bit—was it too slow?") Then the class and teacher responses can build on those perceptions.

STRATEGY 7
Ask Students to Organize Their Work for Your Efficiency

Ask yourself, Where do I waste time in the physical or logistical aspects of grading? Can you instruct students to organize their work for your efficiency? For example, do you hunt through students' papers to see whether all the parts are present? If so, how about requiring a table of contents? Do you have to search for pages caught under someone else's paper clip? Ban paper clips.

If you use a checklist such as the one just shown you can add other efficiency items to it:

_____ This paper is stapled, not paper clipped

_____ On top of the paper, I have included an evaluation of my work.

Take a hint from your gas and electric company. They know that human beings cannot always think of all the little details. On the back flap of the envelope, they give the bill payer a checklist: "Did you write your account number on the check? Did you sign the check?" Podunk Gas and Electric has figured out how to prod the human mind, with its shortcomings, into actions that will save time for the company. You can do the same.

STRATEGY 8
Delegate the Work

Ask yourself, Am I doing things in the grading process that other people could do? We suggested earlier that checklists can be given to students to help them organize their work for your efficiency and can thus help you avoid wasting time on careless work. But checklists can be much more broadly based than the ones we have shown so far, and they can help you delegate much of the work—in this case, to students themselves. Exhibit 8.2 shows several checklists.

Any of the self-checklists could also become a peer checklist so that students could check each other's work. Exhibit 8.3 is a peer checklist that anthropologist Mark Curchak of Beaver College employed to guide students in responding to one another's papers. Notice that Curchak's checklist is a reading guide for student peers. It leads them through the steps of a careful and helpful reading. Without this sort of guidance, students may focus too early on low-level problems such as comma errors, or they may miss some aspects their teacher knows are important, or they may believe they have to give a grade or a judgment on the paper. The checklist guides them toward descriptive suggestions rather than outright judgments, which students find hard to express to their peers. The checklist also guides students in a sequence of questions; it is a guide to the reading-and-responding process. Armed with such a rubric, students should be able to give good help to one another.

When you arrange for student peer response, it is important to consider what kind of response you want to elicit and at what point you want it to be given. A psychologist who was using peer response had organized the process so that students gave each other responses on the basic elements of their psychology papers, then they revised their papers based on those comments, then they received their teachers' comments and revised again before the final grade. However, what happened in a number of cases is that student peers did not critique the papers deeply enough; they often did not catch the most fundamental problems of conceptualization, organization, and evidence. And students did not take seriously their peers' comments on these issues. So the first round of revisions, based on peer responses, tended to be too superficial. In the next round, when the teacher saw the papers, she made those fundamental criticisms and suggestions. By then, however, student writers had already invested a great deal of time in the papers, had revised them once, and were disinclined to make the fundamental changes their teacher suggested. The psychologist came to see that she might better have reversed the order of response, doing it herself on the first round, to get at the most fundamental conceptual problems, and letting peers respond to the smaller-scale problems that were likely to turn up in the further revisions. She also saw ways to improve the checklist she gave students as a guide for their responses.

Exhibit 8.2.   Checklists for Assignments from Three Disciplines.

Example 1: Simple checklist for a chemistry assignment in which students are instructed to describe how they would prepare certain compounds. Students check each item before submitting the paper.

> *Emel Yakali, Chemistry, Raymond Walters College, University of Cincinnati, Cincinnati, Ohio*

_____ Identification of the type of compound the product is

_____ Identification of the C-to-C bond to form to get the product

_____ Identification of the oxygen compound to be used

[other items covering each aspect that must be present]

Example 2: Checklist for a "nursing process" form students complete, based on their clinical work for a course in "Family Adaptation." Students check each item before submitting the form.

> *Patricia Schlecht, Nursing, Raymond Walters College, University of Cincinnati, Cincinnati, Ohio*

_____ Assessment is complete

_____ Nursing diagnosis uses program-approved format

_____ Nursing diagnosis is supported by assessment data

[other items]

Example 3: Checklist for draft and final revision of an essay in a literature class. Students check each item before submitting the draft or final version.

> *Barbara Walvoord*

Draft   Final

_____   _____   I have read the novel at least twice.

_____   _____   The essay presents my own position and does not merely summarize others.

_____   _____   My position is thoughtful; it challenges the reader; it goes beyond the obvious or the trite.

[other items]

Exhibit 8.3.   Curchak's Peer Checklist for First Draft of Term Papers in Sociology.

Author of draft _____   Name of reviewer _____

Directions: By answering the following questions thoughtfully and clearly, be as helpful as possible to the author of this draft. Use complete sentences and specific examples to ensure clarity in your advice. You will be evaluated on the thoughtfulness and helpfulness of your responses.

1. *Overall situation:* How near to completion is this draft? What steps should the author take to complete this term paper? Be both specific and helpful in listing the three most important steps below:

   A.

   B.

   C.

2. *Organization:* Is this draft organized in a standard pattern: an introductory section; the body of the paper, presenting the information in a reasonable sequence; and a summary and analysis of the situation? If there is an alternative organization, say what it is and whether it is effective.

3. *Introductory section:* The first few paragraphs should prepare the reader (another student in the course) for the research that has been done on the topic.

   A. Does the introduction explain the topic and why it is important? Briefly state why you think it is important.

   B. After reading the paper, say whether you think the introduction introduces what you've read. Does it? How?

4. *Body of the paper:* The major portion of the paper should present the collected information in an orderly and clear fashion.

   A. In the space below, outline in some detail the major points established in the body of the paper and the evidence used to support the points.

   B. Is the style of the writing appropriate to the intended audience, you and the others in the class?

   C. Compared with that of the textbook, is the style more or less formal? How?

   D. Has the author thoroughly paraphrased the information from the references so that the writing style is consistent? Remember that inadequate paraphrasing is a common student problem and may even approach plagiarism.

   E. Has the writer organized the information in the most effective way?

      1. If not, suggest improvements.

      2. How would you characterize the organization? Is it a list of equal points, an arrangement of topics and subtopics, a chronological sequence, an argument with two or more opposing viewpoints, or what?

   F. How has the writer handled citations?

      1. Are they in an acceptable style, used consistently?

2. Is the number of citations adequate to the information taken from sources?

3. How has the information from sources been organized?

    a. One source per paragraph (give an example)

    b. Multiple sources for each paragraph (give an example)

G. Are the tables and figures used in the paper

    1. Clear and easy to understand?

    2. Referred to in the text?

    3. Labeled with a title or legend?

    4. Cited (at the end of the title or legend)?

5. *Conclusions:* A conclusion can take several forms: a restatement of the overall argument of the paper, a summary of the key points, a combination of several points to make a final point, an analysis of the data, and so on.

    A. What form has the writer used to conclude the paper?

    B. Does the conclusion seem to be supported by the evidence? How or how not?

6. *Features of the writing:*

    A. Are there any problems in the grammar, spelling, punctuation, paragraph structure, sentence structure, transition? Which one(s) in particular? Do these problems interfere with the meaning the writer is trying to express?

    B. Has the writer acknowledged the help of others?

7. *General evaluation:* In the space remaining, give your general impression of the paper. Did you like it and why? What did you learn from it? What else do you wish you had learned from it? Give any other ideas that you think might help.

Source: Reprinted from Walvoord, 1986, pp. 47–49.

How can you use an assistant other than peers? We described how to use TA graders in Chapter Five. In addition to using the suggestions in that chapter, see whether you can get unpaid "assistants" whom your students locate and "hire" for you. We know a teacher who requires that all students find an "editor" somewhere in the outside world among their friends, children, parents, or spouses. The "editor" reads the paper and makes suggestions before the student hands it in. Students then write an acknowledgments page, just as their teacher does when publishing a book or article. The student might say, "I am indebted to my discussion group, John Anderson, Rafael Ruíz, Lawanda Washington, and Dawn O'Shaughnessy, for helping me work out the ideas for this paper, and to my friend Sandy Eckerd for proofreading it." You may have to give students an example or two of the language of an acknowledgment.

STRATEGY **9**

Use Technology to Save Time and Enhance Results

Here are a few ideas about using technology to make your grading and commenting time more efficient:

- Instead of writing on the student's paper, write the comments on your computer. When you find yourself writing the same thing over and over, create a boilerplate passage you can insert into your comments.

- Give students a handout, or make available to them on computer, your advice on various common problems—for example, your standard advice on a common math error. Then you can give students the handout or the computer file name for students to read your explanation.

- Use a spreadsheet for grading. Can your institution provide you with a class list you can download onto your own computer without rekeying all the student names?

- Record your comments into an audiotape. Students can hand you a blank tape when they submit their work. Record your comments on their tapes and hand back the tape with each person's work. The student can then listen to your comments. You can say more in five minutes than you can write.

- Use e-mail or bulletin boards to help your students respond to each other's work.

- If possible, make yourself thoroughly accessible by e-mail, voice mail, and telephone, so students can quickly get answers to their questions as they work on their assignments. Answering a question as it comes up may save you later having to write a long explanation on the finished work.

ACTIVITY

1. Review this chapter and list suggestions you think you could use.
2. Work out the details of one of your ideas.
3. Discuss your ideas with peers and with students and revise as needed.
4. Keep a record for a week or two, or for a semester if you can, of how you spend your grading time. How could you reduce the time without significantly reducing the quality of your grading and teaching?

CHAPTER 9

Using the Grading Process to Improve Teaching

If you have been using the interactive teaching and assessment recommendations we offer in this book, and if you have produced a PTA scale and used it to score students' work, you will have a great deal of information about your students' strengths and weaknesses and about their learning processes. You can use that information to improve your teaching.

The strategies we recommend in this chapter are based on the grading process, because the book is about grading. But ungraded student work is also highly useful for assessing student learning and improving classroom practice. Angelo and Cross's 1993 book *Classroom Assessment Techniques* can guide you in using strategies such as the "one-minute paper" to assess student work that is not necessarily graded but is used to inform your teaching.

Improving Teaching: Two Case Studies

In this chapter we present two examples of teachers who used information stemming from the grading process to analyze students' learning and to improve their teaching. The first example is Anderson's biology class, for which you saw the assignment sheet in Exhibit 3.5 and the PTA scale in Exhibit 5.3. Here we'll talk about how Anderson used the PTA scale to improve her students' titles and their use of the scientific format (see also Anderson and Walvoord, 1991).

The students' product-comparison titles that appear in Chapter Five were written by students before Anderson constructed her

PTA scale and before she instituted some other changes designed to help her students write better titles.

What Anderson was doing at that time was taking students to the library early in the course for two sessions on biological descriptors, in which students looked at indexed scientific titles and talked about how descriptors are used in science to allow other researchers to find relevant work in the literature.

Also, in the early scenario, students had read five scientific articles that were appropriately titled. Anderson had deleted the abstracts from these articles, and she required the students to write the missing abstracts. So if students had learned about the importance of keywords in the title and had abstracted scientific articles appropriately titled, why was she getting titles such as "The Battle of the Suds"? Analyzing her students' titles in the light of the criteria she had recently spelled out in her PTA scale helped Anderson to diagnose what was going wrong:

1. Students were not applying to their own titles the formats of the titles they read.

2. Students were not applying to their own titles the lessons they had learned about descriptors in the library.

3. Anderson's instructions to her students on the assignment sheet to "write to an audience of your peers" seemed to have been misunderstood: these students appeared to be writing to their peers not as scientists in training, but rather as fellow beer drinkers.

4. Students appeared to be modeling titles after other disciplines and settings. "The Battle of the Suds," for example, might be an appropriately humorous title for a Speech 101 class or an article in the student newspaper. "Research to Determine the Better Paper Towel," like "Book Report on Silas Marner," might have been adequate, if a bit pedestrian, for a high school English class.

What we're saying, then, is that constructing a PTA scale and examining student work in relation to the scale can help the teacher diagnose exactly what is going wrong.

Next, Anderson had to figure out what would amend the situation. She did not want to spend enormous amounts of extra time on titling, because, while titling is important to scientists because of their indexing systems, title was not the most important feature of students' work. So Anderson set out to discover whether, with little additional time, she could improve her students' titles.

The key appeared to lie in helping students define the appropriate audience, apply what they learned in the library and in their reading of scientific titles, and apply Anderson's criteria when examining their own titles.

Here is what she did: after the library sessions and the abstracting of scientific articles were completed, Anderson called the students' attention to one of the articles they had abstracted, entitled "Relative Climbing Tendencies of Gray (*Elaple obsoleta spiloides*) and Black Rat Snakes (*E.o. obsoleta*)." She asked students how they would have felt about the author if the article had been titled "Do Snakes Get High?"

After the laughter, she asked them what they had learned about audience in their English composition classes and how it related to scientific writing. She asked them who they thought their audience was for the original research paper they were working on. They discussed the notion of peers, and she emphasized that she saw them as scientists in training rather than as party animals. As a class, they identified the words *high* and *snake* as descriptors in the title and discussed how little information these "fun title words" could transmit via the keyword indexes in *BioAbstracts* or *Science Citation Index.*

The year after Anderson carried out this ten-minute exercise in class, 90 percent of her students scored 3.0 or better on her PTA for title, according to the scoring of two outside raters (Exhibit 5.3). (We explain systems for using outside raters later in the chapter.) In a previous year (the year of "The Battle of the Suds"), only 50 percent of the students had scored 3.0 or better. Of course, the later year had different students; but in subsequent years, Anderson's students have continued to write titles that meet her expectations at these levels.

Anderson also turned her attention to helping her students with scientific format. In the old days, Anderson had told her students several times, both verbally and in writing, that scientific research reports contained these sections: title, abstract, introduction, methods and materials, results, and conclusions and implications. Early in the course, students were required to read five scientific articles that followed the scientific format. Anderson had deleted the abstracts from these articles, and students had to compose the missing abstracts.

Also, several days after her lecture on the scientific format, Anderson asked her students to bring in three pages from their own Methods and Materials section. That was followed by a forty-minute peer-conferencing session in which students were free to address with each other format or other concerns about their papers.

What did students end up doing in their final reports? A few wrote papers with no sections at all. Some omitted sections. Some invented new sections. Some organized things poorly within sections.

Clearly, Anderson's strategies were not effectively addressing students' format problems. A lecture and handout on the scientific format did not necessarily convey to students the information they needed to arrange their own material into the appropriate headings. Writing abstracts for scientific articles encouraged students to focus not on the "what-goes-where" in the scientific format but rather on the gist of the article. The peer conferences on their Materials and Methods sections might have helped students with organization of material within that section, but it did not help them conceptualize the entire report in terms of the format. Further, Anderson's assignment to write the Materials and Methods section early in their experimental process initiated (or at least perpetuated) the erroneous idea that scientists, from the beginning, write their work in sections. In fact, however, scientists write throughout the planning, piloting, and experimenting stages and not necessarily in the sequence they will eventually use to report their work to the scientific community.

After her Primary Trait Analysis allowed Anderson to separate out the components of poor format and to diagnose more clearly how and why her students were going wrong, she used her in-class time differently. She gave a fifteen-minute lecture on format this time, as before, but in it she emphasized how she and other scientists wrote throughout the research process and then put their writing into the research report format later.

Next, she decided to use one of the articles they had already read and abstracted, but this time to call students' attention specifically to format, which their abstracting task had not done. She cut up copies of one of the articles into separate paragraphs. In class, she put the students into small working groups and gave each group a handful of cut-up paragraphs, which they then had to reassemble into the complete article, with appropriate headings. They had to justify why they placed each paragraph as they did. The activity took fifteen minutes.

At the end of class, Anderson asked students to bring in three pages of text from their research for the next class. When they returned, she had the students assemble in the same small groups and work for fifteen minutes to decide into which scientific format sections the pieces of each person's own three pages of text would fit. As they had for title, the scores of the class on scientific format improved substantially. Anderson's strategies for improving other aspects of her student scientific reports appear in Anderson and Walvoord, 1991.

You will see that between analyzing students' problems on the one hand and implementing appropriate pedagogical strategies on the other lies a philosophy or model of how learning takes place and a prediction about which kinds of pedagogical strategies will successfully address the problems. Being aware of unspoken theories and developing explicit theories helps you predict why one thing will work and another won't (Menges and Rando, 1989). Anderson, as you can see, tends to address students' conceptual problems by hands-on application, actually having them identify descriptors in the snake title or physically rearrange the cut-up paragraphs. She helps students specifically and concretely apply what they have learned in one setting—such as a library visit or a lecture on scientific format—to their own work. Also, she believes strongly in collaboration among students.

If you want to explore further the models and research on student development, student learning, and pedagogical techniques that tend to enhance learning, Resource 9.1 offers suggestions.

Another example of how faculty can use the grading process to analyze their students' learning and improve teaching is provided by Steven Dunbar, who teaches mathematics at the University of Nebraska at Lincoln. Dunbar has a system for analyzing how well each of his students is doing and how well the class as a whole is doing on each of several learning goals. Each goal is assessed on several tests, homework problems, and exams. Dunbar composes the graph shown in Table 9.1, which allows him to identify the strengths and weaknesses (or, in our language, the primary traits) of his students on specific goals over time.

Table 9.1. Dunbar's Graph of Student Progress in a Math Class.

Goal 4: Solve and demonstrate an understanding of a dual problem and its meaning

	Exam #2 Q 14	Exam #2 Q 20	Homework 8	Final exam Q 7	Mean for individual student
Student 1	75	64	63	80	70
Student 2	64	48	44	74	56
Student 3	91	79	89	85	86
And so on					
Mean for each question/problem	76	64	65	80	71

Resource 9.1.

Sources About Student Development, Learning, and Pedagogy.

Schemes of Intellectual and Moral Development

Belenky, Clinchy, Goldberger, and Tarule, 1986. A study of women learning in academic and nonacademic settings, intended to balance and correct Perry's study of academic males.

Kurfiss, 1988. Summarizes Perry, Belenky, and others, pointing out differences and similarities related to the teaching of critical thinking.

Magolda, 1992. With Perry and Belenky as background, reports a new study of students at Miami University, revealing gender similarities and differences to create a more comprehensive picture of students' ways of knowing.

Noddings and Witherell, 1993. Bibliography of publications on moral development.

Perry, 1970. A study of the intellectual development of Harvard male students in the 1950s and 1960s, outlining the stages of development through which they pass.

Stark and Lattuca, 1997. Within a book about curriculum, authors summarize many theories of student development.

Swartz and Perkins, 1990. Summarizes research on how students learn critical and creative thinking and addresses such issues as the transfer of students' thinking skills from one discipline to another, the meaning of learning to think better, and so on.

Welte, 1997. A review of Magolda.

Learning Styles

Davis, 1993. The chapter on students (pp. 60–93) offers a review of the literature and implications for teaching students of different learning styles, races, genders, and so on.

Best Teaching Methods for Higher Education

Angelo, 1993. Fourteen research-based principles.

Astin, 1985. Based on his own and others' research, proposes the "theory of student involvement," which posits involvement as the key to learning.

Bonwell and Eison, 1991. Highly useful review of the literature and suggestions about implementing "active learning," defined as "instructional activities involving students in doing things and thinking about what they are doing."

Chickering and Gamson, 1987. Reports interpretations of the research in the form of seven principles, shaped by a group of national experts.

Frost, 1991. Short summary of contributors to student success; useful bibliography.

Grasha, 1996. Detailed suggestions about how to teach well and develop appropriate skills in each of several different teaching styles.

Kurfiss, 1988. A summary of research and practice in critical thinking for the practitioner. (See pp. 88–89, which summarize the research on teaching methods that enhance critical thinking.)

Light, 1992. A study, with eleven data sources, of faculty and students at Harvard and twenty-four other institutions. The central finding: involvement is the key to learning.

Pascarella and Terenzini, 1991. A literature review. Concludes involvement is the key but offers extensive detail about various outcomes and the factors that appear to encourage them.

While our language may be different, the principle is the same: you can take any trait that you care about and lay out students' performance in a similar graph to identify whole-class weaknesses and strengths. Then guide your teaching by that analysis.

Dunbar reports that he has been able to refine the goals for the course and adjust the relative amounts of time spent on various goals based on the record from previous courses. For example, based on class performance records as in Table 9.1, students' averages were lower, and students had greater dispersion on the problems related to modeling compared with the problems related to deriving the answer from a formulated model. So Dunbar recommended that in a large enrollment course for senior math and actuarial science majors more time be spent on "mathematical modeling" and less time on the algorithmic method used to derive answers from the models. By tracking the progress of individual students on the goals (along a row of the table) Dunbar can deduce whether individual students are having more or less trouble with topics of the course. Occasionally this is helpful in determining whether a particular student has a weakness in background or a gap in prior knowledge. A trend in grades or a consistent pattern of success (or lack of success) across goals for a particular student is helpful in determining a meaningful course grade for the student. This moves course grading in the direction of outcomes-based assessment instead of compiling a lumped or even weighted average of test scores, converted to percentages and then scored by letter grade.

Collecting Additional Data

Sometimes you may find that you would like to have additional data beyond what is generated in your grading process. For example, Dunbar might want to know more about how his students were attacking certain problems or what they remembered from past mathematics classes about basic concepts that were essential to their understanding of dual problems. Anderson might want to know more about her students' past experiences in using the scientific method or about their ability to construct and label graphs.

Classroom research is a name frequently applied to this kind of investigation. It can be highly useful for the teacher, need not necessarily be highly time-consuming, and may result in substantial improvement as well as in publication of your findings. For example, Madan Batra, who teaches international business at Indiana University of Pennsylvania, was using a number of strategies to help his students work effectively in teams to complete semester-long business projects. He wanted to know what students found most and least helpful about his strategies, so that he wouldn't waste his time on strategies they did not find helpful. He designed a questionnaire, gathered this information from his students over several different semesters, tallied the results, used them for changes in his own classroom, and published them (Batra, Walvoord, and Krishnan, 1995; Batra, Walvoord, and Krishnan, 1997). Additional sources for information about classroom research are in Resource 1.1.

ACTIVITY

1. Take an aspect of your own students' performance that does not meet your expectations. Alone or with a colleague, explain as precisely as you can where their difficulties lie. Plan how you might help your students improve.

2. Try to articulate the models of learning and teaching that lie behind your proposed solutions in (1). You might frame your response in the following ways:

   "The problem my students are having is . . ."

   "The problem is caused by . . ."

   "I might help them by . . ."

   "I think this strategy will work because . . ."

   Explaining why you think a strategy will work forces you to articulate your theories of student learning.

3. Pose a question about your students' learning that you believe would help you improve your teaching. Plan how you would gather data to answer your question. Discuss your plan with a colleague and revise if needed.

PART TWO

How Grading Serves Broader Assessment Purposes

CHAPTER 10

Determining Faculty Performance, Rewards, and Incentives

At times in academic life, a faculty member may need to document student learning for promotion and tenure, for grants, or for publication. Often, you are trying to show how student learning changed over time as you implemented particular teaching strategies. We use that situation as a focus of this chapter.

External, standardized tests are one way to measure student learning. But an assignment or test that is a normal part of your course, together with a PTA that reflects your criteria, can be an excellent assessment because it is embedded in the semester-long conversation of the course, with all its tacit understandings, its goals, and its expectations. You're not imposing someone else's goals and assumptions on your students; rather, you are testing whether they have learned what you wanted, in the environment that you constructed.

This chapter presents two examples where faculty members documented their students' learning using classroom assignments or tests and a PTA they constructed to express their criteria and standards. The first example is Gisela Escoe and Philip Way, who teach economics in the University of Cincinnati's College of Arts and Sciences. Escoe and Way received a National Science Foundation grant for, among other things, moving from lecture-based to interactive learning in their microeconomics and macroeconomics courses for undergraduates, which enroll several hundred students per section. They needed a way to compare student performance before and after their pedagogical changes. The standard, nationally normed multiple-choice Test of Understanding of College Economics did not meet their needs because, while the test might be an excellent instrument for measuring students' command over economic knowledge, they judged it might not be a valid measure of students' ability to express economic concepts or ideas, nor students' ability to apply economics to their own situations—two of the important traits Way and Escoe wanted to teach and to measure in their class. Thus they turned to assignments and PTA scales they constructed to help them track differences in student performance. They composed PTA scales for a series of critical-thinking assignments students completed as part of their regular work for the class. You already saw one of the assignments and its PTA scale (Exhibit 5.8). TAs graded the assignments using the PTA scales. In such a situation, one could have the TAs function as outside raters and calculate their rate of agreement. Alternatively, one could import other raters as an additional check.

As this book goes to the printer, the results of Escoe and Way's teaching changes are not yet in. However, for our purposes the magnitude of change is not as important as the fact that they are tracking changes in student performance in a detailed way, for the teacher's own information and also for reporting to a funding agency, for publication, and for Escoe's successful tenure application.

Our second example is Anderson the biologist, who used primary trait scoring to inform her teaching and to document changes in students' performance in her classes over time, as she changed her teaching strategies. She has used her findings for her own improvement and also for conference presentations and for publications. You saw Anderson's assignment in Exhibit 3.5, her PTA scale in Exhibit 5.3, and some of her teaching changes in Chapter Nine.

As Anderson implemented her new teaching strategies, she naturally asked herself, Have student scores improved? That question can be addressed but not conclusively answered because of the small number of students and the fact that the students were different from one semester to the next. But Anderson tried to get some data to address the question of whether her changes were of any benefit. She asked two college-level biology teachers who were otherwise unconnected to her class to act as outside raters. They used Anderson's PTA scale (Appendix C) to score twenty-two original scientific research reports. Although the outside raters believed that all the papers were from one intact class, Anderson actually gave them eleven papers (all that were turned in) from the class before Anderson had made her changes and eleven papers (all that were turned in) from the same class taught after she had made her changes. Demographically, these two Towson University Biology 381 classes were very similar. In each, fifteen students had been enrolled, four dropouts occurred, and eleven completed the research assignment. Both classes had the same number of males and females, the same number of minority students and ESL students, similar age distributions, and equal numbers of transfer students. SAT scores were not available for all the students because Towson does not collect them for transfers; however, Towson's SAT or GPA minimum requirements for enrollment were the same for both groups of students. Both classes had the same assignment (Exhibit 3.5), the same teacher, and the same amount of time to perform the task. Experientially, however, the two classes had become different; Anderson had changed her teaching strategies.

By using outside raters, Anderson had obtained PTA scores that could corroborate her impression that her students' work had improved after her changes. She had two data sets to compare:

1. *Before:* mean scores (derived from the average individual scores of all eleven students) given by the outside raters to each of the primary traits (such as title, designing an experiment, and so on) contained in the original research papers

Table 10.1. Student Scores on PTA for Science Reports, Before and After Pedagogical Changes.

Trait	Before	After	P values*
Title	2.95	3.22	.24
Introduction	3.18	3.64	.14
Scientific format	3.09	3.32	.31
Methods and materials	3.00	3.55	.14
Nonexperimental information	3.18	3.50	.24
Designing the experiment	2.68	3.32	.07
Defining operationally	2.68	3.50	.01
Controlling variables	2.73	3.18	.10
Collecting data	2.86	3.36	.14
Interpreting data	2.90	3.59	.03
Overall	2.93	3.42	.09

*The *P* value given is the probability, under the null hypothesis, that the difference in the two groups are attributable to chance and not to treatment. The probability values calculated were the *P* values of a T distribution within twenty degrees of freedom. The values were determined by interpolation between standard tabulated values for the T distributions (see Fisher and Yates, 1963; Dayton and Stunkard, 1971, Table F.3).

Adapted from Anderson and Walvoord, 1991, p. 247.

written by students in Anderson's class in the semester before she made her changes.

2. *After:* mean scores (derived in the same way) for the same traits in the original research papers written by students in Anderson's class after she had made her changes.

In Table 10.1, the scoring is based on 5 as the best performance and 1 as the worst performance. For example, a class having a mean score of 4.1 on designing experiments and 2.25 on title means that experimental design is good, but titles are not.

Anderson published these findings, together with the pedagogical changes, (Anderson and Walvoord, 1991) and has used them for numerous conference and workshop presentations. In addition, she included them when she applied for full professorship.

We have told Escoe and Way's and Anderson's stories to illustrate how teachers used Primary Trait Analysis as part of classroom research to discover more about how and why their students were learning. They used this information not only for their own classroom improvement but also for promotion, tenure, grants, and publication.

We concentrated here on measuring student improvement over time. It is also possible to contrast sections of the same course taught in different ways. (A helpful model for such a cross-sectional design is Macdonald and Cooper, 1992).

ACTIVITY

1. Identify an aspect of your students' learning that you would like to try to improve.

2. Select an assignment or test you might use to assess that learning.

3. List the traits that you might use for a PTA scale for that test or assignment (or you might use the PTA scale, which you began at the end of Chapter Five).

4. Sketch a design by which you would test student learning over time, or by which you would test student learning between one course section and another.

CHAPTER 11

Strengthening Departmental and Institutional Assessment

The previous chapters concentrated on how to make grading easier and more useful in the classroom and how the individual teacher can document classroom learning. We began there because good assessment must begin in the classroom and end there, too. Now we want to explore how the grading process can be used as the basis of departmental and general education assessment.

Such a plan is based on a theoretical stance that has two parts. The first part holds that critical thinking, problem solving, or whatever learning you're trying to measure is *context-specific*. That is, critical thinking is different in math than in history, and it may been be somewhat different in my history class than in your history class. It is different in an Ivy League university class than in a community college class. While certain commonalities do develop within the academic culture, nonetheless, critical thinking and other kinds of learning may profitably be taught and assessed not just in a standardized exam given outside class but in the context of a particular institution's or department's mission and within a particular teacher's semester-long work with a particular body of knowledge and a particular group of students over time.

This theoretical stance accords well with many of the guidelines for good assessment. Accrediting agencies typically insist strongly that assessment be tied to an institution's mission and to its specific learning goals and objectives. Further the "Principles of Good Practice for Assessing Student Learning" (Appendix A) from the American Association for Higher Education (AAHE) suggests that, among other things, assessment should

- Lead directly to improvement in teaching and learning
- Be embedded in the context of learning
- Take place repeatedly over time

The second part of this theoretical stance holds that critical thinking, problem solving, or whatever type of learning you are trying to assess is not new to your faculty. You are not imposing something in a vacuum; rather, these bodies of knowledge and skills are being taught and assessed on your campus. No one claims they're being taught and assessed perfectly, but it is foolish to pretend they don't exist. When an assessment system acknowledges what faculty are already doing, it can more easily capture the faculty commitment and buy-in that are valuable to institutions and required by regional accrediting agencies. Further, acknowledging what faculty already do can be cost-effective by capitalizing on resources already in place.

Within this two-part theoretical stance, the nature of the assessment task changes in an important way. Instead of having to find externally a definition of the learning you want and a way of assessing it, with the grading process having no relevance, the task is to make systematic, explicit, and public the goals of learning and the assessment of learning that are already happening on campus, often in connection with grading processes. Then, as needed, the task is to improve campus teaching, student learning, and assessment.

For example, if Anystate University adopts this theoretical stance to assess its critical thinking in general education, it asserts that critical thinking at Anystate University is whatever Anystate University faculty make it in their daily, contextualized practice in their classrooms and laboratories and clinics. Classroom grading processes, when well done, produce what ethnographers call artifacts of the culture. In this case, classroom grading produces, or could produce, statements of teacher objectives for learning, course skeletons such as we described in Chapter Three, tests and assignments, PTA scales or other statements of the standards and criteria for student work, student work with teacher grades and comments, and evidence of teacher change based on this information, such as a revised assignment sheet or syllabus. All this material can be used as data to answer assessment questions.

The assessor's task then is to define critical thinking at Anystate University and make it explicit, so outsiders can understand it and practitioners can improve it. The process of faculty examining their own work leads to conversation and to changes in faculty practices and in curricular and programmatic structures. Assessors are not external imposers of something brand new but investigators, ethnographers, and facilitators. The assessor's approach is not to get people to do assessment but to examine how people teach and assess critical thinking and to help them improve. It's an approach that accords deep respect to faculty who are teaching critical thinking and the skills and knowledge of their disciplines. It's an approach that draws upon their wisdom and practice. It's an approach that has a chance to win their participation and commitment.

It's also a stance that can meet external requirements and recommendations for assessment. Accrediting agencies want to see broad faculty participation in the shaping of assessment plans. They want to see, and AAHE recommends, strong feedback loops from assessment back into student learning and into individual teachers' classroom practices (see Appendix A).

Based on this theoretical stance, our approach to departmental, general education or institutional assessment is to make classroom grading practices public and analyzable. Such a strategy, we believe, can be a strategic part of an institution's or department's assessment plan. Your institution may also want to use standardized tests or other external measures of student learning as part of an assessment plan; however, we limit ourselves in this chapter to a discussion of how classroom grading practices can yield good data for answering important assessment questions.

Just how might this be done? What might such an assessment plan look like? Figure 11.1 suggests some of the types of data that faculty might submit to a central assessment committee or other body and then some of the assessment questions that the data might help the committee to address. The data and the questions are illustrative only; an institution can collect whatever data and address whatever questions it decides are needed.

As you can see, the basic assessment plan calls for faculty to submit data that arise from their classroom grading processes. Faculty use the data for improvement in their own classrooms. The central committee or other body uses the data to answer departmental or general education assessment questions. Findings are fed back into the institution for improvement.

Faculty readers may at this point be thinking to themselves, Submitting all that stuff sounds like a lot of work, and it also sounds somewhat dangerous. How do I know how this material will be used? Doesn't this violate academic freedom? As faculty members ourselves, we share those concerns. But we think our plan offers one way to protect those values in the present climate, where assessment and accountability are being imposed from the outside. The challenge now, as faculty practices can no longer remain invisible, is to manage visibility in ways that benefit our students, ourselves, and our institutions.

First, the data that faculty might submit to the committee (listed in the left-hand column of Figure 11.1) can be products of

Figure 11.1.   Using the Classroom Grading Process for Departmental or General Education Assessment.

Basic Assessment Plan:
Collect and Analyze the Data Generated by Faculty's Classroom Grading Processes

Classroom Data	can answer these questions	Departmental or General Education Assessment
1. Teacher's learning goals (individual or collective among group or department) 2. Tests, assignments ("assessment instruments") 3. Teacher criteria and standards (in form of PTA?) 4. Student scores over time ("outcomes") 5. Evidence of feedback into learning and teaching		▪ Is assessment taking place in classrooms? ▪ What kinds of learning are we teaching and assessing? ▪ What are common criteria and standards? ▪ How do assignments, criteria, and standards for sequenced courses relate? ▪ What are trends in student scores over time? ▪ What are areas of weakness and strength in student scores? ▪ How do our assignments, criteria, and standards compare to national tests or to best practices elsewhere?

the grading process or, more broadly, products of the teaching process: statements of what the faculty member wants students to learn; and copies of assignments and tests, as well as grading criteria. We grant that these products might take additional time for faculty to compile for submission to the assessment committee, and we urge that assessment planners realistically plan how faculty are to find that time. But all of the assessment programs now being required of institutions are going to take more time. Our hope is that by collecting data from the classroom teaching and grading processes we can reduce the amount of time needed and can integrate the assessment that faculty already conduct in their classrooms with the broader assessment they conduct for departments and institutions.

Faculty autonomy, academic freedom, and faculty control of the curriculum and of assessment have important uses in a free society. We think our plan offers one way to protect those values in the present climate, where assessment and accountability are often being imposed on faculty and institutions from outside. To protect those values, we believe faculty need to distinguish between making what they do more public and giving up control of it. In our system, the criteria and standards, the tests and exams, remain under faculty control, but are made public in new ways.

It's not as though everything faculty do in classroom grading has been totally secret up to now. In the academy supported by public funds, there has always been a mixture of faculty autonomy and public accountability. Faculty have been sharing certain aspects of their classroom assessment for a long time. Audiences for grades have included the student, the employer, graduate schools, and administrators who have access to computerized records of grades.

Though grades are shared in these ways, what has not been so routinely or broadly shared are the learning goals, the assignments and tests, and the criteria and standards on which the grades are based. Even here, though, there has been sharing—with promotion and tenure committees, in annual review by department heads, or among faculty who are team teaching or planning curriculum or participating in faculty development workshops. In the hundreds of faculty workshops we have led, where faculty shared their learning goals, assignments, and criteria, no one has ever claimed that academic freedom was being violated by such sharing.

And then there's the student grapevine. Have you ever asked students in your class, on the first day, to write anonymously what they've heard about your class before coming to it? You may find that they know (or think they know) quite a lot about your tests and papers, your grading criteria, and your expectations. In some institutions, students even publish such information.

The visibility we're talking about, then, is not brand new; it is an extension to new audiences with new purposes. The alternative, we believe, is to let external forces impose external tests graded by external raters and thus to force faculty to teach to those tests. While that situation may be desirable in some instances and is already happening in fields where there are licensure exams, we believe that, in the main, faculty and institutions will want to work hard to keep course content, tests, assignments, criteria, and standards largely under the control of their own faculty—individually and as faculty work together in departments, curriculum committees, and the like.

We might consider faculty research as a useful paradigm. In that arena, one must make one's goals, standards, methods, and criteria public, and one is expected to follow practices established by peers in one's discipline. In teaching, as in research, we want to establish visibility together with faculty peer control, rather than allow others to impose standards, criteria, and methods for assessing student learning. The challenge now, as classroom grading practices can no longer remain invisible, is to control visibility in ways that benefit our students, ourselves, and our institutions.

In sum, then, we recognize that the plan we outlined in Figure 11.1 may give rise to questions about faculty time and faculty control. We have tried to address those concerns, but there is no perfect system. Our assessment model, like any other, has tradeoffs. Our system requires wide participation from faculty, and it requires faculty time to reevaluate their classroom practices, improve them as needed, and make them visible in new ways. In exchange, we hope to maintain maximum faculty control over curricular content; over the teaching, learning, and grading process in classrooms; and over the tests, assignment, criteria, and standards by which faculty assess student learning. We believe our system offers a chance for institutions to integrate the assessment they conduct through grading with their other "assessment plans." We believe our system offers a strong chance that many faculty will participate and that assessment will affect teaching and learning in classrooms.

Addressing Assessment Goals Through Grading Process Data

This section offers hypothetical examples of how a department or general education program might use data that emerge from classroom grading to address assessment goals. For each assessment example below, we address three questions:

1. Who needs to know, and why?
2. Which data are collected from the chosen classrooms?
3. How does the assessment committee (or other body) analyze data and present findings?

We have supplied hypothetical samples, types and sizes, data, and details of analysis; individual institutions will adapt those practices to their own situations.

The examples that follow progress in complexity. They are not mutually exclusive. Institutions, departments, and general education programs may want to combine them or to begin with the more simple and work up to the more complex.

Example 1: Assuring That Effective Classroom Assessment Is Taking Place

Who Needs to Know, and Why?   This is the most simple and basic of our examples. It posits that the institution wants to know for itself and to demonstrate, for its accrediting agency and similar audiences, that assessment is taking place in classrooms and that those classroom assessment practices adhere to certain criteria. Based on accrediting agency and institutional needs, and on what AAHE recommends (Appendix A), the committee might establish criteria to ensure that

1. Student learning is being assessed in classrooms.
2. Assessment in those classrooms is connected to the teacher's learning goals and objectives and to the departmental and institutional mission.
3. Assessment instruments (tests, exams, and assignments) in those classrooms are measuring student achievement of the teacher's goals in a valid and reliable way.
4. Criteria and standards for the tests and assignments are being stated in writing.
5. Student work is being assessed against those criteria and standards.
6. The results of assessment are being fed back into student learning and into teacher planning.

In this example, there is no attempt to aggregate the results of classroom assessment. The only goal is to make sure that healthy assessment practices are taking place in classrooms. The assessors are content to make sure the faculty have the outcomes of their own classroom assessment and that they use those outcomes for improvement. In later stages, an institution or department may want to aggregate data in ways we explain in our subsequent examples. But this first, basic step—documenting that good classroom assessment is occurring—may well be a good place for an institution to start. Further, we believe that without healthy classroom assessment as the bedrock, other forms of assessment have only a shaky foundation.

Which Data Are Collected from Classrooms?   In order to achieve the necessary faculty commitment, a committee will undoubtedly have to articulate very carefully how access to the data will be handled, how and to whom results will be reported, and how privacy and academic freedom will be protected. (Chapter Twelve will explain how one college achieved this commitment.)

Assuming the commitment has been gained, the committee then decides upon the sample of courses from which it will collect data and the specific data it will request:

- Data from each class in the sample:
  - Statements of course goals and objectives
  - Major tests and assignments that assess those goals

- A PTA scale showing criteria and standards on the major tests and assignments
- Evidence of how the teacher is feeding back that information into teaching and learning—perhaps a sample of teacher comments on drafts or a revised assignment sheet (items 1, 2, 3, and 5 in Figure 11.1)

The committee disseminates to the sample faculty its guidelines for submission of data. The committee decides to offer help to faculty in compiling and submitting the data (through workshops, consultation, and secretarial services). Once faculty have submitted the data, the committee analyzes them.

How Does the Assessment Committee (or Other Body) Analyze Data and Present Findings?   After examining the collected data, the assessment committee might report something like this:

> To determine whether classroom assessment is being conducted and whether it conforms to the six criteria listed earlier, the committee requested information from a random sample of 20 percent of the courses being taught in fall semester 2001. The information was submitted in each case by the instructor of that course. (*Instructor* may include an adjunct teacher or a TA if that person is the instructor of record. In case of multiple sections of the course, only one section, selected at random, was used.)

> - A teacher's written statement of learning objectives for the course
> - Copies of what the teacher judged to be the two to three most central tests, exams, and assignments that assessed student achievement of those goals
> - Written statements of the criteria being used to assess students' performances on the tests, exams, and assignments
> - Evidence (such as teacher comments on student tests and assignments, revised syllabus or handouts) that assessment results were being fed back into student learning and into the teacher's own practice

> The committee offered a workshop for faculty in the sample, to explain the criteria and the data needed, to help faculty prepare the data, and to help faculty implement classroom changes spurred by their own examination of their data against the criteria. The workshop met for two days prior to the beginning of the fall semester and for a two-hour session three times during the fall semester.

> Fifty-seven percent of the faculty sample attended the workshop. End-of-workshop evaluations showed that 96 percent of faculty attenders agreed or strongly agreed that "The workshop helped me to prepare materials for submission," and 88 percent agreed or strongly agreed that this workshop would help them improve stu-

dent learning in their classrooms. In open-ended comments, faculty reported they strongly appreciated the colleague interaction and the opportunity to re-evaluate their courses during the workshop. Workshop leaders observed that many teaching changes were implemented or planned for the next semester by faculty as a result of the workshops. In addition to the workshop attendance, twenty-three of the sample faculty individually requested and received help from committee members as they prepared their data.

The committee recognizes that once members of the faculty sample had participated in the workshop, they were no longer representative of the total faculty, although they had originally been chosen randomly. The committee nonetheless chose to offer the workshop for two reasons:

1. Faculty chosen for the sample strongly requested help in preparing the data and in using the data collection process for their own self-improvement.
2. The committee reasoned that, as the goal of the assessment project is to improve teaching and student learning, the faculty's strong desire for help represented a unique opportunity to help faculty improve assessment practices.

Thus this study measures the practices of a random sample of faculty, 57 percent of whom participated in a workshop subsequent to their selection for the sample.

For 76 percent of the sample courses, faculty submitted all the data listed earlier; for an additional 13 percent, faculty submitted partial data.

Professor John Jackson of Highlands University acted as consultant to the committee for data analysis. He conducted two half-day training sessions for the committee. In the first session, before data were requested, committee members constructed explicit definitions for each criterion and composed explicit requests for data. At the second workshop, after data had been collected, committee members practiced analyzing data against the criteria.

Then data were divided among the committee members. Data for each class were reviewed twice. Committee member raters scored each class's data against each of the six criteria, using the following 3-point scale: (3) clearly meets this criterion, (2) unclear whether it meets the criterion, and (1) clearly does not meet the criterion. When the members' ratings were disparate, those data were read by a third committee member.

The lowest mean scores occurred for the criteria 3, 4, and 5. This suggests that the areas most difficult for faculty were constructing tests and assignments that were valid and reliable, stating criteria and standards clearly, and evaluating student work according to those criteria and standards.

Faculty who attended the workshop scored significantly higher on criteria 3, 4, and 5 than faculty who did not. Responses from workshop participants and observation by the workshop leader suggest that the workshops were a powerful force for faculty change.

The workshop leader observed that when they first came into the workshop, many faculty were unaware of the college's mission statement or of mission statements for their own departments.

Based on these findings, the committee makes these recommendations:

1. Offer workshops of a similar nature and try to get as many faculty into them as possible.
2. Offer follow-up workshops for those in the sample who have already attended and submitted their data, to help them continue their growth as teachers. (Both types of workshops should give special emphasis to criteria 3, 4, and 5, as these were problematic to faculty in the sample.)
3. Work with departments to ensure that institutional and departmental mission statements are better known to faculty.
4. After four or five years, collect similar data from a sample of faculty who have and have not attended the workshops, to see whether the two groups differ and whether the scores for faculty as a whole have risen.

Many readers of this book could improve on the research design we have outlined for the hypothetical college. We tried to propose a research design that would be rigorous enough to offer usable information but not too daunting for a college assessment committee to conduct.

An interesting problem raised by this case is that you are likely to change faculty practices just by asking for certain data. If you tell faculty what criteria you are going to use to evaluate their classroom data, as this committee did, then faculty may change their practices to bring them closer to the criteria. If you offer faculty some guidance in preparing their course objectives, tests, exams, assignments, criteria, and standards, and if you teach them PTA scoring, and if you do so in a workshop setting where interaction is rich and stimulating, faculty are likely to change their practices. You have begun to do what you most wanted to do—change faculty practice in ways that are quite possibly more effective for student learning. But now your sample of faculty is no longer representative of the unobserved, unsupported faculty. Our hypothetical committee decided to hold the workshops anyway. In their report they acknowledged this dilemma and explained their reasoning.

Methodologically, the committee has moved from a paradigm in which the prime value is to keep the sample representative and untainted to a paradigm in which the prime value is to help faculty improve. The literature on "action science" (Argyris, Putnam, and Smith, 1985) or on participatory modes of evaluation (Guba and

Lincoln, 1989) will be helpful to theorize and explain how this paradigm may be followed in a responsible and defensible way.

Example 2: Finding Common Expectations

In this example, the goal is not merely to establish that classroom assessment is being conducted but to aggregate the findings to answer questions about courses as a group. The assessment committee wanted to identify common expectations among courses.

Who Needs to Know, and Why? In this hypothetical case, the general education committee needs to know what is being taught to and expected of students in general education courses. The committee would like to make recommendations to general education faculty and to the faculty senate about enhancing the cohesiveness of the general education experience for students. Further, the college would like to describe more specifically for external audiences what it teaches in general education. It also wants to show its accrediting agency that it has a general-education assessment plan in place. As in all of our examples, substantial effort may be necessary to get the faculty on board for this assessment plan. Once that has been done, the committee selects its sample of faculty and gathers the data from them.

Which Data Are Collected from Classrooms? The hypothetical sample here is all general education courses taught in spring 2002. Data collected include (1) one major assignment, test, or exam that the teacher believes assesses critical thinking as defined and taught in the course and (2) for that assignment, test, or exam, a PTA scale for the traits that the faculty member defines as critical thinking in the course. In other words, the data are items 2 and 3 in Figure 11.1.

How Does the Assessment Committee (or Other Body) Analyze Data and Present Findings? The committee selects its sample of general education courses and asks the faculty teaching them to submit their major assignments, tests, and exams, plus the PTA scales. When the committee receives these data, it engages a qualitative researcher to analyze the types of learning being expected of students, as revealed in the data.

The researcher's greatest challenge is to arrive at common terms to categorize the types of learning. If the committee has, ahead of time, provided faculty with guidelines about terminology, the task may be somewhat easier. Even if the committee has allowed all faculty to use their own terminology, however, the researcher's training offers methods and experiences to address this challenge. The researcher presents the following report to the committee:

> Usable data were submitted for 82 percent of the general education courses in the sample. Examination of these assignments, tests, exams, and PTA scales reveals the following common types of learning being required of students in general education. The following categories were derived from terms that were listed as traits on the faculty members' PTA scales. Assignment instructions and other submitted data were used to help clarify the meaning of the traits listed by faculty on the PTA scales. [A key to terminology might be included here.] Following are the types of learning and the frequency with which they were included in the traits:
>
>> *Problem-solving:* used as a trait for at least one PTA in 46 percent of the courses
>> *Generalizing from data:* used in 42 percent of the courses
>> *Questioning assumptions:* used in 39 percent of the courses
>> *Analyzing a text:* used in 79 percent of the courses

In aggregating materials from various faculty and disciplines, a major challenge is to decide on common terminology. For example, an assignment may call for analysis of text but not use those words. The researcher, then, must interpret the terminology on the PTA scales and arrive at a common set of traits in order to aggregate the data. The assignments or tests will help the assessors understand what is being asked and to classify PTA language appropriately.

Divergences of terminology may be reduced if faculty develop their PTA scales in a workshop or collaborative setting, or if they have common models or mission statements to work from, or if the committee establishes guidelines for common language.

Because of the difficulty of aggregating terminology from various disciplines and classrooms, and to illustrate another way of proceeding, we imagined in the preceding example that the committee hired an outside researcher to examine the data and write the report. However, if it wishes, the committee could do this task itself.

Example 3: Checking the Sequence of Skills Taught in a Department

Who Needs to Know, and Why?   In this hypothetical situation, an English department wants to find out whether skills taught and assessed at lower levels build consistently toward skills required for its senior seminar, which requires students to produce a significant essay of literary analysis. Further, the department wants to describe to its prospective students, and to those who employ its students, which skills the students have been taught. Finally, the department wants to show the institution's assessment office that it has constructed an assessment plan as requested.

Which Data Are Collected from Classrooms?   The sample is a random 50 percent of lower level courses plus all sections of the three senior seminars (all students are required to take one) taught in fall and spring 2003. Data collected are (1) major assignments, tests, and exams and (2) PTA scales for those assignments, tests, and exams (items 2 and 3 on Figure 11.1).

How Does the Assessment Committee (or Other Body) Analyze Data and Present Findings?   Two members of the department analyze the data. Their goal is to identify the most significant skills required for completion of the senior seminars and then to discover whether and where those skills are being taught in lower-level majors courses. They prepare the following report:

> Usable data were obtained from 82 percent of the sample of lower-level majors courses and from 100 percent of senior seminar sections. Examination of tests, exams, assignments, and PTA scales from this sample indicates the criteria being used to evaluate student work in the senior seminars and the lower-level courses.
>
> The following skills are required in all the senior seminar sections. An asterisk following an item indicates those skills that are also required in at least 75 percent of the lower-level courses.
>
> - Stating a position in an analytical essay*
> - Backing the position with evidence from the literary work*
> - Acknowledging alternative points of view
> - Using the library to find literary critical works
> - Integrating others' work smoothly into one's own interpretations
> - Avoiding overreliance on sources
> - Organizing an essay in a logical fashion*

A report such as this may lead to a discussion by the department about whether appropriate skills are being required in the senior seminars, about whether lower-level courses are building those skills in a appropriate ways, and about how suggested changes can best be made. Members of the department may now build a grid to show which of the senior-level criteria are addressed in each lower-level course. Results of this discussion are reported to the assessment office as evidence that assessment is being used to enhance teaching and learning in the department.

Example 4: What Is Required of Graduates?

Who Needs to Know, and Why?   In this hypothetical situation, a department wants to know what is being required of its graduates. It wants this information for its own use, for employers and prospective students, and for the institution's assessment office, which has requested an assessment plan from the department. This investigation goes a step beyond the previous ones because it attempts not merely to name the criteria that are being used as traits on the PTA scales but also to ascertain the standards that are being applied—that is, the level of performance that students must reach if they are to receive a certain grade.

Which Data Are Collected from Classrooms?   The sample is all sections taught in fall and spring of 2003–04, of all three courses that juniors and seniors in the major must all take. Data come from (1) the final exam and one important assignment and (2) statements of criteria and standards necessary for a C grade on the exam and on the assignment (adaptations of items 2 and 3 in Figure 11.1).

How Does the Assessment Committee (or Other Body) Analyze Data and Present Findings?   The committee's job is difficult because it is not just listing traits from faculty members' PTA scales. Rather, the committee is trying to aggregate statements of standards—the level of performance students must reach to earn at least a C grade. To reduce and simplify the data, the committee decides to include only four of the most common criteria that appear in the data the teachers submit. These four criteria are listed along the top of the following chart. Then, for each course, the committee writes a shortened version of the standards each teacher requires for a C on that trait. The assessment committee presents this report to the department:

> An examination of assignments and of requirements for C grades in the sample courses indicates that four traits are most commonly included in descriptions of criteria for a C grade: (1) statement of a position or thesis, (2) analysis of literary devices, (3) synthesis of literary critical sources, and (4) evidence to support claims. For each of these four traits, we summarized the level of performance required for a C grade by each teacher [Table 11.1].

The major challenge of data analysis in this case is to deal with the sometimes long and complex descriptions of standards for a C grade. The committee might initially offer faculty some guidelines for consistency in naming the criteria and the standards. Or per-

Table 11.1. Most Common Traits and Standards for *C* Grade.

	Position	*Analysis*	*Sources*	*Evidence*
101	Must state a position that is not trite or obvious	Not mentioned	Not used	Must support position with evidence
102	Must state a position clearly	Must refer to named literary devices	Must cite sources	Must support position with evidence from the work of literature
204	Must organize around a clear thesis	Not mentioned	Must cite sources; must integrate effectively	Must support position with evidence

haps pilot data would be submitted first and then, working from the pilot, the department as a whole would discuss ways to state the criteria and standards in common forms and common language.

If the data reveal little consistency in the standards required for a *C*, the department may want to conduct a series of conversations to clarify what it expects from *C* students in those senior-level courses.

Example 5: Strengths and Weaknesses in Student Performance at a Single Point in Time

With this example, we move from cases that would require a committee to examine only the course objectives, assignments, tests, exams, and PTA scales to a case where the committee might also examine student scores (item 4 in Figure 11.1). The teachers would have to submit these scores in the aggregate or with students' privacy protected, to the committee. Remember that the scores are not the same as the grades. It is possible to score a piece of student writing only for the traits that the committee wants to look at. For example, a faculty member might submit students' PTA scores only for certain traits such as skill in initiating the therapeutic relationship and skill in leading the client to consider multiple options, whereas the grade might be determined by additional characteristics such as recording data in the appropriate format, submitting the material on time, editing for grammar and punctuation, and so on.

Who Needs to Know, and Why?   Let us suppose that the English faculty presented earlier, having identified the skills being assessed in their three senior courses, now decide they want to track over time how well their students do on these skills. They need not institute an external test for this, as long as the teachers of the three senior courses will submit student scores over time.

Which Data Are Collected from Classrooms?   The sample is a random 40 percent of all sections of the three required junior and senior courses. Data collected include (1) final exam and major assignments for each of the three required senior courses, taught in spring 1998 and spring 2002, (2) PTA scales for each exam and assignment, and (3) student scores (mean and distribution) on the PTA scales, with the number of students for whom scores are being submitted.

How Does the Assessment Committee (or Other Body) Analyze Data and Present Findings?   After examining the data from the required courses, the committee finds that

- Among all the PTA traits, and in both 1998 and 2002, students consistently scored lowest on "acknowledging alternative viewpoints."
- Student scores on "analysis of literary devices" and "evidence to support claims" have remained fairly constant.
- Student scores on "synthesis of literary critical sources" have risen significantly over the four years.

An analysis such as this might lead the department to ask why scores in the various traits have risen or stayed the same and why students consistently score lowest on "acknowledging alternative viewpoints." The department might move to help students more directly with alternative viewpoints in lower-level courses. Or the teachers of the senior courses might agree to work harder or differently with that trait. Analysis of further scores over time could determine whether students were doing better.

Example 6: Tracking Student Performance Over Time

Who Needs to Know, and Why?   In this hypothetical example, the college has been working hard to improve instruction in critical thinking in general education courses. The general education committee wants to know whether their efforts have produced any changes in students' performance on assignments that assess critical thinking.

Which Data Are Collected from Classrooms?   The sample is a random sample of all general education courses taught in spring 2001 and spring 2005. Data collected are (1) final exams and one major assignment from each general education course in the sample, (2) PTA scales for those, containing only traits the faculty member has identified as central to critical thinking in that discipline. The committee requests that each PTA scale contain five levels, labeled 1 through 5, with 1 as the lowest score, (3) the class mean score on each of those traits for spring semester 2001 and 2005, and (4) the number of students for whom the scores are being submitted (items 2, 3, and 4 from Figure 11.1).

How Does the Assessment Committee (or Other Body) Analyze Data and Present Findings?   The committee has several choices: it might decide to establish common traits and ask each faculty to use those traits and submit student scores on those traits. However, it is perfectly possible for the committee to accept each teacher's PTA traits as discipline-specific and not to insist that all teachers use common traits or terminology. What the committee reports, then, is whether, on those critical thinking traits named by the teachers, student scores in that class have risen over time. The report might read like this:

> The committee finds that students' scores in critical thinking, as defined in each discipline through the PTA scales, have risen significantly in 48 percent of the courses, remained the same in 27 percent, and fallen significantly in 25 percent.

The committee might follow with further information about the areas of rise and fall, suggestions about contributing factors, recommendations, and so on.

This kind of comparison among various disciplines is possible because critical thinking, though defined differently in each course, is labeled as such by the teachers and is formatted as a PTA scale with five points. That is, the chemistry teacher constructs a five-point scale for traits related to critical thinking as she defines it; the history teacher constructs a five-point scale on traits related to critical thinking as he defines it. The committee is comparing students' movement across those scales. For example, let's say the chemistry teacher is asking students for research proposals that require the traits of hypothesization and experimental design. The chemistry

Table 11.2. Mean Primary Trait Score for Students on Teacher-Defined Critical Thinking Traits.

Course	2001	2005
Chemistry 312	3.4	3.0
History 103	2.8	3.2

chemistry: $n = 208$ in 2001; 235 in 2005

history: $n = 42$ in 2001; 38 in 2005

teacher defines those as critical thinking. She constructs a five-point scale for each trait. She (and outside raters if needed) scores student work on those five-point scales, and the chemistry teacher turns in those aggregated scores to the committee along with the assignment and the PTA scale. The history teacher is asking students for essays that require the traits of evidence and counterargument. He defines those as critical thinking and constructs a five-point scale for each trait. He (and outside raters if needed) scores student work on those five-point scales, and he turns in that material just as the chemistry teacher did. Now the committee sees a configuration such as the one shown in Table 11.2.

This is the only information the committee needs if it wants merely to determine the direction of scores over time on critical thinking as defined in the disciplines. The committee sees that scores have fallen in chemistry and risen in history. The actual critical thinking traits can remain a "black box," specific to the teacher and the discipline.

These last few examples we have presented are the most difficult because once faculty members are asked to submit not just their criteria but their standards and their students' scores, assessment becomes more contentious and threatening. A faculty member may be afraid that she or he will be revealed as not having appropriately high standards or that his or her students will not do as well as others' students. Even faculty members who believe they will look good in such comparisons may be philosophically opposed to reported data that is teacher-specific.

Walvoord and others (forthcoming), as part of a larger research project on change in academic departments, have been studying in detail a department at one university where these issues are being thrashed out. The department was undecided about whether to adopt a new teaching method in its introductory course. Some teachers were using one method; some were using another method. The department wanted to know whether the method made a difference in student learning, and if so, which method was better. After much discussion, they agreed to give a common portion of the final exam. To answer their research question, sections had to be individually identified in the data. However, the department members did not want individual sections or teachers to be identified in the reports of the data to the chair or to the department as a whole. After much discussion, they solved the dilemma by hiring an outside researcher who collected the data and assigned a code number to each section, known only to the researcher. The department could thus find out whether significant differences occurred among sections and whether the sections taught by one method produced better exam performances than the sections taught by the other method, but individual sections and teachers were not identified.

In small departments or in courses with only a few sections, even that strategy might not work to protect anonymity. But the basic approach used by the sample department seems wise: allow plenty of time for open discussion, keep everyone in the loop, and, especially at first, be ready to sacrifice information you may have wanted in order to safeguard peoples' participation and trust in the process.

Limitations of Our Grading Process Assessment Model

Widespread faculty participation is both a strength and a limitation of our assessment model. Grading-based assessment cannot just be passed off to some administrator or committee. Nor can it be handled by an external test that someone else administers and scores. If the majority of the faculty is not willing to make their grading processes public in at least some of the ways we have suggested, and if they are willing to give to others their traditional control of the assessment of student learning, then our assessment model is probably not right for that campus. However, if at least a small percentage of faculty on a given campus is willing to pilot our methods, then our assessment model may be useful. We describe in Chapter Twelve how, at Raymond Walters College of the University of Cincinnati, a group of fourteen faculty piloted a general education assessment program, built on our model, that eventually won a faculty vote and a commitment by the faculty as a whole to submit assignments and PTA scales.

A strength and a limitation of our method is its grounding in the diversity of individual classrooms. Our approach allows a great deal of room for individual faculty or small groups of faculty to set their own assignments, tests, criteria, and standards for assessing student learning. Our approach in its purest form asks only that those tests, criteria, standards, and other classroom data be made public in new ways, that they be analyzed along with similar materials from other classes, and that they provoke discussion about common goals and standards. The opposite end of the spectrum would be a method in which tests, criteria, and standards to be used by every faculty member are established by the department as a whole, by a university committee, or by another external body, thereby enforcing faculty unanimity in testing, criteria, and standards.

A number of institutions are defining middle ground between these two ends of the spectrum. For example, faculty at a university or college might agree that all general education courses would teach and test three particular aspects of critical thinking but leave faculty free to teach and assess other aspects according to their own judgment and their disciplines. The committee would then collect information about faculty practices and analyze it as we have suggested. The report and the faculty conversations generated as these data were discussed would undoubtedly lead to collaboration and change, but the university would not try to impose unanimous practice on all faculty. Or a department might decide together which knowledge and skills it wanted its graduating seniors to possess and then assign the teaching and testing of those skills to various courses, but leave to the individual teacher the decision about the criteria, standards, and pedagogy, with the proviso that these be shared for discussion. These patterns all represent combinations of centrally determined and individually determined tests, criteria, and standards for assessing student learning. (Useful models are found in Farmer, 1988 and Seybert, 1997. Also, you might consult Banta, 1996 for ideas that might work in your setting.)

Another kind of middle ground is for the department or the general education committee, before it sets its common tests and standards, to collect from its faculty some of the information we listed in Figure 11.1, as a way of finding out what faculty are already doing, as a basis for setting the new requirements. The standards and criteria are then binding on all, but they have been informed by data about the faculty's current practice.

Our model, then, which begins in the classroom and gathers careful data about current classroom practice and which tends to value faculty diversity, can be integrated with more centrally determined, top-down models. You should find the mix that fits your own needs and institutional culture.

Another limitation to grading-based assessment is that it is hard to compare student scores at one institution or department with scores at another, because the classroom tests and assignments are not universal and neither are the criteria and standards. Our model does not produce a nationally normed score for a group of students. If a nationally normed score is the highest value of your assessment plan, then external standardized tests are probably your instrument of choice. Standardized tests can, however, be combined with our model of classroom-embedded assessment in an institution's total assessment plan.

Though a single standardized test score is not available with our method, one can compare assignments and tests, PTA traits, criteria, standards, and student scores across classes, departments, and institutions. To conduct these comparisons, we suggest the concept of *benchmarking,* or comparing one's own practice against examples of effective practice in other settings. For example, suppose that Anystate University's history department compared a sample of its classroom assignments, tests, criteria, and student scores to examples of best practice at other institutions. Faculty teaching those courses could get good ideas from one another, and the department could get some sense of whether its own courses were assessing the same kinds of learning, applying the same kinds of criteria, and achieving the same kinds of student performances as those at other schools.

Nationally normed scores are achieved at a price, literally and figuratively. They are expensive to administer and score. But further, they may not closely match what faculty believe ought to be taught and learned. They may not offer detailed diagnostic information that teachers and students can use for improvement in the classroom. They may encounter faculty suspicion or resistance. Faculty may make it a point not to teach to the test and thus widen the gap between what is taught and what is tested. There may be little way to create a tight feedback loop from the test back into the classroom. You can discover that your students score low on a national exam, but if there is no way to make faculty believe in the exam, take it seriously, and do in their classrooms what is necessary to help students learn better, then you have no way to improve those low scores. You can only weep to see them on the table at a board meeting or featured in the local newspaper ("Anystate University Students Score in 37th Percentile on Critical Thinking"), and you are powerless because your faculty will not do in their classrooms what is necessary to raise the scores on that critical thinking test. Our approach, which builds on the classroom grading process and on faculty-determined criteria and instruments, helps you counter these disadvantages of standardized tests—but it also denies you the external credibility and comparability of the standardized scores.

Every assessment method, then, is a trade-off. Accrediting agencies and assessment experts wisely recommend that an assessment program include multiple methods. Our argument is that classroom grading processes are highly valuable as part of an assessment program.

The final question for this book is, Now that we've presented what a developed assessment program might do, how would an institution get started? That is the subject of the final chapter.

CHAPTER 12

A Case Study of Grading as a Tool for Assessment

One College's Story

LESTA COOPER-FREYTAG, BARBARA E. WALVOORD,
and JANICE DENTON

At various points throughout this book we have mentioned Raymond Walters College of the University of Cincinnati as one institution that has begun an assessment program based on our model. Their story is by no means finished, but they have made a very strong start. This chapter has been collaboratively constructed by Cooper-Freytag, professor of biology, former Interim Associate Dean (1992–94), and member of the Academic Assessment Committee at Raymond Walters College (RWC); Denton, associate professor of chemistry and chair of the Academic Assessment Committee at RWC; and Walvoord, a consultant to the college whose role will be further explained.

Throughout the story, we offer principles we think can help other schools as they launch an assessment program based on our model. Exhibit 12.1 outlines the chronology of events.

Background

The University of Cincinnati (UC) is a large, urban university which has, as part of its diverse community, several two-year, open-access colleges. Ohio lacks the network of public community colleges that characterize many other states, so UC's open-access colleges serve many of the same purposes. Raymond Walters College (RWC), named after a past president of the University of Cincinnati, is one of those two-year, open-access colleges. It is

Exhibit 12.1   Brief History of General Education Assessment at Raymond Walters College.

1967	Raymond Walters College (RWC) opened as a state-supported two-year college of a municipally owned university.
1992	State and North Central Association (NCA) mandates turned RWC's attention to functional mission statement and assessment planning.
1992	RWC formed Academic Assessment Committee which, in turn, formed several subcommittees, including one on general education.
1993–94	Pilot study of Education Testing Service standardized test was met with concern by RWC faculty.
1995	Walvoord met with the General Education Subcommittee to discuss possible use of classroom-based assessment as a means of assessing critical thinking and quantitative reasoning skills as part of the overall general education assessment plan.
1995	Group of fourteen faculty members took part in a pilot study of PTA for use in the classroom and as a general education assessment tool for the college.
1995	RWC fall faculty convocation devoted to PTA scoring.
1995	At a college faculty meeting, the college faculty passed a motion that course-embedded classroom assessment would be used to assess students' critical thinking and quantitative reasoning skills.
1995–96	Follow-up session held November 14, with a "poster session" in January, featuring completed PTA scales from many disciplines.
1996	On October 5, the Academic Assessment Committee attended a workshop conducted by Walvoord to develop a document that would guide departmental discussions of PTA scoring.
1996	By October, 90 percent of the faculty had submitted a PTA scale for one of their assignments that measured critical thinking in their classroom.
1996–97	PTA data were discussed within each department, and members discussed actions they would take to enhance student learning, thus creating a feedback loop. Departments wrote reports about their discussion and submitted these reports to the Academic Assessment Committee for collegewide analysis and feedback.
Future 1997–98	▪ Individuals, departments, and the Academic Assessment Committee act on the feedback gained through the process. ▪ The cycle begins again, with individual faculty collecting data, which are then presented and discussed in spring departmental meetings and reported to the Academic Assessment Committee. This time, the departments must also report on the successes of the strategies they had decided upon the previous year.
Summer 1998	Academic Assessment Committee synthesizes the department reports into a college document. The college summary describes the process used to measure general education outcomes and the application of the assessment results to improve student critical thinking/quantitative reasoning skills and learning.
1998–99	North Central Association accreditation site visit.

located in a suburb about fifteen miles from the main campus. Its student enrollment is 2,100 full-time equivalent (FTE), 3,800 head count. Mean age of an RWC student is 29. Faculty number about 105 full-time and 130 adjunct.

When RWC opened its doors in 1967, offering both transfer programs and technical programs, the University of Cincinnati was a municipally owned institution with some state affiliation. Consequently, RWC came into being as a state-supported two-year college of a municipally owned university. Although UC became a fully state-supported institution at a later date, RWC continues to maintain a high degree of autonomy. As part of the unionized UC faculty, RWC faculty share its culture of strong suspicion toward central administrative initiatives and a fierce determination to preserve faculty autonomy. UC faculty voted "no-confidence" in their president in 1991 and went on strike in 1993, largely over governance issues.

During these years, also, RWC was embroiled in a divisive struggle over whether the open-admissions colleges of UC were to be separated from the university and combined in a separately governed system with its own board. The RWC campus's chief academic officer (dean) also shifted during this time, with three deans in two years. Finally, in the fall of 1993, the current dean, Barbara Bardes, was appointed.

In the same years, the early 1990s, the college was wrestling with severe budget cuts, new state mandates for accountability (including a list of "service expectations" to the community), a mandate for annual faculty performance review, and board initiatives to institute "performance funding" to be based on institutions' functional mission statements.

First Steps

In this climate of uncertainty and turmoil, the college faced the North Central Accreditation process, looking toward the required submission of an assessment plan in 1995 and a full accreditation visit in 1998–99. In line with its historical autonomy, RWC has its own separate timetable for accreditation (separate from the UC main campus), and RWC was to come up first. The immediacy it felt about accreditation was thus not felt with the same urgency on the main campus. Main campus was itself experiencing turmoil, with severe budget constraints and two provosts leaving between 1991 and 1995.

The small size of the college, its physical setting on a lovely suburban campus, its relative autonomy from main campus interference, the stability and cohesiveness of its faculty, and the presence of strong faculty leaders were positive characteristics during this chaotic time. Thus RWC was able to move positively and early to deal with the upcoming accreditation requirements. Under a widely respected external consultant, the college devised a functional mission statement in March of 1994 and committed itself to outcomes assessment that would enable it to communicate to the public at large (including the state and the North Central Association) the value of its educational programs.

In January of 1993 then Interim Associate Dean Cooper-Freytag asked each department chair or a departmental representative to serve on an Academic Assessment Committee. The large numbers of well-respected faculty for this committee turned out to be a key element in subsequent developments. The committee was led, successively, by two strong chairs: first, in 1993–94, Don O'Meara, a sociologist, who became associate dean, and then, from 1994 to the present, Janice Denton, a chemist. The committee structure allowed the college to build upon its faculty's cohesion, dedication, and leadership capabilities. In the absence of a strong dean figure prior to the fall of 1993, the committee was positioned to take strong leadership. The committee's twenty-four members in turn formed several subcommittees, including one on general education assessment.

Lessons Learned

So far, we derive from this story four principles that may be helpful to other colleges and universities:

- Assessment can be carried on despite considerable turmoil and hardship in an institution, provided the institution builds upon its strengths.
- Assessment structures must be built upon an understanding of the institution's culture.
- A strong faculty committee, with strong leadership, is an important asset.
- Establishing an institutional mission statement, when well done, can be a unifying and positive initiation for an assessment effort.

Dilemmas

The general education subcommittee faced a puzzling difficulty: there was no separate, prescribed general education requirement for students at RWC. The college's functional mission statement had stated a set of lofty and ambitious general education learning goals: "Ultimately, the College works toward the creation of an informed citizenry with the ability to think critically, communicate effectively and solve problems. The College strives to provide a general education which promotes tolerance, lifelong learning and a devotion to free inquiry and free expression, to assure its graduates are individuals of character more sensitive to the needs of community; more competent to contribute to society and more civil in habits of thought, speech and action."

However, rather than being limited to specific general education courses, these goals were to be achieved through "an appropriate general education component in all degree programs as an essential part of the students' learning experience." The North Central Association states that all programs must have a coherent component of general education with articulated outcomes for student academic achievement, that faculty should have ownership and control over general education, and that faculty should systematically and comprehensively review the general education curriculum. It very quickly became obvious to the General Education Subcommittee that, without a specific general education curriculum, the college could have a problem conducting outcomes assessment in this area.

Taking Action

The General Education Subcommittee now made what we believe to have been a wise move: it sharply limited what it would assess in the first cycle of assessment, and it constructed language more specific than the language of the functional mission statement. The subcommittee decided to assess students' skills in writing, quantitative reasoning, and critical thinking.

Having limited its initial concern to these three skills, once again the subcommittee moved to limit its task in practical, achievable ways. First, it sought to take advantage of assessment procedures already in place within the curriculum. Accordingly, the assessment of writing skills was assigned to the English department, and a separate committee began to revise current procedures for that assessment. The assessment of quantitative reasoning skills was combined with the assessment of critical thinking, because some faculty argued strenuously that in some disciplines, critical thinking was quantitative reasoning. Denton and the subcommittee agreed to incorporate quantitative reasoning as part of critical thinking. Denton believes that without this concession, the entire project would have collapsed. This concession, she says, "kept us trucking."

Critical thinking, however defined, was a difficult case because there was no department that could assume responsibility and no defined set of courses. We focus this story now on critical thinking, as the committee members, the new dean, and the faculty at large struggled to find effective ways to assess that skill, embedded as it was within the total curriculum.

A basic problem was that one must be able to define something in order to assess it. The committee avoided one possible pitfall into which general education efforts on other campuses had been known to slide: spending a year trying, and failing, to come up with a campus-wide definition of *critical thinking* that would satisfy everyone and still be specific enough to serve as the basis for assessment. Rather than try to fashion a uniform definition of critical thinking in the abstract, the RWC subcommittee began to look at standardized tests of critical thinking. The subcommittee went quite far down this road. Some of the subcommittee members themselves took the standardized tests. They conducted a pilot administration, to students, of the ETS Academic Profile test. The results of the pilot were flattering to the college, in terms of students' ranking against national norms. However, many faculty believed that this test was not a good assessment of general education as perceived and taught by faculty at RWC. The subcommittee feared that the test would not be acceptable to faculty as a whole and that the college would be unable to integrate the test results into a feedback loop to improve general education. Given the bottom-up, inclusive way they had worked so far, the subcommittee was unwilling to force on the faculty a plan about which a substantial number had serious reservations. Yet the committee could not envision workable alternatives to standardized testing.

At this point, another alternative did offer itself. It came through someone already known and trusted by RWC faculty. Since 1991, Walvoord had been director of several faculty development programs on the main campus and leader of a number of workshops that many RWC faculty had attended and liked. RWC's Assessment Committee chair, Janice Denton, heard that Walvoord was working with classroom-embedded assessment, though that was not Walvoord's official title or responsibility at UC. Denton called Walvoord, who explained her ideas. The two of them met for further discussion, and then Walvoord came to address the entire General Education Subcommittee, expanded for the occasion by invited representatives from a number of departments. Walvoord was, herself, still developing her ideas.

Exhibit 12.2 is the plan the committee had in writing at the time Walvoord arrived, and which they shared with her as a preparation for her meeting with them. Note how the ambiguous language of the mission statement and the functional mission statement are wisely simplified and limited in the middle column as we have explained. Note too, in the right-hand column, how much this committee had so far depended on a single standardized test. Mailing this statement to the subcommittee members, Denton penned at the bottom, "Barbara Walvoord has agreed to meet with the subcommittee to help us investigate the development of further measures."

About eighteen people attended that initial two-hour meeting—virtually the entire subcommittee as well as representatives from various departments whom Denton had specifically invited,

Exhibit 12.2.   General Education Subcommittee's Plan for Assessment as of February 1995.

Mission (from the faculty handbook)	Outcomes Statements	Measures
To offer courses in general education as an essential part of student's learning experience.	1. Upon graduation, students will demonstrate effective writing skills.	1a. Freshman English Exit Exam.
		1b. Education Testing Service (ETS) Academic Profile test. This is a criterion referenced score.
Goal (from the functional mission, pp. 3,4)	2. Upon graduation, students will demonstrate effective quantitative reasoning skills.	
Ultimately, the college works toward the creation of an informed citizenry with the ability to think critically, communicate effectively, and solve problems. The college strives to provide a general education that promotes tolerance, lifelong learning, and devotion to free inquiry and free expression to ensure that its graduates are individuals of character, more competent to contribute to society, and more civil in habits of thought, speech, and action.	3. Upon graduation, students will demonstrate they can think critically about issues and arguments presented in the humanities and in the behavioral and social sciences.	2a. ETS Academic Profile test. This is a criterion referenced score.
		3a. Graduation survey.
		3b. ETS Academic Profile test. This is a criterion referenced score.

in line with her basic philosophy that this had to be a ground-up project, with the widest possible involvement of faculty at every point. Attenders included a number of highly respected and influential faculty. Walvoord presented herself as a faculty member, not as an assessment expert. She had personally nothing to gain or lose whether RWC adopted her ideas or not. Walvoord reiterated and affirmed the problems with the standardized test that had been bothering faculty, both within and outside of the subcommittee. Many heads were nodding at this point. Then Walvoord proposed that RWC could build upon the definitions and assessments of critical thinking that were already embedded in the curriculum. She proposed that faculty could submit assignments and PTA scales for those assignments to allow the college to identify how faculty currently defined critical thinking and how they were assessing it in their own classes, within their own disciplines. She proposed that, eventually, classroom tests and exams could be scored, and student scores used to answer questions about students' performance on these classroom-based assessments of critical thinking. For the faculty audience at that meeting, the opportunity to define and assess critical thinking *"in my class* and *in my discipline"* were, as Cooper-Freytag observed, "the core that sold this thing."

By the end of the meeting, the subcommittee decided to conduct a *pilot program*—the same term they used when investigating standardized testing. Fourteen faculty, including most of the subcommittee members and some department heads, volunteered to choose one test or assignment in one of their own courses—a test or assignment they thought assessed critical thinking as defined in their classrooms and disciplines. They would submit to subcommittee colleagues the assignment or test and a PTA scoring scale for it. They would, in other words, first do themselves what they might eventually ask all faculty to do. A series of meetings was established at which Walvoord would return to help with construction of PTAs.

At the subsequent five two-hour meetings, across that spring of 1993, Walvoord returned. Meeting in a vacant classroom with their chairs in a circle, faculty members shared with the group their developing PTA scales. Walvoord and the group helped each member to improve his or her scale. There were always tasty snacks brought by faculty members.

Lessons Learned

We can offer several more principles that may be helpful to other colleges and universities:

- The quality, commitment, and cohesiveness of the committee are crucial to the success of the program.
- The committee must be willing to do themselves what they ask other faculty to do.
- Widespread inclusiveness of faculty at all stages is crucial.
- It is helpful to use assessment procedures already in the system.
- Plans should be limited to what is feasible.
- Compromise may be necessary in order to "keep on trucking."
- A mission statement may have to be narrowed, made more concrete, or amended as the institution begins to apply it to specific situations and to use specific assessment measures.
- It takes time for a committee to work through options, detours, and dead-ends.
- An idea must arrive at a propitious time, when people see a need for it, perhaps when previous ideas have not worked or the committee is searching for alternatives to a controversial plan.
- It helps if the bearer of the idea enjoys the trust of the faculty and has no stake in making the faculty do anything.
- The concept of the pilot is valuable because it allows a committee or an institution to "try out" an idea without needing to commit to it forever.

Surprises and Difficulties

As these five two-hour meetings progressed, and faculty members slowly constructed and revised their PTA scales, Walvoord was surprised by several things: first, by how often it was necessary, in those meetings, to reiterate the basic approach and philosophy of classroom-based assessment, the basic aims of assessment, and the basic outline of what the subcommittee was trying to do. Despite the fact that this subcommittee of sophisticated and intelligent faculty leaders had been meeting for two years, the most basic questions continued to arise and needed to be addressed: "What are we really trying to do here?" "What do the NCA accreditors require?" "What is classroom-based assessment?"

The second thing that surprised Walvoord was the difficulty some faculty members experienced in constructing a PTA scale. Part of the problem was that faculty in some disciplines were not accustomed to thinking in terms of specific outcomes. Another "problem" that turned out not to be a problem at all was that other aspects kept intruding, such as plans for teaching critical thinking, instructions to students about assignments and tests, or the sequencing of preliminary assignments. The fact that many subcommittee members were excellent teachers who taught in rich and provocative ways sometimes at this stage complicated the process of constructing a scale, within the standard format, that would state the traits as nouns and the scales under each trait as descriptions of student work. It was hard for faculty to distinguish the criteria and standards they held for the final version of an assignment from the criteria and standards they used to evaluate ongoing preliminary work.

A third surprise, and this appeared to be a surprise to everyone, was the enjoyment these meetings provided and the richness of the conversations about teaching that developed. The PTA drafts engendered rich and provocative discussions of teaching methods. Faculty discovered they were teaching similar critical thinking skills and began to collaborate. People immediately began taking what they learned back into their teaching. As Cooper-Freytag put it, "To our amazement, faculty from different disciplines were talking about teaching and having a heck of a good time."

Although the PTA scales emerged slowly, the fourth surprise for Walvoord was the amount of change and improvement in the PTA scales that occurred through group response and revision. Some scales that were, in Walvoord's view, quite far off the mark in early drafts changed radically for the better from one meeting to the next.

An unexpected difficulty arose in disciplines where critical thinking was tested by multiple-choice tests. Patricia Schlecht, professor of nursing, undertook to work on this problem. She demonstrated that multiple-choice exam questions could be classified as to the level of critical thinking they demanded, and that such classification was situation-specific, depending on how much the student relied on material presented in class or readings and how much the student was required to reason on his or her own. Schlecht's work paved the way for constructing PTA scales even for exams using multiple-choice questions.

Lessons Learned

From these developments, we deduce several more principles that may be helpful for other institutions:

- Faculty development, faculty collaboration, comradeship, and good food are crucial aspects of assessment.

- Linking discussion of assessment to discussion of individual faculty members' teaching may temporarily delay the establishment of a narrow focus upon constructing PTA scales in standard format, but the discussion should not be hurried or passed over, because it promotes a rich and powerful conversation for faculty, and it leads to a strengthened sense of commitment on their part—a sense that all this "assessment stuff" is linked to their classroom teaching in meaningful ways.

- Unexpected difficulties will arise. Their solution is facilitated when dedicated faculty members undertake to solve the problems themselves.

Adopting the Plan

At the end of spring 1995, twelve subcommittee members had completed PTA scales for one of their assignments or tests. They had received no special remuneration or released time for this effort. The subcommittee now decided to adopt classroom-embedded assessment for assessing critical thinking in general education. They wanted every faculty member to hand in an assignment, test, or exam that assessed critical thinking in one of their courses, together with a PTA scale for that assignment, test, or exam.

Those data would be analyzed to answer assessment questions. The exact nature of those questions and the methods for analysis were left open; Walvoord and the committee were very much developing the model as they went. An institution that uses our model now would, we believe, have a better idea ahead of time how the data could be analyzed and used.

The full committee and the dean agreed with the subcommittee's plan. The dean had attended most of the committee and subcommittee meetings, but in a very participatory way, not a directive way. The large size of the subcommittee plus its additional participants, and their standing among the faculty, meant that the work of the subcommittee had become well known throughout the faculty. Subcommittee members prepared carefully for faculty buy-in to their plan.

Their first move was to schedule a day-long faculty convocation (planned by the Faculty Development Committee), in early fall 1995, for the entire faculty. Led by Walvoord and members of the subcommittee, the meeting drew about sixty of RWC's one hundred full-time faculty and a number of adjuncts. The leaders of the meeting included Bill Marsh, a widely respected mathematics faculty member who had been at the college for many years and was known for his steady, conservative wisdom, and Ruth Benander, a new faculty member in English who had gained attention for her teaching and leadership abilities. Several of the committee members showed the PTA scales they had developed. The chair of the Academic Assessment Committee, Janice Denton, summarized the history of assessment deliberations at RWC. It was, in short, very much a faculty show. The dean spoke briefly, stayed for the whole event, showed her support and enthusiasm, but clearly was not running the show. Postconvocation evaluations by the faculty were very high. About 30 percent of the faculty in attendance indicated they wished to learn more about doing PTA scales.

A few weeks later, at a meeting attended by about 75 percent of the full-time faculty and a number of adjuncts, the faculty passed the following motion: "The faculty is committed to using course-embedded classroom assessment to measure students' critical thinking and quantitative reasoning skills."

As a first phase, the subcommittee asked each full-time faculty member to select one test or assignment that they believed measured critical thinking in one of their courses and to develop a PTA scale for that test or assignment. These were to be submitted by September 1996.

At this point (December 1995) the committee foresaw a general procedure for handling the data. Cooper-Freytag, recording events for the coauthors of this chapter, wrote, "The next step will be to organize these results in a meaningful way and to share these so that the feed-back loop to improve teaching will occur. Files will have to be organized within departments and the Office of Academic Affairs so that results can be made public and used to support the college's assessment presentation to the NCA."

Faculty Development

To aid the faculty in fulfilling the first phase of the plan—constructing PTA scales for one test or assignment—several activities were planned by the College Faculty Development Committee and the Assessment Committee. At the end of the fall quarter, a PTA workshop drew about 15 percent of the faculty. During the winter quarter of 1996, a poster session featured PTAs that faculty in various disciplines had already developed. This was well attended and appreciated. In early spring 1996, Walvoord led a day-long workshop in downtown Cincinnati, open to faculty from the entire university and neighboring institutions. About twelve RWC faculty attended that workshop, working to develop or refine their PTA scales. The associate dean of academic affairs, Don O'Meara, worked closely with departments and department chairs concerning PTAs. He was a widely respected faculty member in sociology, former department head, and former chair of the Academic Assessment Committee who at that time had been associate dean for a year and still retained close ties among the faculty. In her December 1995 record, Cooper-Freytag wrote about these faculty development activities: "At this moment in time, the college faculty appears energized and highly interested in pursuing Primary Trait Analysis as a tool for part of our general education assessment. We have found that PTAs are student-oriented and faculty-controlled, that they are discipline-specific and give concrete, usable results, and that they continue to spark discussion and debate among our faculty. It is just possible that we may have found our way to measure the immeasurable."

All these faculty development activities, plus the widespread support the plan enjoyed among the faculty, had a gratifying result: by fall of 1996, 90 percent of the RWC full-time faculty (representing all departments) had submitted a PTA scale for one of their tests or assignments in one of their courses.

Analyzing the Data

Now the issue of exactly how to analyze and use these data was pressing. The committee scheduled a planning day with Walvoord in late summer 1996. Wisely, the committee asked a number of key department chairs to join the session. The committee's earlier idea that these data would be first discussed by faculty in their departments, with department then reporting to the central committee, was now worked out in greater detail. Walvoord decided to focus the workshop on preparing the document necessary for this purpose (Exhibit 12.3). The document contained (1) a set of instructions and suggestions to departments about how to handle and analyze the data and (2) a form to guide departments in reporting the results of their deliberations to the Academic Assessment Committee. The group of about twenty faculty subcommittee members, the department heads, and the dean worked all day, with blackboards and two overhead projectors, to outline the contents of the document. Along the way, many thorny issues had to be resolved. At the end of the day, the documents were outlined, and many issues decided. The group felt they had accomplished much more than they expected. They left half an hour early, feeling justifiably proud of themselves.

During the academic year 1996–97, departments used the guidelines to discuss the classroom data that faculty had presented. Each department composed a report to the committee.

Exhibit 12.3.   Guidelines for Writing the Department Report on Critical Thinking–Quantitative Reasoning Skills Assessment.

[The document opens with a review of the history of general education assessment at the college, a reminder of the key general education learning goals the Academic Assessment Committee is trying to assess {writing, critical thinking/quantitative reasoning}, and a time line for general education assessment aiming toward the North Central Association site visit in 1998–99. Next, the document recommends that, in their discussions preceding the writing of the report, departments might meet as a whole, or in small groups first and then as a whole. The document recommends that these meetings give each person a chance to discuss his or her goals, assignment, PTA scale, results, and possible strategies for next year to improve student critical thinking/quantitative reasoning skills. The department would then discuss "the results and possible strategies to improve student critical thinking/quantitative reasoning skills specifically and learning in general. The meeting concludes with the report form being completed."]

Department: _____   Prepared by: _____

1. Number of full-time faculty (excluding those on leave) _____

2. Number of part-time faculty teaching courses this academic year _____

3. How many full-time faculty members used a PTA assignment to evaluate students' critical thinking/quantitative reasoning skills? _____

4. How many, if any, part-time faculty members used a PTA assignment to evaluate students' critical thinking/quantitative reasoning skills? _____

5. Please list the course numbers and titles in which a PTA assignment was used. (It is not necessary to include specific section numbers.)

6. Which of the following scenarios did your department use for reporting/sharing critical thinking/quantitative reasoning skills assessment results?

    ___ Individual presentations

    ___ Small group presentations

    ___ Other (please specify)

7. How many full-time faculty participated in the department meeting in which the critical thinking/quantitative reasoning skills assessment results were presented/shared? _____

8. How many, if any, part-time faculty participated in the department meeting in which the critical thinking/quantitative reasoning skills assessment results were presented/shared? _____

9. Based on the above meeting(s), please answer the following:

    a. Overall, were your department's expectations for student critical thinking/quantitative reasoning skills met? That is, are students performing as expected?

        ___ Yes, most students perform as expected

        ___ About half of the students perform as expected

        ___ No, most students do not perform as expected

    b. What would faculty cite as the specific critical thinking/quantitative reasoning skills in which students demonstrate mastery?

    c. What would faculty cite as the specific critical thinking/quantitative reasoning skills in which students need improvement?

10. What strategies are faculty members intending to use to improve student critical thinking/quantitative reasoning and learning skills in the future? Please check all that apply.

    __ Revise the amount of written/oral/visual/clinical or similar work

    __ Increase in-class critical thinking discussion and activities

    __ Increase student collaboration and/or peer review

    __ Provide more frequent or fuller feedback on student progress

    __ State critical thinking goals or objectives more explicitly

    __ State criteria for grading more explicitly

    __ Increase guidance of students as they work on assignments

    __ Use methods of questioning that encourage critical thinking

    __ Increase interaction with students outside of class

    __ Ask a colleague to critique critical thinking assignment/activities

    __ Collect more data on critical thinking activities

    __ Revise the content of critical thinking assignment/activities

    __ Nothing, assessments indicate no improvements are necessary

    __ Other (please describe)

11. What will the department do to help faculty members improve student critical thinking/quantitative reasoning skills and learning? Check all that apply.

    __ Offer and/or encourage attendance at seminars, workshops, or discussion groups about teaching methods

    __ Consult teaching and learning experts about teaching methods

    __ Encourage faculty to share their exercises/activities that foster critical thinking

    __ Write collaborative grants to fund departmental projects to improve teaching

    __ Provide articles/books on college teaching and critical thinking

    __ Visit classrooms to provide feedback (mentoring)

    __ Examine course curriculum to determine what critical thinking skills are taught, so the department can build a progression of critical thinking skills as students advance through courses

    __ Nothing, assessments indicate no improvements are necessary

    __ Other (please describe)

12. Additional comments, if any:

Department meetings varied widely in their tone and content. Departments accustomed to external accreditation by their disciplinary associations were more comfortable with the departmental discussion. But to some departments, this kind of self-evaluation of teaching and learning was unusual. A member of one department said, "Our department functions best as an anarchy. We tend to immerse ourselves in our individual work. . . . We had not really addressed these issues before the meeting." Another faculty member said, "As the department meeting facilitator, my goal was to keep the department meeting non-threatening and encouraging."

Despite the differences among departments in tone and content of the meetings, one overarching theme emerged: the departmental meetings spurred further thought and action. A member of one department said that the list of teaching strategies in Exhibit 12.3, question 10 "was good for provoking people to think and react against." Some faculty felt enthusiastic about what the data-collection process had done for them as teachers but skeptical of its value to the department as a whole. "I see this whole process working out at the classroom level," said one.

The departmental discussion spurred individual action. One faculty member, for example, went away from the meeting and sat down to write a list of "reasoning skills" he thought necessary to students in his courses and in the department. "We could only really work on this after we'd had the meeting," he said. Some departments worked inductively during the meeting to arrive at a list of departmental learning goals. One department did it by listing all the traits that appeared on everyone's level-five PTA scores. Thus they finished the meeting with a list of what all of their faculty were expecting as highest-level work. In another department, one group of teachers had worked out a common scale together for a course they all taught. Aside from that group, however, the department discovered that there was little unanimity in their scales.

Although all department discussions were productive, the following issues emerged and will have to be addressed in order to keep the assessment process moving forward. First, many departments had concerns about how they would expand the primary trait activities and discussions to include adjunct faculty. The greater the percentage of adjunct faculty in the department the more urgent was this issue.

Second, many faculty felt overwhelmed at having yet another meeting at the end of the spring quarter. The Academic Assessment Committee had developed an in-class assessment process that had not increased workload, but the timing of the department discussions stretched a number of departments. One faculty member said, "There is finally a realization that assessment is an ongoing process and that department reporting will be an annual event."

Third, faculty who use multiple-choice assignments and tests are still very unsure of how to construct PTA scales to assess student learning.

Fourth, this was the first time the departmental report form had been used, and faculty had differing interpretations of what the questions were asking. In response to Exhibit 12.3, question 9a, one department reported that student work was "as expected" because they had expected to see a range of student skills, and they did. Another department interpreted "expected" to refer to their ideals, and they thought their students did not meet these ideals. Question 10 was the focus of concern in another department. Some members believed that to say that the department wanted to do something was to imply that they were not currently doing it, and would make the department look bad. Said a member of another department, "We were afraid to commit ourselves" to a course of action, because the department could not fully predict the future uses or consequences of its answers.

Fifth, while some departments are familiar with pedagogical methodology, others are less so. All faculty are comfortable with discipline-specific content, but some struggle with designing alternative ways to present the content to enhance student learning.

Sixth, the Academic Assessment Committee had forced departments to deal with the assessment issue head-on, and internal departmental dynamics influenced how the issues were discussed. There were also a few cynical faculty members who said that the report would never be read and so was a waste of time. Some faculty were critical of the method of sharing "apples and oranges" and questioned the usefulness of the information.

For the first round, the committee was happy to have the department reports in hand. Members of the Academic Assessment Committee were not dismayed by the elements of confusion and cynicism. The fact that 90 percent of the faculty had submitted reports indicated a great deal of classroom examination and thought. The committee members had recognized that the department-level discussions would be challenging and they were heartened by the fact that these kinds of conversations had taken place for the first time ever, that departments had been forced to address key issues of learning and teaching, and that the process had been deeply embedded in classrooms and departments—the places where real change must be located. The required report, as one committee member said, "facilitated a conversation that didn't want to happen."

The next step, as this book goes to the printer, is for the Academic Assessment Committee to analyze the departments' reports and to use that information in their attempts to enhance student learning. It seems clear that the report form (Exhibit 12.3) will change somewhat as a result of this first year's experience. But the departments know that from now on, each year, as part of Raymond Walters College's ongoing assessment program, they will be asked to collect classroom data, engage in the same kind of conversation, and submit a report. They must use the information they have shared to enhance student learning.

Web page for updated information about Raymond Walters College's progress: www.rwc.uc.edu/phillips/index_assess.html.

AAHE's Principles of Good Practice for Assessing Student Learning

1. **The assessment of student learning begins with educational values.** Assessment is not an end in itself but a vehicle for educational improvement. Its effective practice, then, begins with and enacts a vision of the kinds of learning we most value for students and strive to help them achieve. Educational values should drive not only what we choose to assess but also how we do so. Where questions about educational mission and values are skipped over, assessment threatens to be an exercise in measuring what's easy, rather than a process of improving what we really care about.

2. **Assessment is most effective when it reflects an understanding of learning as multidimensional, integrated, and revealed in performance over time.** Learning is a complex process. It entails not only what students know but what they can do with what they know; it involves not only knowledge and abilities but values, attitudes, and habits of mind that affect both academic success and performance beyond the classroom. Assessment should reflect these understandings by employing a diverse array of methods, including those that call for actual performance, using them

This document was developed under the auspices of the AAHE Assessment Forum with support from the Fund for the Improvement of Postsecondary Education with additional support for publication and dissemination from the Exxon Education Foundation. Copies may be made without restriction.

over time so as to reveal change, growth, and increasing degrees of integration. Such an approach aims for a more complete and accurate picture of learning, and therefore firmer bases for improving our students' educational experience.

3. **Assessment works best when the programs it seeks to improve have clear, explicitly stated purposes.** Assessment is a goal-oriented process. It entails comparing educational performance with educational purposes and expectations—those derived from the institution's mission, from faculty intentions in program and course design, and from knowledge of students' own goals. Where program purposes lack specificity or agreement, assessment as a process pushes a campus toward clarity about where to aim and what standards to apply; assessment also prompts attention to where and how program goals will be taught and learned. Clear, shared, implementable goals are the cornerstone for assessment that is focused and useful.

4. **Assessment requires attention to outcomes but also and equally to the experiences that lead to those outcomes.** Information about outcomes is of high importance; where students "end up" matters greatly. But to improve outcomes, we need to know about student experience along the way—about the curricula, teaching, and kind of student effort that lead to particular outcomes. Assessment can help us understand which students learn best under what conditions; with such knowledge comes the capacity to improve the whole of their learning.

5. **Assessment works best when it is ongoing, not episodic.** Assessment is a process whose power is cumulative. Though isolated, "one-shot" assessment can be better than none, improvement is best fostered when assessment entails a linked series of activities undertaken over time. This may mean tracking the process of individual students, or of cohorts of students; it may mean collecting the same examples of student performance or using the same instrument semester after semester. The point is to monitor progress toward intended goals in a spirit of continuous improvement. Along the way, the assessment process itself should be evaluated and refined in light of emerging insights.

6. **Assessment fosters wider improvement when representatives from across the educational community are involved.** Student learning is a campus-wide responsibility, and assessment is a way of enacting that responsibility. Thus, while assessment efforts may start small, the aim over time is to involve people from across the educational community. Faculty play an especially important role, but assessment's questions can't be fully addressed without participation by student-affairs educators, librarians, administrators, and students. Assessment may also involve individuals from

beyond the campus (alumni/ae, trustees, employers) whose experience can enrich the sense of appropriate aims and standards for learning. Thus understood, assessment is not a task for small groups of experts but a collaborative activity; its aim is wider, better-informed attention to student learning by all parties with a stake in its improvement.

7. **Assessment makes a difference when it begins with issues of use and illuminates questions that people really care about.** Assessment recognizes the value of information in the process of improvement. But to be useful, information must be connected to issues or questions that people really care about. This implies assessment approaches that produce evidence that relevant parties will find credible, suggestive, and applicable to decisions that need to be made. It means thinking in advance about how the information will be used, and by whom. The point of assessment is not to gather data and return "results"; it is a process that starts with the questions of decision-makers, that involves them in the gathering and interpreting of data, and that informs and helps guide continuous improvement.

8. **Assessment is most likely to lead to improvement when it is part of a larger set of conditions that promote change.** Assessment alone changes little. Its greatest contribution comes on campuses where the quality of teaching and learning is visibly valued and worked at. On such campuses, the push to improve educational performance is a visible and primary goal of leadership; improving the quality of undergraduate education is central to the institution's planning, budgeting, and personnel decisions. On such campuses, information about learning outcomes is seen as an integral part of decision making, and avidly sought.

9. **Through assessment, educators meet responsibilities to students and to the public.** There is a compelling public stake in education. As educators, we have a responsibility to the publics that support or depend on us to provide information about the ways in which our students meet goals and expectations. But that responsibility goes beyond the reporting of such information; our deeper obligation—to ourselves, our students, and society—is to improve. Those to whom educators are accountable have a corresponding obligation to support such attempts at improvement.

Authors: Alexander W. Astin, Trudy W. Banta, K. Patricia Cross, Elaine El-Khawas, Peter T. Ewell, Pat Hutchings, Theodore J. Marchese, Kay M. McClenney, Marcia Mentkowski, Margaret A. Miller, E. Thomas Moran, and Barbara D. Wright

Types of Assignments and Tests

Abstract

Advertisement

Annotated bibliography

Biography or autobiography (of the student or of some real or hypothetical character)

Briefing paper or "white paper"

Brochure, poster

Budget with rationale

Case analysis

Chart, graph, visual aid

Client report for an agency

Cognitive map, web, or diagram

Contemplative essay

Court brief

Debate

Definition

Description of a process

Diagram, table, chart

Dialogue

Diary of a fictional or real historical character

Essay exam

Executive summary

Fill-in-the-blank test

Flowchart

Group discussion (One English faculty member asks students in groups of seven to discuss a piece of short fiction for thirty minutes without her intervention, while she watches and takes notes. The group is graded on the quality of discussion and group dynamics.)

Horoscope

"I Search" (first-person narrative account of an inquiry) (Macrorie, 1980)

Instructional manual

"Introduction" to an essay or scientific report (rather than the full report)

Inventory

Laboratory or field notes

Letter to the editor

Matching test

Materials and methods plan

Mathematical problem

Memo

"Micro-theme" (a tight, coherent essay typed on a 5 x 8 note card) (Bean, 1996; Bean, Drenk, and Lee, 1982)

Multimedia or slide presentation

Multiple-choice test

Narrative

News or feature story

Notes on reading

Nursing care plan

Oral report

Outline

Personal letter

Plan for conducting a project

Poem, play

Question

Regulations, laws, rules

Research proposal addressed to a granting agency

Review of book, play, exhibit

Review of literature

Rough draft or freewrite (writer writes freely, with no constraints for a certain amount of clock time) (Elbow, 1981)

"Start" (a thesis statement and outline or list of ideas for developing)

Statement of assumptions

Summary or precis

Summit conference (One historian has the class divide into teams representing nations; they must negotiate a treaty that would have prevented World War I.)

Taxonomy or set of categories

Technical or scientific report

Term paper, research paper

Thesis sentence (sentence that expresses author's main point)

Word problem

Work of art, music, architecture, sculpture

Examples of Primary Trait–Based Scales Developed by Faculty

Example 1   Biology: Original Scientific Experiment

Virginia Johnson Anderson, Towson University, Towson, Maryland

Assignment: Semester-long assignment to design an original experiment, carry it out, and write it up in scientific report format. Students are to determine which of two brands of a commercial product (such as two brands of popcorn) is best. They must base their judgment on at least four experimental factors. (For example, "percentage of kernels popped" is an experimental factor, but price is not, because price is written on the package.)

Title

5   Is appropriate in tone and structure to science journal; contains necessary descriptors, brand names, and allows reader to anticipate design.

4   Is appropriate in tone and structure to science journal; most descriptors present; identifies function of experimentation, suggests design, but lacks brand names.

3   Identifies function and brand name but does not allow reader to anticipate design.

2   Identifies function or brand name, but not both; lacks design information or is misleading.

1   Is patterned after another discipline or missing.

Introduction

5   Clearly identifies the purpose of the research; identifies interested audiences; adopts an appropriate tone.

4   Clearly identifies the purpose of the research; identifies interested audiences.

3   Clearly identifies the purpose of the research.

2   Purpose present in Introduction, but must be identified by reader.

1   Fails to identify the purpose of the research.

Scientific Format Demands

5   All material placed in the correct sections; organized logically within each section; runs parallel among different sections.

4   All material placed in correct sections; organized logically within sections, but may lack parallelism among sections.

3   Material placed in proper sections but not well organized within the sections; disregards parallelism.

2   Some materials are placed in the wrong sections or are not adequately organized wherever they are placed.

1   Material placed in wrong sections or not sectioned; poorly organized wherever placed.

Materials and Methods Section

5   Contains effective, quantifiable, concisely organized information that allows the experiment to be replicated; is written so that all information inherent to the document can be related back to this section; identifies sources of all data to be collected; identifies sequential information in an appropriate chronology; does not contain unnecessary, wordy descriptions of procedures.

4   As in 5, but contains unnecessary information or wordy descriptions within the section.

3   Presents an experiment that is definitely replicable; all information in document may be related to this section; but fails to identify some sources of data or presents sequential information in a disorganized, difficult way.

2   Presents an experiment that is marginally replicable; parts of the basic design must be inferred by the reader; procedures not quantitatively described; some information in Results or Conclusions cannot be anticipated by reading the Methods and Materials section.

1   Describes the experiment so poorly or in such a nonscientific way that it cannot be replicated.

Nonexperimental Information

5   Student researches and includes price and other nonexperimental information that would be expected to be significant to the audience in determining the better product, or specifically states nonexperimental factors excluded by design; interjects these at appropriate positions in text or develops a weighted rating scale; integrates nonexperimental information in the Conclusions.

4   As in 5, but is less effective in developing the significance of the nonexperimental information.

3   Student introduces price and other nonexperimental information but does not integrate them into Conclusions.

2   Student researches and includes price effectively; does not include or specifically exclude other nonexperimental information.

1   Student considers price and other nonexperimental variables as research variables; fails to identify the significance of these factors to the research.

Experimental Design

5   Student selects experimental factors that are appropriate to the research purpose and audience; measures adequate aspects of these selected factors; establishes discrete subgroups for which data significance may vary; student demonstrates an ability to eliminate bias from the design and bias-ridden statements from the research; student selects appropriate sample size, equivalent groups, and statistics; student designs a superior experiment.

4   As in 5, but student designs an adequate experiment.

3   Student selects experimental factors that are appropriate to the research purpose and audience; measures adequate aspects of these selected factors; establishes discrete subgroups for which data significance may vary; research is weakened by bias or by sample size of less than 10.

2   As above, but research is weakened by bias and inappropriate sample size.

1   Student designs a poor experiment.

Operational Definitions

5   Student constructs a stated comprehensive operational definition and well-developed specific operational definitions.

4   Student constructs an implied comprehensive operational definition and well-developed specific operational definitions.

3   Student constructs an implied (though possibly less clear) comprehensive operational definition and some specific operational definitions.

2   Student constructs specific operational definitions but fails to construct a comprehensive definition.

1   Student lacks understanding of operational definition.

Control of Variables

5   Student demonstrates, by written statement, the ability to control variables by experimental control and by randomization; student makes reference to or implies factors to be disregarded by reference to pilot or experience; superior overall control of variables.

4   As in 5, but student demonstrates an adequate control of variables.

3   Student demonstrates the ability to control important variables experimentally; Methods and Materials section does not indicate knowledge of randomization or selectively disregards variables.

2   Student demonstrates the ability to control some but not all of the important variables experimentally.

1   Student demonstrates a lack of understanding about controlling variables.

Collecting Data and Communicating Results

5   Student selects quantifiable experimental factors and defines and establishes quantitative units of comparison; measures the quantifiable factors and units in appropriate quantities or intervals; student selects appropriate statistical information to be utilized in the results; when effective, student displays results in graphs with correctly labeled axes; data are presented to the reader in text as well as graphic forms; tables or graphs have self-contained headings.

4   As in 5, but the student did not prepare self-contained headings for tables or graphs.

3   As in 4, but data reported in graphs or tables contain materials that are irrelevant or not statistically appropriate.

2   Student selects quantifiable experimental factors or defines and establishes quantitative units of comparison; fails to select appropriate quantities or intervals or fails to display information graphically when appropriate.

1   Student does not select, collect, or communicate quantifiable results.

Interpreting Data

5   Student summarizes the purpose and findings of the research; student draws inferences that are consistent with the data and scientific reasoning and relates these to interested audiences; student explains expected results and offers explanations or suggestions for further research for unexpected results; student presents data honestly, distinguishes between fact and implication, and avoids overgeneralizing; student organizes nonexperimental information to support conclusion; student accepts or rejects the hypothesis.

4   As in 5, but student does not accept or reject the hypothesis.

3   As in 4, but the student overgeneralizes or fails to organize nonexperimental information to support conclusions.

2   Student summarizes the purpose and findings of the research; student explains expected results but ignores unexpected results.

1   Student may or may not summarize the results but fails to interpret their significance to interested audiences.

Example 1 adapted from Anderson and Walvoord, 1991, Appendix A. Copyright 1991 by the National Council of Teachers of English. Reprinted with permission.

Example 2   Nursing and Occupational Therapy: Group Activities

Judith Bloomer, Occupational Therapy and Evelyn Lutz, Nursing, Xavier University, Cincinnati, Ohio

Assignment: Group projects in occupational therapy and nursing.

Group Project: _____   Member being assessed: _____

Instructions
Using the key that follows, circle the number that represents your opinion on the group member's performance on each item.

    3   Outstanding
    2   More than satisfactory
    1   Satisfactory
    0   Less than satisfactory
  N/O Inadequate opportunity to observe

Work-Related Performance	
Comprehension: Seemed to understand requirements for assignment	0 1 2 3 N/0
Problem identification and solution: Participated in identifying and defining problems and working toward solutions	0 1 2 3 N/0
Organization: Approached tasks (such as time management) in systematic manner	0 1 2 3 N/0
Acceptance of responsibility: Shared responsibility for tasks to be accomplished	0 1 2 3 N/0
Initiative/motivation: Made suggestions, sought feedback, showed interest in group decision making and planning	0 1 2 3 N/0
Creativity: Looked at ideas from viewpoints different than the usual ways	0 1 2 3 N/0
Task completion: Followed through in completing own contributions to group project	0 1 2 3 N/0
Attendance: Attended planning sessions, was prompt, and participated in decision making	0 1 2 3 N/0

Work-Related Interactions with Others	
Collaboration: Worked cooperatively with others	0 1 2 3 N/0
Participation: Contributed "fair share" to group project, given the nature of individual assignment	0 1 2 3 N/0
Attitude: Displayed positive approach and made constructive comments in working toward goal	0 1 2 3 N/0
Independence: Carried out tasks without overly depending on other group members	0 1 2 3 N/0
Communication: Expressed thoughts clearly	0 1 2 3 N/0
Responsiveness: Reacted sensitively to verbal and nonverbal cues of other group members	0 1 2 3 N/0

Add total score   Total: _____

Divide by number of items scored with a number   Average: _____

Comments (use back of paper):

Name of evaluator: _____   Date: _____

Permission granted to Xavier University Departments of Occupational Therapy and Nursing to use instrument in nursing and occupational therapy courses only.

Example 3   Economics: Analysis of a Proposed Law

Philip Way, Department of Economics, University of Cincinnati, Cincinnati, Ohio

Assignment: For your employer, a congresswoman, research and analyze a proposed law to raise the minimum wage. (The full assignment is in Exhibit 3.6.)

Executive Summary

5   Clearly states the position of the researcher; summarizes the main reasons for this conclusion.

4   Clearly states the position of the researcher; provides information as to why the conclusion was reached.

3   Clearly states the position of the researcher.

2   Position of the researcher is present in the Summary but must be identified by the reader.

1   Fails to identify the position of the researcher

Criteria

3   Student clearly and correctly defines the criteria used to assess the implications of the research question.

2   Student provides definitions of the criteria used to assess the implications of the research question, but the presentation is unclear or at least one definition is not factually correct.

1   Student fails to define correctly the criteria used.

Relative Weighting of Criteria

3   Student indicates the relative weighting (importance) of the criteria.

2   Student's weighting scheme, although present, is unclear.

1   Student fails to identify the relative weighting (importance) of the criteria.

Production Possibility Diagram

5   Student clearly presents and fully explains the impact of the proposed change in terms of a production possibility frontier (PPF) diagram. Graph is appropriately drawn and labeled. Discussion is in terms of identified criteria.

4   Student presents and explains the impact of the proposed change in terms of a PPF diagram. Either the explanation or the graph is less than clear, although they do not contain factual errors.

3   Student presents and explains the impact of the proposed

change in terms of a PPF diagram, but the presentation contains some factual errors.

2   Student presents and explains the impact of the proposed change in terms of a PPF diagram. Presentation contains serious factual errors.

1   Student does not present the impact of the proposed change in terms of a PPF diagram.

Supply-and-Demand Diagram

5   Student clearly presents and fully explains the impact of the proposed change in terms of a supply-and-demand diagram. Graph is appropriately drawn and labeled. Discussion is in terms of identified criteria.

4   Student presents and explains the impact of the proposed change in terms of a supply-and-demand diagram. Either the explanation or the graph is less than clear, but they do not contain factual errors.

3   Student presents and explains the impact of the proposed change in terms of a supply-and-demand diagram, but presentation contains factual errors.

2   Student presents and explains the impact of the proposed change in terms of a supply-and-demand diagram. Presentation contains serious factual errors.

1   Student does not present the impact of the proposed change in terms of a supply-and-demand diagram.

Production Costs/Supply Diagram

5   Student clearly presents and fully explains the impact of the proposed change in terms of a production costs/supply diagram. Graph is appropriately drawn and labeled. Discussion is in terms of identified criteria.

4   Student presents and explains the impact of the proposed change in terms of a supply-and-demand production costs/supply diagram. Either the explanation or the graph are less than clear, but they do not contain factual errors.

3   Student presents and explains the impact of the proposed change in terms of a production costs/supply diagram, but presentation contains factual errors.

2   Student presents and explains the impact of the proposed change in terms of a production costs/supply diagram. Presentation contains serious factual errors.

1   Student does not present the impact of the proposed change in terms of a production costs/supply diagram.

Supporting Data

5   Student provides an analysis of economic data that supports the student's position. Quantitative and qualitative information concerning the effect of the increase are presented accurately; differences of opinion are noted where they exist.

4   Student provides an analysis of economic data that support the student's position. Either quantitative or qualitative information concerning the effect of the increase is presented accurately; differences of opinion are noted where they exist.

3   Student provides an analysis of economic data that support the student's position. However, the discussion is unclear or contains factual errors.

2   Student provides an analysis of economic data that support the student's position. However, the discussion is very unclear or contains serious factual errors.

1   Student fails to provide an analysis of economic data that supports the student's position.

Integration

3   Student provides a clear link between the theoretical and empirical analyses and the assessment criteria.

2   Student provides some link between the theoretical and empirical analyses and the assessment criteria.

1   Student does not provide a link between the theoretical and empirical analyses and the assessment criteria.

Conclusions

3   Student's conclusion is fully consistent with student's analysis.

2   Student's conclusion is generally consistent with student's analysis.

1   Student's conclusion is not consistent with student's analysis.

Original Thought

3   Paper shows evidence of original thought: that is, analysis is not simply a summary of others' opinions or analyses but rather an evaluation of the proposals in light of the criteria and weighting scheme chosen by the student.

2   Paper shows some evidence of original thought but is mostly a summary of others' opinions or analyses rather than an evaluation of the proposals in light of the criteria and weighting scheme chosen by the student.

1   Student's paper fails to show evidence of original thought.

Miscellaneous

5   Student appropriately cites sources. The paper is typewritten, neat, and easy to read.

4   The student's paper is generally professional and includes citations, but it contains minor stylistic errors.

3   The paper is legible and includes some citations. However, it contains serious stylistic errors.

2   The student's paper lacks citations and is sloppy or otherwise unprofessional.

1   The student's work is not professionally presented.

Example 4   Art History: Hypothetical Newspaper Article

Christine Havice, Art History, University of Kentucky, Lexington.

Assignment: For a hypothetical "newspaper" in the ancient Assyrian empire, write a news report on the unveiling of the palace relief titled "Ashurnasirpal II at War."

Criteria for Evaluation (Possible Fifteen Points)

14–15   Describes work concisely
Relates message to artist's choices and use of various devices
Develops how message affects beholder
Considers audience in writing
Clearly organized and presented
Well-imagined
Legible
No problems with mechanics, grammar, spelling, or punctuation

11–13   Good description
Relates message to artist's choices and use of various devices
Some consideration of effect on beholder
Considers audience
Perhaps could be better organized or presented
Adequately imagined
Legible
Few problems with mechanics, grammar, spelling, or punctuation

8–10   Adequate description
Less thorough analysis of how artist conveys message and devices
Audience not necessarily kept in mind
Needs significant improvement in organization or presentation
Needs better imagination
Problems with legibility, mechanics

6–7   Lacking substantially in either description or analysis;
Problems with audience, organization, presentation, or mechanics interfere with understanding

0–5   Substandard on more than two of these: description, analysis of choices and devices, effects on beholder
Major problems with audience, organization, presentation, or mechanics

Example 5   *Career Planning: Field Observation*

Cheryl Cates, Division of Professional Practice, University of Cincinnati

Assignment: Students research a career field they are interested in and write a report. Assignment includes conducting an interview with a professional employed in the field of students' interest.

Content/Format

5   Report offers information that relates to the assignment and leads the reader through the information in a logical and interesting way.

4   Report covers many of the content issues required by the assignment but is not arranged in a format that provides for interesting reading.

3   Information is incomplete, confusing, and arranged in such a way that it is difficult to judge how it relates to the assignment.

2   Information does not relate to the assignment.

1   Information is absent.

Research

5   Report sufficiently answers most of the questions listed in the assignment through both secondary library research and formal interview.

4   Student answers at least half the questions through both secondary research and informational interview.

3   Student makes an attempt through secondary research and informational interview.

2   Student conducts no secondary research and does little to address questions asked in the assignment.

1   Student has in no way answered the relevant questions (no secondary research and no interview).

Interview

5   Student conducts a formal in-person interview with someone the student considers to be a potential employer.

4   Student conducts an informal or telephone interview with someone that the student considers to be a potential employer.

3   Student conducts a formal interview with another (senior) student in the same discipline.

2   Student conducts an informal interview with another student (for example, the student catches a senior after co-op information night and asks a few quick questions).

1   Student did not conduct a personal interview for the project.

Example 6   Education: Poster Presentation

Suzanne Wegener Soled, Associate Professor, Division of Educational Studies, University of Cincinnati

Assignment: Students asked to develop a poster to illustrate how they have demonstrated certain themes in their internships.

Distinguished

_____ A variety of multiple intelligences are addressed in the poster.

_____ Creativity is evident; you explain why you chose to present the way you did.

_____ Risk taking is evident; includes explanation of what worked, what didn't, and why.

_____ You clearly and concisely explain how you used assessment materials.

_____ You meet the needs of diverse learners.

_____ Statistical concept included, and its use clearly and concisely explained.

_____ Reflection provides explicit documentation of the theme.

_____ Reflection is written in professional language; no convention errors.

Proficient

_____ Several multiple intelligences addressed in poster presentation.

_____ Some creativity evident; some explanation of why you chose to present the way you did.

_____ Some risk taking evident; includes explanation of what worked, what didn't, and why.

_____ How you used the assessment materials is clearly explained.

_____ Meeting the needs of diverse learners is fairly evident.

_____ Statistical concept is included and its use clearly explained.

_____ Reflection provides fairly clear documentation of the theme.

_____ Reflection written in professional language; one convention error.

Apprentice

_____ Multiple intelligences addressed minimally in poster presentation.

_____ Creativity partially evident: partial explanation of why you chose to present the way you did.

_____ Minimal or no risk taking evident. Does not include explanation of what worked, what didn't, and why.

_____ How you used assessment materials partially explained.

_____ Meeting the needs of diverse learners partially evident.

_____ Statistical concept included and its use partially explained.

_____ Reflection provides partial documentation of the theme.

_____ Reflection written with some errors in professional language; some convention errors.

Total number of points earned out of fifteen possible: _____

Example 7   Business Management: Team Project

Lawrence D. Fredendall, Management, Clemson University

Assignment: Student teams work with a firm to identify problems and offer recommendations. To be completed by members of the business firms in which student teams work, this sheet is given to students and to members of the firm from the very beginning of the project.

Team's Customer Satisfaction Skills		
Punctuality Some team members missed appointments or did not return phone calls. 0 1 2 3	All team members arrived on time for appointments and returned all phone calls promptly. 4 5 6 7	All team members were always early. 8 9 10
Courtesy Some team members were not respectful of some firm employees. 0 1 2 3	All team members were always courteous and respectful of all firm employees. 4 5 6 7	All employees felt that the team members were very respectful and courteous and fully elicited their ideas. 8 9 10
Appearance Sometimes some team members were inappropriately dressed. 0 1 2 3	All team members were always appropriately dressed. 4 5 6 7	All team members adjusted their attire to match the attire used in our firm. 8 9 10
Enthusiasm Some team members did not seem interested in the project. 0 1 2 3	All team members appeared enthusiastic and eager to work on the project. 4 5 6 7	The enthusiasm of the team members to complete the project was contagious and inspired others at our firm. 8 9 10

Communication		
Some team members did not communicate clearly during meetings or phone calls.	The team members always communicated clearly with employees during meetings and phone calls.	The team members always made an extra effort to make sure they understood us and that we understood them during meetings and phone calls.
0 1 2 3	4 5 6 7	8 9 10
Team's Project Management Skills		
Plan Awareness		
No team member ever presented a plan to the firm about how to complete the project.	The team presented a plan, but some team members did not seem to follow it.	All the team members seemed to be aware of the plan and following it.
0 1 2 3	4 5 6 7	8 9 10
Problem Definition		
The team's definition of the problem was absent or vague.	The problem was clearly defined. Data were provided measuring the scope of the problem.	The problem's importance and relationship to the firm's goals were clearly stated.
0 1 2 3	4 5 6 7	8 9 10
Plan Feasibility		
The plan that was presented was not feasible.	The plan that was presented was feasible but needed improvement.	The plan was feasible and was regularly updated as necessary during the project.
0 1 2 3	4 5 6 7	8 9 10
Plan Presentation		
A written plan was not presented.	A clear plan with a Gannt chart was presented.	The team was able to explain clearly why it collected certain data and did not collect other data.
0 1 2 3	4 5 6 7	8 9 10

Team's Data Analysis		
Data Collection		
The team did not use any apparent method to determine which data to gather.	The data were gathered in a systematic manner.	The team was able to explain clearly why it collected certain data and did not collect other data.
0 1 2 3	4 5 6 7	8 9 10
Collection Method		
The team's data collection method was haphazard and random.	The team had a clear plan they followed to collect the data.	The data collection methods simplified the data analysis.
0 1 2 3	4 5 6 7	8 9 10
Analysis Tools		
The team used no tools to analyze the data, or the tools seemed to be randomly selected.	The team used all the appropriate tools for data analysis	The team fully explained why it selected certain tools and did not use others for data analysis.
0 1 2 3	4 5 6 7	8 9 10
Results Analysis		
The team did no evaluation of the validity of its data analysis results.	The team validated its results by checking with the appropriate staff for their insight.	The team validated its results by conducting a short experiment.
0 1 2 3	4 5 6 7	8 9 10
Team's Recommendations		
Clarity		
The team had no recommendations, or they were not understandable.	The team's recommendations were reasonable given the problem examined.	The recommendations logically emerged from the problem statement and data analysis.
0 1 2 3	4 5 6 7	8 9 10

Impact		
The impact of implementing the recommendation was not examined or was completely wrong.	The recommendations are specific enough to serve as the basis for decisions by management.	The recommendations include an implementation plan that is feasible to implement.
0 1 2 3	4 5 6 7	8 9 10
Qualities of Team's Paper		
Executive Summary		
There was no executive summary.	The executive summary was well written and captured key goals, problems, analysis, steps, and recommendations.	The executive summary is as good as those usually presented in our firm.
0 1 2 3	4 5 6 7	8 9 10
Organization		
The paper is difficult to follow.	The paper is easy to follow and read.	All relationships among ideas are clearly expressed by the sentence structures and word choice.
0 1 2 3	4 5 6 7	8 9 10
Writing Style		
The paper is sloppy, has no clear direction, and looks as if it were written by several people.	The format is appropriate with correct spelling, good grammar, good punctuation, and appropriate transition sentences.	The paper is well written and is appropriate for presentation in the firm.
0 1 2 3	4 5 6 7	8 9 10

Team Members' Personal Skills		
Self-Confidence Some team members' mannerisms made them look as if they were not confident of their abilities. 0 1 2 3	All the team members always seemed confident. 4 5 6 7	All team members were confident and would be able to lead in this organization. 8 9 10
Knowledge Some team members did not seem to understand what they were doing. 0 1 2 3	All team members seemed to have adequate knowledge or ability to learn the necessary material. 4 5 6 7	All team members were proactive about identifying skills they needed and obtaining them in advance. 8 9 10
Reliability Some team members did not follow through with their commitments. 0 1 2 3	All team members fulfilled all commitments they made to staff here. 4 5 6 7	The work the team completed more than met my expectations. 8 9 10
Your Satisfaction with the Product		
Project Completion The team did not do a reasonable amount of work on the project. 0 1 2 3	The team completed a reasonable amount of work on the project. 4 5 6 7	The work the team completed more than met my expectations. 8 9 10
Project Recommendations The recommendations provide no insight. 0 1 2 3	The recommendations are useful and will be examined in detail by our firm. 4 5 6 7	The recommendations will be implemented in full or in part. 8 9 10

Satisfaction		
We are not satisfied.	We are completely satisfied.	We are more than satisfied, we are delighted with the team's work!
0 1 2 3	4 5 6 7	8 9 10

Your name: _____

Would you sponsor another team project? _____

What do you recommend that the department do to improve the project?

Example 8   Architecture: Architectural Program

Cara Carroccia, Architecture, University of Notre Dame

Assignment: To construct an architectural program

Program: Plan

4   The assigned program is carefully analyzed and developed. The architect has not omitted any portion of the program and has in fact added to the program.

3   The architect provides some insight or depth of understanding to the assigned program. However, the internal logic and character of the work need to be more clearly established and developed.

2   The development of the program is generalized and lifeless. Mainly surface relationships are provided. The program has not been developed much beyond the level of bubble diagram.

1   The architect communicates no real understanding or development of the assigned program.

Clarity of Concept and Design Objectives

4   The architect's concept is organized and unified and has logical transitions between the urban and intimate scale.

3   The design objective is mainly clear to the viewer because the architect has tried to order the objectives. The link between the urban and architectural realms is not fully explained graphically.

2   Although there may be some attempt at presenting design objectives in a thoughtful manner, the work is confused and disjointed.

1   The project has no discernible concept.

Style

4   The architect demonstrates a quality of imagination and rigor that results in a distinctive project. The work shows a personal exploration.

3   The architect includes refining details, but a portion of the work remains general. The overall composition is pleasing.

2   The architect does not invest himself or herself into the work. The style seems bland, guarded, flat, and not very interesting.

1   The architect demonstrated no recognizable individualistic or historic style.

Development of the Small Scale; Detailed Information

4   Character, detail, and scale are clearly expressed in plan and section.

3   Some details are thoughtful and vivid. However, the character of the plan or section is not developed.

2   Simplistic details are used in a typical way. Repetition of these details distracts from the work. The plan and section together describe a reasonable, believable building, but little information about or attention to detail is developed.

1   Development of the character of the plan or section is limited and immature.

Development of the Urban Scale

4   The development of the urban scale shows a confident control of the project and communicates a clear parti. The work "reads" smoothly from urban scale to the intimate scale. Coherent development at this level makes the project clear and easy to understand.

3   The architect shows some control in the development of an urban parti, and has only a few elements at the urban scale that are awkward or perfunctory.

2   The architect has definite problems with parti: in simplistic terms, the big idea. Most of the urban plan is simplistic in conception and immature in its development.

1   There is no discernible urban idea. All is perfunctory.

Knowledge of Construction

4   There are no obvious errors in construction. The architect shows familiarity with the building materials and their appropriate use.

3   A few errors in construction practices appear in the project, showing the architect is still learning about the building materials that were chosen. These errors do not substantially detract from the overall impression of the work.

2   Errors or omissions in the use of the chosen building materials are so numerous that they are distracting to the viewer.

1   Errors or omissions in standard building practices are serious enough and frequent enough to interfere with meaning.

Graphic Presentation

4   The project is presented in a complete and compelling manner.

3   The project is compelling but incomplete.

2   Required drawings are missing, and the presented work is not legible due to the lightness of the drawings or the haphazard method of presentation.

1   Little effort was invested in the graphic communication of the assigned project.

Example 9 Statistics: Statistical Investigation

William Marsh, Mathematics, Physics, and Computer Science, Raymond Walters College of the University of Cincinnati

Assignment: Conduct a statistical investigation, including identifying a problem, developing an hypothesis, obtaining a random sample, measuring variables, analyzing data, and presenting conclusions.

Methodology

5   Correct statement of problem with accompanying null and alternative hypothesis. Well-defined population with appropriate random sample. Data collection is free of bias or contamination.

4   One part of the 5 level is not as high as it should be, and overall the quality of the methodology is just slightly lower than the highest level.

3   All the necessary parts of the methodology are present, but the quality level is only adequate.

2   There is a serious deficit in the methodology in the form of poorly performed tasks or some portions simply omitted. The results are compromised and may be unusable.

1   There is total failure to understand the task. The results will be invalidated because the methodology is erroneous.

Data Analysis

5   Uses appropriate statistical test with correct results. Provides an interval estimation of the values of the parameter. Includes a hypothesis test and gives accompanying p-level stating probability of type 1 error.

4   Provides most of level 5, but one of the characteristics is missing or unclear.

3   Uses correct statistical test, but estimation or interpretation is omitted.

2   Uses correct statistical test, but there are errors in calculation and other work.

1   Incorrect statistical test: data are erroneous or missing.

Note: This PTA scale identifies only three critical thinking traits. It does not include all the traits that would be included in the student's grade.

Conclusions

5   A complete presentation of results with conclusions, estimations, and p-levels for type 1 errors. Identifies possible threats to the study and also any areas in need of additional study.

4   As in 5, but one characteristic could be improved.

3   The presentation is only adequate. Conciseness and clarity are lacking.

2   Conclusions are vague and inaccurate. There has been an effort by the student, but there is an obvious lack of understanding and thoroughness.

1   A failure to make the necessary conclusions and implications.

Example 10   Office Administration: Spreadsheet

Maureen Margolies, Office Administration, Raymond Walters College of the University of Cincinnati

Introduction

5	4	3	2	1
Identifies the purpose of the application, who will be the primary user, how the application will be used.	Identifies the purpose of the application and how it will be used.	Identifies the purpose of the application.	Purpose of the application is unclear.	Fails to identify the purpose of the application.

Construction of spreadsheet

5	4	3	2	1
Based on chosen application, student constructs a spreadsheet in a logical, clearly understood format using appropriate labels, values, and formulas, including two or more logical and statistical functions and a data table or lookup table.	Based on chosen application, student constructs a spreadsheet in a logical, clearly understood format using appropriate labels, values, and one logical or statistical function.	Based on chosen application, student constructs a spreadsheet in a logical, clearly understood format using basic mathematical formulas and functions.	Based on chosen application, student constructs a spreadsheet in a logical, clearly understood format using basic mathematical formulas and functions.	Spreadsheet is not based on application, nor is it logically or clearly understood by the reader or other user.

Application of formulas and functions and testing for accurate results

5	4	3	2	1
Student works through the application, testing formulas and functions for accurate results. Debugs if necessary and corrects. Makes decisions about changing formulas or functions to achieve desired results.	Student works through the application, testing formulas and functions for accurate results. Debugs if necessary and corrects.	Student works through the application, testing formulas and functions for accurate results. Corrects obvious mistakes but fails to debug.	Student works through the application, testing formulas and functions for accurate results; but no corrections are made.	Student fails to test the application or correct any miscalculations or formulas.

Data analysis, reporting, and summarizing

5	4	3	2	1
Creates three graphs from the spreadsheet that compare, contrast, or show percentage of the whole to help analyze the data. Queries the spreadsheet to extract data that would be used in a planning report.	Same as 5, except creates only two graphs.	Creates two graphs from the spreadsheet that compare, contrast, or show percentage of the whole to help analyze the data, or queries the spreadsheet to extract data that would be used in a planning report.	Creates one graph from the spreadsheet that compares, contrasts, or shows percentage of the whole to help analyze the data.	Creates a graph but fails to show how it compares, contrasts, or shows a percentage of the whole.

Analysis of purpose, findings, and conclusions

5	4	3	2	1
Summarizes purpose and findings, draws conclusions on usefulness in fulfilling user goals, explains results, and offers explanations.	Summarizes purpose and findings, draws conclusions on usefulness in fulfilling user goals, but fails to explain results or offer explanations.	Summarizes purpose and findings but fails to draw conclusions on usefulness.	Vaguely summarizes the purpose or findings and fails to draw conclusions.	Summary statement either does not summarize purpose or findings and is merely a restatement of purpose, or there is no summary at all.

Example 11   Mathematics: Journals

Assignment: Drake and Amspaugh developed this list of items to illustrate the kinds of criteria that might be used for journal entries.

Criteria	5	4	3	2	1
Thoroughness of comments: Are the comments just superficial, or do they demonstrate deeper processing? Do your writings appear to be a restatement of someone else's words, or an interpretation in your own words? Have you mentioned applications or relationships to other material?					
Completeness: Have all important points been discussed? Are there omissions of information?					
Understanding: Are the ideas correctly understood? What evidence illustrates that understanding?					
Personal connections: Is the information connected to your personal observations and experiences?					
Growth: Is there evidence that your understanding has increased? Did you learn something that you didn't know before?					
Inquiry: Have you thought of other questions? Have you asked any additional questions not yet answered?					
Problem completion: Does it appear that problems have been attempted, or have they merely been skimmed over?					
General quality: What is the overall quality of your work in this journal?					

Reprinted by permission from Drake, B. M., and Amspaugh, L. B. "The *Write* to Learn Mathematics." *Literacy: Issues and Practices*, 1993, *10*, 28–34.

Example 12   Business Management: Case Analysis

Daniel Singer, Towson University, Towson, Maryland

Assignment: Students write a case analysis.

Part One of the Paper: The Strategic Statement

1. The following four elements are present: (1) analysis of the firm's goals, (2) resources, (3) environment, and (4) past, present, or planned strategy.   1 2 3 4 5

2. The analysis of the firm's goals:

   The statement about goals is consistent with the material in the case.   1 2 3 4 5

   The writer presents sufficient and clearly organized evidence for the summary of the firm's goals.   1 2 3 4 5

   The writer has chosen the most important or primary goals.   1 2 3 4 5

   The goals are stated specifically enough to be the basis for decisions by management.   1 2 3 4 5

3. The analysis of the firm's resources:

   The statement about resources is consistent with the material in the case.   1 2 3 4 5

   The writer presents sufficient and clearly organized evidence for the summary of the firm's resources.   1 2 3 4 5

   The writer has chosen the most important or primary resources.   1 2 3 4 5

4. The analysis of the firm's environment:

   The statement about environment is consistent with the material in the case.   1 2 3 4 5

   The writer presents sufficient and clearly organized evidence for the summary of the firm's environment.   1 2 3 4 5

   The writer has chosen the most important or primary environmental features.   1 2 3 4 5

5. The analysis of how the firm expects to achieve its goals:

   The statement about *how* is consistent with the material in the case.   1 2 3 4 5

The writer presents sufficient and clearly organized evidence for the summary of the *how*.   1 2 3 4 5

The writer chose the actual strategies rather than being misled by what an individual in the firm may think is the *how*.   1 2 3 4 5

Part Two of the Paper: The Strategic Fit

6. The writer analyzes the fit and the appropriateness of the firm's present and planned strategy in light of the firm's goals. The writer tells how probable it is that the firm will achieve its goals by those means.   1 2 3 4 5

7. The writer supports the analysis of strategic fit by logical reasoning and by evidence from the case.   1 2 3 4 5

Part Three of the Paper: The Recommendations

8. The recommendations grow logically out of the first two sections of the paper.   1 2 3 4 5

9. The recommendations are specific enough to serve as the basis for decisions by management.   1 2 3 4 5

10. The recommendations are clearly stated and explained.   1 2 3 4 5

Part Four: Qualities of the Entire Paper

11. Within the paper is a clear statement of the writer's thesis (the summary of the main idea that guides the entire analysis).   1 2 3 4 5

12. The voice of the writer is appropriate for a consultant addressing a board of directors.   1 2 3 4 5

13. The paper is interesting and fresh.   1 2 3 4 5

14. The relationships among ideas are clearly reflected in sentence structure and word choice.   1 2 3 4 5

15. Important ideas are given appropriate emphasis.   1 2 3 4 5

16. The word choice is precise.   1 2 3 4 5

17. The paper is economically written: every word pulls its weight.   1 2 3 4 5

18. Paper is accurate in spelling.   1 2 3 4 5

19. The writer properly punctuates sentence
    boundaries.   1 2 3 4 5

20. The writer correctly uses apostrophes and
    plurals.   1 2 3 4 5

21. The writer observes "standard English"
    forms of noun-verb agreement and pronoun-
    antecedent agreement.   1 2 3 4 5

22. The writer observes "standard English"
    forms of verbs, pronouns, and negatives.   1 2 3 4 5

23. The writer correctly uses other punctuation
    such as commas within sentence boundaries,
    colons, semicolons, quotation marks,
    capitals, and so on.   1 2 3 4 5

Example 13 First-Year Composition: Essay

Barbara E. Walvoord, University of Notre Dame, Notre Dame, Indiana

Assignment: To write an essay that explores an idea or insight. Students are to use external sources as needed, but this is not a term paper.

A Range

Originality of thesis: The author develops an authentic, fresh insight that challenges the reader's thinking. The paper shows a complex, curious mind at work.

Clarity of thesis and purpose: The thesis and purpose are clear to the reader.

Organization: The essay is organized in a way that fully and imaginatively supports the thesis and purpose. The sequence of ideas is effective, given the writer's thesis and purpose. The reader always feels that the writer is in control of the organization, even when the organizational plan is complex, surprising, or unusual. The subpoints serve to open up and explore the writer's insight in the most productive way.

Support: The writer offers the best possible evidence and reasoning to convince the reader. No important pieces of available evidence and no important points or reasons are omitted. It is clear that the writer is very well informed, has searched hard and effectively for appropriate evidence, and has thought about how evidence may be used for the argument. Evidence presented is always relevant to the point being made. Through telling detail, the writer helps the reader to experience what the writer is saying.

Use of sources: The writer has used sources to support, extend, and inform the ideas but not to substitute for the writer's own development of an idea. The writer has effectively combined material from a variety of sources, including, as relevant and needed, personal observation, scientific data, authoritative testimony, and others. (This is not to say that the writer must use a certain number or type of sources. Need and relevance should be the determining factors.) The writer uses quotations to capture a source's key points or turns of phrase but does not overuse quoted material to substitute for the writer's own development of an idea. Quotations, paraphrase, and citation are handled according to accepted scholarly form.

Ethos: The writer creates a "self" or "ethos" that sounds genuine, that is relevant to the writer's purpose, and that is consistent throughout the essay.

Style: Language is used with control, elegance, and imagination to serve the writer's purpose. The essay, when read aloud, pleases the eye and ear.

Edited Written Standard English (ESWE): Except for deliberate departures (the quoted speech of a person, a humorous purpose, and so on), the writer uses ESWE forms of grammar, punctuation, spelling, and syntax.

Presentation: The essay looks neat, crisp, and professional.

B Range

Falls short of the *A* range in one or more ways.

C Range

Originality of thesis: The thesis may be obvious or unimaginative.

Clarity of thesis and purpose: The thesis and purpose are clear to the reader.

Organization: The essay is organized in a way that competently supports the thesis and purpose. The sequence of ideas is effective, given the writer's thesis and purpose. The reader almost always feels that the writer is in control of the organization, even when the organizational plan is complex, surprising, or unusual. The subpoints serve to open up and explore the writer's insight in a productive way.

Support: The writer offers solid evidence and reasoning to convince the reader. No important pieces of available evidence and no important points or reasons are omitted. It is clear that the writer is well informed and has thought about how evidence may be used for the argument. Evidence presented is usually relevant to the point being made.

Use of sources: The writer has used sources to support, extend, and inform the ideas but not to substitute for the writer's own development of an idea. The writer uses quotations to capture a source's key points or turns of phrase but does not overuse quoted material to substitute for the writer's own development of an idea. Quotations, paraphrase, and citation are handled with reasonable consistency, according to accepted scholarly form.

Ethos: The writer creates a "self" or "ethos" that sounds genuine, that is relevant to the writer's purpose, and that is generally consistent throughout the essay.

Style: Language is used competently, though it may be awkward at times. There are few or no sentences that confuse the reader or are incomprehensible.

Edited Written Standard English (ESWE): Except for deliberate departures (the quoted speech of a person, a humorous purpose, and so on), the writer generally uses ESWE forms of grammar, punctuation, spelling, and syntax. There are no more than an average of two departures from ESWE per page in any combination of the following areas: sentence boundary punctuation, spelling and typos, use of apostrophe and plural, ESWE verb and pronoun forms, ESWE agreement between subject-verb and pronoun-antecedent.

Presentation: The essay looks neat, crisp, and professional.

D–F Range

Any one of the following may result in a *D* or *F:*

The thesis is obvious, cut-and-dried, trite.

The reader cannot determine the thesis and purpose.

The organization is not clear to the reader.

The organizational plan is inappropriate to the thesis; it does not offer effective support or explanation of the writer's ideas.

The writer offers little or no effective support for the ideas.

The writer has neglected important sources that should have been used.

The writer has overused quoted or paraphrased material to substitute for the writer's own ideas.

The writer has used source material without acknowledgment. (This may also result in the kinds of penalties attached to plagiarism. See Student Handbook.)

The language is so muddy that the reader is frequently at a loss to understand what the writer is trying to say.

The use of ESWE falls below the standard established above for a *C.*

REFERENCES

Abramson, L. Y., Seligman, M., and Teasdale, J. "Learned Helplessness in Humans: Critique and Reformulation." *Journal of Abnormal Psychology,* 1978, *87,* 49–74.

Adelman, C. (ed.). *Signs & Traces: Model Indicators of College Student Learning in the Disciplines.* Office of Educational Research and Improvement, Publication OR89–538. Washington, D.C.: U.S. Department of Education, 1989.

American Association for the Advancement of Science. *Project 2061: Benchmarks for Science Literacy.* New York: Oxford University Press, 1993.

Ames, C. "Classrooms: Goals, Structures, and Student Motivation." *Journal of Educational Psychology,* 1992, *84,* 261–271.

Anderson, S. B., Ball, S., Murphy, R. T., and Associates. *Encyclopedia of Educational Evaluation.* San Francisco: Jossey-Bass, 1975.

Anderson, V. J., and Walvoord, B. E. "Conducting and Reporting Original Scientific Research: Anderson's Biology Class." In B. E. Walvoord, L. P. McCarthy, and others, *Thinking and Writing in College: A Naturalistic Study of Students in Four Disciplines.* Urbana, Ill.: National Council of Teachers of English, 1991.

Angelo, T. A. "Introduction and Overview: From Classroom Assessment to Classroom Research." In T. A. Angelo (ed.), *Classroom Research: Early Lessons from Success.* New Directions for Teaching and Learning, no. 46. San Francisco: Jossey-Bass, 1991a.

Angelo, T. A. "Ten Easy Pieces: Assessing Higher Learning in Four Dimensions." In T. A. Angelo (ed.), *Classroom Research: Early Lessons from Success.* New Directions for Teaching and Learning, no. 46. San Francisco: Jossey-Bass, 1991b.

Angelo, T. A. "A Teacher's Dozen: Fourteen General Research-Based Principles for Improving Higher Learning in Our Classrooms. *AAHE Bulletin,* April, 1993, *45*(8), 3–7, 13.

Angelo, T. A. "Improving Classroom Assessment to Improve Learning: Guidelines from Research and Practice." *Assessment Update,* 1995, *7*(6), 1–2, 12–13.

Angelo, T. A. "Transforming Assessment." *AAHE Bulletin,* 1996, *48*(8), 3–4.

Angelo, T. A., and Cross, K. P. *Classroom Assessment Techniques: A Handbook for College Teachers.* (2nd ed.) San Francisco: Jossey-Bass, 1993.

Argyris, C., Putnam, R., and Smith, D. M. *Action Science.* San Francisco: Jossey-Bass, 1985.

Association of American Colleges. *Integrity in the College Curriculum: A Report to the Academic Community.* Washington, D.C.: AAC, 1985.

Astin, A. W. *Achieving Educational Excellence.* San Francisco: Jossey-Bass, 1985.

Astin, A. W. *What Matters in College: Four Critical Years Revisited.* San Francisco: Jossey-Bass, 1993.

Astin, A. W. "Involvement in Learning Revisited: Lessons We Have Learned." *Journal of College Student Development,* 1996, *37*(2), 123–134.

Baird, J. S., Jr. "Perceived Learning in Relationship to Student Evaluation of University Instruction." *Journal of Educational Psychology,* 1987, *79*, 90–91.

Bandura, A. *Social Foundations of Thought and Action: A Social Cognitive Theory.* Englewood Cliffs, N.J.: Prentice-Hall, 1986.

Banta, T. (ed.). *Assessment in Practice: Putting Principles to Work on College Campuses.* San Francisco: Jossey-Bass, 1996.

Barnet, S. *A Short Guide to Writing About Art.* (3rd ed.) Glenview, Ill.: Scott, Foresman, 1989.

Batra, M. M., Walvoord, B. E., and Krishnan, K. S. "Effective Pedagogy for a Collaboratively-Authored Student Writing Project in a University-Level International Marketing Class." Proceedings of the Western Marketing Educators' Association Annual Conference, San Diego, Calif., April 1995.

Batra, M. M., Walvoord, B. E., and Krishnan, K. S. "Effective Pedagogy for Student-Team Projects." *Journal of Marketing Education,* 1997, *19*(2), 26–42.

Bean, J. C. *Engaging Ideas: The Professor's Guide to Integrating Writing, Critical Thinking, and Active Learning in the Classroom.* San Francisco: Jossey-Bass, 1996.

Bean, J. C., Drenk, D., and Lee, F. D. "Microtheme Strategies for Developing Cognitive Skills." In C. W. Griffin (ed.), *Teaching Writing in All Disciplines.* New Directions for Teaching and Learning, no. 12. San Francisco: Jossey-Bass, 1982.

Belenky, M. F., Clinchy, B. M., Goldberger, N. R., and Tarule, J. M. *Women's Ways of Knowing: The Development of Self, Voice, and Mind.* New York: Basic Books, 1986.

Black, L., Daiker, D. A., Sommers, J., and Stygall, G. (eds.). *New Directions in Portfolio Assessment: Reflective Practice, Critical Theory, and Large-Scale Scoring.* Portsmouth, N.H.: Boynton-Cook, 1994.

Bloom, B. S. (ed.). *Taxonomy of Educational Objectives.* 2 vols. New York: David McKay Co., 1956.

Bloom, B. S., Hastings, J. T., and Madaus, G. F. *Handbook on Formative and Summative Evaluation of Student Learning.* New York: McGraw-Hill, 1971.

Boice, R. *First-Order Principles for College Teachers: Ten Basic Ways to Improve the Teaching Process.* Bolton, Mass.: Anker, 1996.

Bonwell, C. C., and Eison, J. A. *Active Learning: Creating Excitement in the Classroom.* ASHE-ERIC Higher Education Report, no. 1. Washington, D.C.: The George Washington University, School of Education and Human Development, 1991.

Bosworth, K., and Hamilton, S. J. (eds.). *Collaborative Learning: Underlying Processes and Effective Techniques.* New Directions for Teaching and Learning, no. 59. San Francisco: Jossey-Bass, 1994.

Boud, D., Dunn, J., and Hegarty-Hazel, E. *Teaching in Laboratories.* SRHE/NFER-Nelson, Open University, Milton Keynes, England, 1986.

Bowen, H. R. *Investment in Learning: The Individual and Social Value of American Higher Education.* San Francisco: Jossey-Bass, 1977.

Brown, D. G., and Ellison, C. W. "What Is Active Learning?" In S. R. Hatfield (ed.), *The Seven Principles in Action: Improving Undergraduate Education.* Bolton, Mass.: Anker, 1995.

Carey, L. M. *Measuring and Evaluating School Learning.* (2nd ed.) Boston: Allyn and Bacon, 1994.

Cashin, W. E. *Improving Essay Tests.* IDEA Paper, no. 17. Kansas State University: Center for Faculty Evaluation and Development, 1987.

Cashin, W. E. *Student Ratings of Teaching: A Summary of the Research.* IDEA Paper, no. 20. Kansas State University: Center for Faculty Evaluation and Development, 1988.

Cashin, W. E. *Student Ratings of Teaching: The Research Revisited."* IDEA Paper, no. 32. Kansas State University, Center for Faculty Evaluation and Development, 1995.

Centra, J. A. *Reflective Faculty Evaluation: Enhancing Teaching and Determining Faculty Effectiveness.* San Francisco: Jossey-Bass, 1993.

Chickering, A. W., and Gamson, Z. F. "Seven Principles for Good Practice in Undergraduate Education." *AAHE Bulletin,* 1987, *39*(7), 3–7.

Clegg, V. L., and Cashin, W. E. *Improving Multiple Choice Tests.* IDEA Paper, no. 16. Kansas State University, Center for Faculty Evaluation and Development, 1986.

Cochran-Smith, M., and Lytle, S. L. (eds.). *Inside/Outside: Teacher Research and Knowledge.* Columbia University: Teachers College Press, 1993.

Cooper, J., and others. "Cooperative Learning and College Instruction: Effective Use of Student Learning Teams." California State University Foundation on behalf of California State University Institute for Teaching and Learning, Office of the Chancellor, 1990. In-house guide for faculty.

Cross, K. P. "Classroom Research: Helping Professors Learn More about Teaching and Learning." In P. Seldin (ed.), *How Administrators Can Improve Teaching: Moving from Talk to Action in Higher Education.* San Francisco: Jossey-Bass, 1990.

Cross, K. P. "Teaching and Learning: The Tradition and Transformation of a Teaching Faculty." *The Independent,* Dec. 1995, pp. 6–8.

Cross, K. P., and Angelo, T. A. *Classroom Assessment Techniques: A Handbook for Faculty.* Ann Arbor, Mich.: National Center for Research to Improve Postsecondary Teaching and Learning, University of Michigan, 1988.

Cross, K. P., and Steadman, M. H. *Classroom Research: Implementing the Scholarship of Teaching.* San Francisco: Jossey-Bass, 1996.

Davis, J. R. *Better Teaching, More Learning: Strategies for Success in Postsecondary Settings.* Phoenix, Ariz.: American Council on Education and the Oryx Press, 1993.

Davis, T. M., and Murrell, P. H. *Turning Teaching into Learning: The Role of Student Responsibility in the Collegiate Experience.* ASHE-ERIC Higher Education Report, no. 8. Washington, D.C.: George Washington University, School of Education and Human Development, 1994. (HE 027 588)

Dayton, C. M., and Stunkard, C. L. *Statistics for Problem Solving.* New York: McGraw-Hill, 1971.

Dressel, P. L. *Handbook of Academic Evaluation.* San Francisco: Jossey-Bass, 1976.

Eisenhart, M., and Borko, H. *Designing Classroom Research: Themes, Issues, and Struggles.* Boston: Allyn and Bacon, 1993.

Elbow, P. *Writing with Power.* New York: Oxford University Press, 1981.

El-Khawas, E. *Campus Trends.* Panel Report, no. 73. Washington, D.C.: American Council on Higher Education, 1986.

Ennis, R. H. "A Taxonomy of Critical Thinking Dispositions and Abilities." In J. Baron and R. Sternberg (eds.), *Teaching Thinking Skills.* New York: W. H. Freeman, 1987.

Ewell, P. T. "Feeling the Elephant: The Quest to Capture 'Quality.'" *Change,* 1992, *24*(5), 44–47.

Facione, P. T. *Critical Thinking: A Statement of Expert Consensus for the Purposes of Educational Assessment and Instruction.* 1990. (ED 315 423)

Farmer, D. W. *Enhancing Student Learning: Emphasizing Essential Competencies in Academic Programs.* Wilkes-Barre, Pa.: King's College Press, 1988.

Feinberg, L. "Multiple-Choice and Its Critics: Are the 'Alternatives' Any Better?" *College Board Review,* 1990, *17,* 12–17, 30.

Feldman, K. A. "Identifying Exemplary Teaching: Using Data from Course and Teacher Evaluations." In M. Svinicki and R. Menger (eds.), *Honoring Exemplary Teaching.* New Directions in Teaching and Learning, no. 65. San Francisco: Jossey-Bass, 1996.

Felstehausen, G., *Authentic Assessment for Occupational Competency for Career and Technology Education. Final Report. Year Two.* Lubbock, Tex.: Texas Technological University, 1995. (ED 388 857)

Ferris, D. R. "Student Reactions to Teacher Response in Multiple-Draft Composition Classrooms." *TESOL Quarterly,* 1995, *29*(1), 33–53.

Fisher, R. A., and Yates, F. *Statistical Tables for Biological, Agricultural, and Medical Research.* New York: Hafner, 1963.

Flower, L. S. "The Role of Task Representation in Reading-to-Write." In L. S. Flower and others, (eds.), *Reading-to-Write: Exploring a Cognitive and Social Process.* New York: Oxford University Press, 1990.

Forsyth, D. R., and McMillan, J. H. "Practical Proposals for Motivating Students." In K. A. Feldman and M. B. Paulsen (eds.), *Teaching and Learning in the College Classroom.* Needham Heights, MA.: ASHE Reader Series, 1994.

Frost, S. H. "Contact, Involvement, and Persistence: Contributors to Students' Success." In *Academic Advising for Student Success: A System of Shared Responsibility.* ASHE-ERIC Higher Education Report, no. 3. Washington, D.C.: George Washington University, School of Education and Human Development, 1991.

Gardiner, L. F. *Redesigning Higher Education: Producing Dramatic Gains in Student Learning.* ASHE-ERIC Higher Education Report, no. 7. Washington, D.C.: George Washington University, Graduate School of Education and Human Development, 1994.

Gardner, H. *Frames of Mind: The Theory of Multiple Intelligences.* New York: Basic Books, 1983.

Geisler, C. *Academic Literacy and the Nature of Expertise: Reading, Writing, and Knowing in Academic Philosophy.* Hillsdale, N.Y.: Lawrence Erlbaum, 1994.

Gibbs, G., Habeshaw, S., and Habeshaw, T. *53 Interesting Ways to Assess Your Students.* Plymbridge Distributors Ltd., Estover Rd., Plymouth, PL67PZ, U.K., 1986.

Gibbs, G., and Jenkins, A. (eds.). *Teaching Large Classes in Higher Education.* London: Kogan Page, 1992.

Gilbert, R. *Living with Art.* (3rd ed.) New York: McGraw-Hill, 1992.

Gilbert, R., and McCarter, W. M. *Living with Art.* (2nd ed.) New York: Knopf, 1988.

Goodsell, A., and others (eds.). *Collaborative Learning: A Sourcebook for Higher Education.* University Park, Pa.: National Center on Postsecondary Teaching, Learning, and Assessment, 1992.

Grasha, A. E. *Teaching with Style: A Practical Guide to Enhancing Learning by Understanding Teaching and Learning Styles.* Pittsburgh, Pa.: Alliance Publishers, 1996.

Greenwood, A. (ed.) *The National Assessment of College Student Learning: Identification of the Skills to Be Taught, Learned, and Assessed: A Report on the Pro-*

ceedings of the Second Study Design Workshop, Nov. 1992. Research and Development Report NCES 94-286. Washington, D.C.: U.S. Dept. of Education, Office of Educational Research and Improvement, National Center for Education Statistics, 1994.

Guba, E. G., and Lincoln, Y. S. *Fourth Generation Evaluation.* Newbury Park, Calif.: Sage, 1989.

Haladyna, T. M. *Developing and Validating Multiple-Choice Test Items.* Hillsdale, N.J.: Erlbaum, 1994.

Halpern, D. F., and Associates. *Changing College Classrooms: New Teaching and Learning Strategies for an Increasingly Complex World.* San Francisco: Jossey-Bass, 1994.

Hamp-Lyons, L., and Condon, W. "Questioning Assumptions About Portfolio-Based Assessment." *College Composition and Communication,* 1993, *44,* 176–190.

Harrow, A. J. *A Taxonomy of the Psychomotor Domain: A Guide for Developing Behavioral Objectives.* New York: Longman, 1972.

Hubbard, R. S., and Power, B. M. *The Art of Classroom Inquiry: A Handbook for Teacher-Researchers.* Portsmouth, N.H.: Heinemann, 1993.

Hunt, L. L. *Writing Across the Curriculum.* Spokane, Wash.: Whitworth College, 1992.

Jacobi, M., Astin, A. W., and Ayala, F., Jr. *College Student Outcomes Assessment: A Talent Development Perspective.* ASHE-ERIC Higher Education Report, no. 7. Washington, D.C.: Association for the Study of Higher Education, 1987.

Jacobs, L. C., and Chase, C. I. *Developing and Using Tests Effectively: A Guide for Faculty.* San Francisco: Jossey-Bass, 1992.

Johnson, D. W., and Johnson, R. T. *Meaningful and Manageable Assessment Through Cooperative Learning.* Edina, Minn.: Interaction, 1996.

Johnson, D. W., Johnson, R. T., and Smith, K. A. *Cooperative Learning: Increasing College Faculty Instructional Productivity.* ASHE-ERIC Higher Education Report, no. 4. Washington, D.C.: George Washington University, School of Education and Human Development, 1991.

Jones, E., and others. *National Assessment of College Student Learning: Identifying College Graduates' Essential Skills in Writing, Speech and Listening, and Critical Thinking: Final Project Report.* Washington, D.C.: U.S. Department of Education, Office of Educational Research and Improvement, National Center for Education Statistics, 1995.

Kantz, M. *Shirley and the Battle of Agincourt: Why It Is So Hard for Students to Write Persuasive Researched Analyses.* Occasional Paper, no. 14. University of California, Berkeley, and Carnegie Mellon University, Pittsburgh, Pa.: Center for the Study of Writing, 1989.

Karabenick, S. A., and Collins-Eaglin, J. "College Faculty as Educational Researchers: Discipline-Focused Studies of Student Motivation and Self-Regulated Learning." In P. R. Pintrich (ed.), *Understanding Self-Regulated Learning.* New Directions for Teaching and Learning, no. 63. San Francisco: Jossey-Bass, 1995.

Kennedy, D. "Another Century's End, Another Revolution for Higher Education." *Change,* May/June, 1995, pp. 8–15.

Knowles, M. J. *Using Learning Contracts: Practical Approaches to Individualizing and Structuring Learning.* San Francisco: Jossey-Bass, 1986.

Kurfiss, J. G. *Critical Thinking: Theory, Research, Practice, and Possibilities.* ASHE-ERIC Higher Education Report, no. 2. Washington, D.C.: Association for the Study of Higher Education, 1988.

Lawson, A., Abraham, M., and Renner, J. *A Theory of Instruction: Using the*

Learning Cycle to Teach Science Concepts and Thinking Skills. Monograph, no. 3. Atlanta: National Association for Research in Science Teaching, 1989.

Light, R. J. *The Harvard Assessment Seminars: Explorations with Students and Faculty about Teaching, Learning, and Student Life: Second Report.* Boston: Harvard University, Graduate School of Education, 1992.

Linn, R. L. *Educational Measurement.* Phoenix, Ariz.: Oryx, 1993.

Lloyd-Jones, R. "Primary Trait Scoring." In C. Cooper and L. Odell (eds.), *Evaluating Writing: Describing, Measuring, Judging.* Urbana, Ill.: National Council of Teachers of English, 1977.

López, C. L. "Classroom Research and Regional Accreditation: Common Ground." Paper presented at 11th American Association for Higher Education Conference on Assessment and Quality, Classroom Assessment and Classroom Research, Washington, D.C., June 1996.

Lowman, J. *Mastering the Techniques of Teaching.* (2nd ed.) San Francisco: Jossey-Bass, 1995.

Lowman, J. "Assignments That Promote and Integrate Learning." In R. J. Menges, M. Weimer, and Associates, *Teaching on Solid Ground: Using Scholarship to Improve Practice.* San Francisco: Jossey-Bass, 1996.

MacDonald, S. P., and Cooper, C. R. "Contributions of Academic and Dialogic Journals to Writing About Literature." In A. Herrington and C. Moran (eds.), *Writing, Teaching, and Learning in the Disciplines.* New York: Modern Language Association, 1992.

Macrorie, K. *Searching Writing.* Rochelle Park, N.J.: Haydon, 1980.

Magolda, M. B. *Knowing and Reasoning in College: Gender-Related Patterns in Students' Intellectual Development.* San Francisco: Jossey-Bass, 1992.

Matthews, R. S. "Collaborative Learning: Creating Knowledge with Students." In R. J. Menges, M. Weimer, and Associates (eds.), *Teaching on Solid Ground.* San Francisco: Jossey-Bass, 1996.

McKeachie, W. J. *Teaching Tips: A Guidebook for the Beginning College Teacher.* (9th ed.) Lexington, Mass.: D. C. Heath, 1994.

McKeachie, W. J., and others. *Teaching and Learning in the College Classroom: A Review of the Research Literature.* (rev. ed.) Ann Arbor, Mich.: University of Michigan, National Center for Research to Improve Postsecondary Teaching and Learning, 1990.

McMillan, J. H., and Forsyth, R. D. "What Theories of Motivation Say About Why Learners Learn." In R. J. Menges and M. D. Svinicki (eds.), *College Teaching: From Theory to Practice.* New Directions for Teaching and Learning, no. 45. San Francisco: Jossey-Bass, 1991.

Menges, R. J., and Rando, W. C. "What Are Your Assumptions? Improving Instruction by Examining Theories." *College Teaching* Spring, 1989, 37(2), 54–60.

Mentkowski, M., and Strait, M. A. "Longitudinal Study of Student Change in Cognitive Development, Learning Styles, and Generic Abilities in an Outcome-Centered Liberal Arts Curriculum." Milwaukee, Wis.: Alverno College Productions, 1983.

Meyers, C. *Teaching Students to Think Critically: A Guide for Faculty in All Disciplines.* San Francisco: Jossey-Bass, 1986.

Meyers, C., and Jones, T. B. *Promoting Active Learning: Strategies for the College Classroom.* San Francisco: Jossey-Bass, 1993.

Millis, B. J., and Cottell, P. G., Jr. *Cooperative Learning for Higher Education Faculty.* Phoenix, Ariz.: Oryx, 1997.

Milton, O., Pollio, H. R., and Eison, J. A. *Making Sense of College Grades.* San Francisco: Jossey-Bass, 1986.

National Center for Education Statistics. *National Assessment of College Student Learning: Identifying College Graduates' Essential Skills in Writing, Speech and Listening, and Critical Thinking.* Washington, D.C.: U.S. Department of Education, 1995.

National Standards Project. (Information continually updated—for more information, call 1-800-USA-LEARN or contact Office of Educational Research and Improvement/FIRST Office, U.S. Department of Education, 555 New Jersey Ave. NW, Washington, D.C. 20208-5524.)

Noddings, N., and Witherell, C. *Moral Development/Moral Education Bibliography.* 1993. (ED 400 214)

O'Neill, K. L., and Todd-Mancillas, W. R. "An Investigation into the Types of Turning Point Events Affecting Relational Change in Student-Faculty Interactions." *Innovative Higher Education,* 1992, *16*(4), 277–290.

Owens, R. E., and Clegg, V. L. *Tips for Writing Tests.* Manhattan, Kans.: Kansas State University, Graduate Services and Publications, 1984.

Palmer, P. *To Know As We Are Known.* New York: HarperCollins, 1983.

Palmer, P. "Community, Conflict, and Ways of Knowing." *Change,* 1987, *19*(1), 20–25.

Palmer, P. J. "Good Teaching: A Matter of Living the Mystery." *Change,* 1990, *22*(1), 11–16.

Palmer, P. J. "Good Talk About Good Teaching: Improving Teaching Through Conversation and Community." *Change,* 1993, *25*(6), 8–13.

Pascarella, E. T., and Terenzini, P. T. *How College Affects Students.* San Francisco: Jossey-Bass, 1991.

Paulsen, M. B., and Feldman, K. A. "Taking Teaching Seriously: Meeting the Challenges of Instructional Improvement." ASHE-ERIC Higher Education Report No. 2. Washington, D.C.: Graduate School of Education and Human Development, George Washington University, 1995.

Perry, R. P., Menec, V. H., and Struthers, C. W. "Student Motivation from the Teacher's Perspective." In R. J. Menges, M. Weimer, and Associates (eds.), *Teaching on Solid Ground: Using Scholarship to Improve Practice.* San Francisco: Jossey-Bass, 1996.

Perry, W. *Forms of Intellectual and Ethical Development in the College Years.* New York: Holt Rinehart, 1970.

Powers, D. E., and Enright, M. K. "Analytical Reasoning Skills in Graduate Study: Perceptions of Faculty in Six Fields." *Journal of Higher Education,* 1987, *58*(6), 658–682.

Rest, J. R., and Narvaez, D. (eds.). *Moral Development in the Professions: Psychology and Applied Ethics.* Hillsdale, N.J.: Erlbaum, 1994.

Rock, D. A. *Development of a Process to Assess Higher Order Thinking Skills for College Graduates.* Washington, D.C.: National Center for Education Statistics, 1991. (ED 340 765)

Rowland, S., and Barton, L. "Making Things Difficult: Developing a Research Approach to Teaching in Higher Education." *Studies in Higher Education,* 1994, *19*(3), 367–374.

Sayre, H. M. *Writing About Art.* Englewood Cliffs, N.J.: Prentice-Hall, 1989.

Schratz, M. "Crossing the Disciplinary Boundaries: Professional Development Through Action Research in Higher Education." *Higher Education Research and Development,* 1993, *12*(2), 131–142.

Schultz, L. M., and Laine, C. H. "A Primary Trait Scoring Grid with Assessment and Instructional Uses." *Journal of Teaching Writing,* 1986, *5*(1), 77–89.

Schunk, D. "Self-Efficacy and Classroom Learning." *Psychology in the Schools,* 1985, *22*(2), 208–223.

Schwegler, R. A., and Shamoon, L. K. "The Aims and Process of the Research Paper." *College English,* 1982, *44,* 817–824.

Scriven, M. *Multiple-Rating Items.* 1991. (ED 340 768)

Seybert, J. A., and O'Hara, K. A. "Development of a Performance-Based Model for Assessment of General Education." *Assessment Update,* 1997, *9*(4), 5–7.

Shavelson, R. J. "Performance Assessment in Science." *Applied Measurement in Education,* 1991, *4*(4), 347–362.

Slavin, R. E. *Cooperative Learning.* Boston: Allyn and Bacon, 1995.

Sommers, N. "Responding to Student Writing." *College Composition and Communication,* 1982, *33*(2), 148–156.

Sormunen, C. *Critical Thinking in Business Education.* Paper presented at the American Vocational Society Convention, St. Louis, Mo., December 1992. (ED 354380)

Sperling, M., and Freedman, S. W. "A Good Girl Writes Like a Good Girl." *Written Communication,* 1987, *4*(4), 343–369.

Stark, J. S., and Lattuca, L. R. *Shaping the College Curriculum: Academic Plans in Action.* Boston: Allyn and Bacon, 1997.

Swartz, R. J., and Perkins, D. N. *Teaching Thinking: Issues and Approaches.* (rev. ed.) Pacific Grove, Calif.: Midwest Publications, 1990.

Thinking Together: Collaborative Learning in Science. Boston: Derek Bok Center for Teaching and Learning, Harvard University, 1992. Videotape.

Tittle, C. K., Hecht, D., and Moore, P. "Assessment Theory and Research for Classrooms: From 'Taxonomies' to Constructing Meaning in Context." *Educational Measurement: Issues and Practice,* 1993, *12*(4), 13–19.

Tobias, S. "The Contract Alternative: An Experiment in Testing and Assessment in Undergraduate Science." *AAHE Bulletin,* 1994, *6*(6), 3–6.

Tobias, S. "In-Class Exams in College-Level Science: New Theory, New Practice." *Journal of Science and Technology Education,* 1996, *5*(4), 311–320.

Walvoord, B. E. *Helping Students Write Well: A Guide for Teachers in All Disciplines.* (2nd ed.) New York: Modern Language Association, 1986.

Walvoord, B. E., and Anderson, V. J. "An Assessment Riddle." *Assessment Update,* 1995, *7*(6), 8–11.

Walvoord, B. E., and Breihan, J. "Arguing and Debating: Breihan's History Course." In B. E. Walvoord, L. P. McCarthy, and others, *Thinking and Writing in College: A Naturalistic Study of Students in Four Disciplines.* Urbana, Ill.: National Council of Teachers of English, 1991.

Walvoord, B. E., and Sherman, A. K. "Managerial Decision Making: Sherman's Business Course." In B. E. Walvoord, L. P. McCarthy, and others, *Thinking and Writing in College: A Naturalistic Study of Students in Four Disciplines.* Urbana, Ill.: National Council of Teachers of English, 1991.

Walvoord, B. E., and Williams, L. *Making Large Classes Interactive.* Cincinnati, Ohio: University of Cincinnati, 1995. Videotape.

Walvoord, B. E., and others. *Academic Departments: How They Work, How They Change.* ASHE-ERIC Report. Washington, D.C.: Graduate School of Education and Human Development, George Washington University, forthcoming.

Walvoord, B. E., McCarthy, L. P., and others. *Thinking and Writing in College: A Naturalistic Study of Students in Four Disciplines.* Urbana, Ill.: National Council of Teachers of English, 1991.

Weimer, M. G. (ed.). *Teaching Large Classes Well.* New Directions for Teaching and Learning, no. 32. San Francisco: Jossey-Bass, 1987.

Weiner, B. *An Attributional Theory of Motivation and Emotion.* New York: Springer-Verlag, 1986.

Weinstein, C. E., Goetz, E. T., and Alexander, P. (eds.). *Learning and Study Strategies: Issues in Assessment, Instruction, and Evaluation.* San Diego, Calif.: Harcourt Brace Jovanovich, 1988.

Welte, S. L. "Transforming Educational Practice: Addressing Underlying Epistemological Assumptions." *Review of Higher Education,* 1997, *20*(2), 199–213.

Yagelski, R. P. "The Role of Classroom Context in the Revision Strategies of Student Writers." *Research in the Teaching of English,* 1995, *29*(2), 216–238.

Yelon, S. L., and Duley, J. S. *Efficient Evaluation of Individual Performance in Field Placement.* East Lansing, Mich.: Michigan State University, 1978.